James' Journey

by Helen Lundström Erwin

Publisher: Powersimple, LLC
New York, NY – USA

ISBN: 978-0-9862666-3-8

Cover design and photography by Ben Erwin.

Acknowledgements

I want to thank the New York Historical Society and the numerous professors and librarians at Harvard, Princeton, Columbia, New York, Kentucky State and other universities who kindly took the time to assist me in my research by answering my many questions.

I would like to thank my husband Ben for his amazing support, encouragement and for all his technical help.

Thanks to my family, Marcia Carter for your invaluable input. David and Shannon Erwin for your support and for making your cottage available for my cover photo.

I also want to thank my editors Todd Barselow and brother in law Bob Erwin, and Pariah Burke for his invaluable expertise in e-book publishing.

To my friends: thank you Anne Andersson for your friendship, for your support, encouragement and faith in me.

Thank you, Mary, Carol, Naaja, Courtney and, Nola, you have all inspired me to keep writing even when I felt like giving up.

Preface

James' Journey is about a man who grew up in a world where slavery was the norm. Everyone he knew, including his parents and his neighbors, owned slaves. His world was dependent on it and he never thought to question it.
James left his environment and had a chance to look at things from a different perspective. His views did not change overnight, but he did eventually come to understand and even embrace abolitionism.

When I began to do the research for *James' Journey* I wanted to understand the minds and attitudes of the people who lived during the antebellum period.

Some of what I discovered was hard to read. I did not expect that the scholars of their time would be so successful at convincing everyone that slavery was actually good for the slaves themselves. In fact, many believed it the best thing that could happen to them since they were "saved" from living as "uncivilized savages" in Africa and brought to the United States so that they could wear "proper" clothes and learn about the Bible. The understanding of diverse cultures and religions that we have today was a foreign concept then. The European-American view was considered superior to other cultures, as was the idea that modern humans consisted of different races and that those of European descent were the most intelligent. Even New York, that had a fair share of abolitionists, was one of the most pro-slavery states in the North.

Many insisted that African Americans were unable to learn to read, handle basic mathematics or learn other skills conducive to an independent life, and argued that it would be cruel to emancipate them.

At the same time, it is important to mention that black literacy was illegal in many states. The most oppressive law came about after Nat Turner's revolt in 1831. People became afraid that the slaves would read abolitionist material. Both the sense that African Americans were not capable to live as equal members of society, and the fear that they might learn too much existed simultaneously.

Another example that sheds light on what many thought during this time are the "Anti-Tom" novels, written by people who were indignant over Harriet Beecher Stowe's portrayal of slavery in her book *Uncle Tom's Cabin.*
Uncle Robin in His Cabin in Virginia, and Tom Without One in Boston, by J.W. Page is one such novel.

In the present information age, it is easy to cherry pick the information that we *want* to have that supports our world view without critical thinking. People preach to the choir, while keeping a closed mind to anything that threatens their status quo, whether it is on Facebook, on TV or at a village townhouse meeting. It is not easy to change the views that you have had your whole life, especially not if they are still supported not only by your family and your society but also by law. It takes enormous courage to speak out.

I want to honor the many, many heroes who have done this in the past, and those who still do today.

James, his family and the township of Woodbank are fictive as are the slaves on his plantation, though their names are names of real enslaved people living during this time. There is no connection to these names and the story.

Several characters are based on real people, but used fictively.

Doctor James McCune Smith was the first African American to hold a medical degree. He graduated at the top of his class at the University of Glasgow, Scotland. He was the first African American to run a pharmacy in the United States.

Henry Ward Beecher was an abolitionist preacher at Plymouth Church in Brooklyn. He and his congregation helped runaways hide and escape to Canada. He had mock slave auctions during his services where runaway slaves waited on the podium as the congregation collected money to send them north. He was the brother of Harriet Beecher Stowe, the author of *Uncle Tom's Cabin*.

Harriet Tubman was an escaped slave who made many trips back south to rescue her family and other slaves and bring them north. She was a nurse for the Union Army and later a spy and an armed scout. Many called her Moses. Some slaveholders thought she was a white man stealing slaves from them.

Moncure Conway grew up with slaves, was briefly pro slavery and later became a Unitarian Minister and an abolitionist who helped his father's slaves escape.

John Brown was an abolitionist who tried to raid the armory at Harper's Ferry, Virginia. He was caught and tried for treason, murder and inciting a slave insurrection. He was convicted and sentenced to death by hanging.

The many stories of amazing resilience and strength of the abolitionists who ran "stations" on the Underground Railroad provided inspiration to write this book, as did a personal discovery of an heirloom book that included an estate manifest from Mississippi dated 1853. It included a detailed inventory of the deceased man's property. It had human beings listed next to tools and broken crockery. One mother was sold with her infant child. A man, most likely her husband was sold to someone else. A six-year-old boy whom I assume was their oldest child was sold to yet a third party.
Reading this had a profound effect on me. I could feel the sadness from this list written over 150 years earlier. Who were they? Did they ever see each other and their children again? It broke my heart and inspired me to tell this story.

Note on terminology

The word Negro was used to describe a person of African descent. Sometimes "colored" was used, as well as other names. It is easier to devalue someone's life, such as to justify owning someone, if you tell yourself that the person you own is something completely different than yourself.

None of the slave traders, planters or slave merchants advertised selling people. They sold "Negroes." It illustrates how deep this Us and Them concept went, and how it was taken full advantage of by those who had the power.

James knew it wasn't a question any longer.
He knew in his heart whom he had to join,
and they'd name him a traitor too,
no better than John Brown.

PART I

Waynewright Plantation Virginia 1855

Chapter 01

It was hot, hotter than it had been all summer, and James felt as if he could barely breathe. He got up to move the rocking chair closer to the wall where it was always cooler. The sun never hit that part of the porch and it retained a cooler atmosphere even on hot days like this. Their negroes were convinced that a ghost lived there and always hurried when they passed so as not to disturb it.

James smiled to himself at the thought and sat down. He closed his eyes and had just begun to drift off when he heard the crunching of worn out shoes running on the gravel in front and a familiar voice, though he couldn't quite tell whom the voice belonged to.

"Massa Jr., Massa Jr., please come!"

James abruptly sat up and saw Johnnie standing before him, sweat pouring down his face.

"What is the matter, Johnnie?"

"Oh Massa Jr., it's the Overseer; he ain't letting my wife go home, the baby is coming," he stopped for a second and looked as if he was about to cry, but he got a hold of himself and said, "she is doubling over from pain, but he says...Mr. Overseer says the tobacco has to come in before it rains."

"He has her working in this heat, when the baby is about to come?"

James was annoyed at having his midday rest bothered with and even more annoyed that his father wasn't here to deal with this.

"Yes, Massa Jr. Please hurry. He says he is going to get the lash, please hurry!"

With that, James stood up and for the first time felt really alert.

"The lash, surely you are exaggerating."

"No, Massa Jr., I tell you the truth."

James opened the porch gate, took the stairs in one leap and ran side by side with Johnnie down to the tobacco fields. Johnnie ran fast and seemingly without trouble, whereas James was laboring to breathe in the hot stale air. His boots made a clunking sound on the dry dirt. He wished he had taken the time to get a horse.

As soon as they approached the tobacco, he could tell that something was amiss. None of the field hands were working, but stood in small groups staring at Mr. Loch and something on the ground. Johnnie had noticed as well and sped past him and was over there in what seemed like seconds. By now James was breathing so hard that he had to slow down or he would not be able to speak.

As he tried to catch his breath, Mr. Loch turned toward him, smiled apologetically and started to walk over.

"Afternoon, Mr. Waynewright. I apologize, sir. I didn't see the buck run to get you. I certainly didn't mean to disturb you on a hot day like this."

James swallowed hard and tried to collect his thoughts, again wishing that his father were home so that he didn't have to be responsible for this. James was only nineteen and had never really had to deal with Mr. Loch who was 20 years older.

His father had hired Mr. Loch earlier in the year, telling James that he had upped the revenue on several plantations in the area and had come highly recommended.

James tried to sound confident and asked, "What seems to be the problem, Mr. Loch?"

Mr. Loch smiled disarmingly, "Really sir, ain't nothin' you need bother yourself with. Again, I apologize for having the buck run and bother you, but since you are here, it's the pregnant girl pretending to have labor pains so that she doesn't have to work. It looks like rain is coming," Mr. Loch looked toward the sky that did indeed look dark as if a thunderstorm was approaching. "It's important that all hands help to get the harvest inside."

"With all due respect to your professional opinion *Mr.* Loch, my mother looked at her just a couple of days ago and she confirmed that it would be her time soon. In fact, I remember overhearing her telling my father that she should stop working in the fields and rest since two days back. She should not have been in the field at all since Friday. Why is she here?" James said, regretting that he brought his mother into this; it made him sound like a child.

Mr. Loch looked taken aback, "Surely you jest. You don't really have them resting when they are days away from birthing? You lose a lot of work that way. That *is* why your father hired me I believe, to get your harvest yield up and well, this is one of the ways it's done."

"Overworking a female as she is about to give birth can't be good for her *or* the baby and might well kill them both. *Then* we would really lose a valuable slave and her production," James said, hoping he sounded like he was in control.

“A couple of lashes would certainly get her to work another hour or two until the rain comes. It’s her first. It could take days. She is a *negro*, not a *lady*! But, as you wish, Mr. Waynewright, take her to her cabin. I assume it’s *you* who’s gotten her into this situation and you have feelings for her. It’s only natural the first time. You are young yet. Soon you get used to it and do it to add more hands to the workforce.”

Before James could stop himself, he had struck the man. Mr. Loch fell backwards as if he was a felled tree and landed on his back with a surprisingly loud thump.

The anger was surging through his body, but James took a deep breath and looked at the field hands. He caught Martha’s eye as she sat on the ground. She was clutching her belly looking miserable but relieved. The rest of them were staring at him in shock. James saw relief but also fear in their eyes.

Will spoke up first, “Massa Jr., you don’t need to worry none; we’ll get the harvest in before it rains, by my word.”

James nodded gratefully and tried to smile. He was very close to Will. They had played together as children and Mother even let him play in the house instead of having James run down to the slave quarters every chance he got.

“Thank you, Will. You do that.” He looked at the girls and nodded, “One of you take her home so she can have the baby and someone run and get a horse so we can get the overseer to the main house. After the harvest is in, I’ll send one of you to town to get my father.”

Chapter 02

"It's a healthy girl; she is cute as a button with lots of kinky hair on top of her little head." Mrs. Waynewright smiled as Auntie Ellen pulled the wet coat off her shoulders. "That will do, Auntie Ellen, why don't you run on down and see her. You are done here for the evening."

"Thank you, Missus," Auntie Ellen said and quickly disappeared out the door.

When they were alone, Mrs. Waynewright turned to James and her smile was gone.

Her voice sounded like ice. "There, James, Father is waiting in the parlor for you. I'll get us some wine."

Mr. Waynewright was sitting in his favorite armchair. He sighed when James came in and motioned for him to sit on the sofa.

"James, I barely know what to say. I'm astounded. Will told me everything when he came all the way to pick me up several days too early. For God's sake, the meetings are almost all the way to Charlottesville. I still have business to attend to and I have to journey back at first light tomorrow morning. Not to speak of having the horses exhaust themselves having to make the journey back and forth twice. The valuable work lost when Will was absent getting me. I don't know what Mr. Loch told you, as I have not yet spoken to him, but surely you cannot hit a man to protect a *negro*! I have never heard of such nonsense. Utter nonsense. Clearly you could have spoken to Mr. Loch and explained that we want things done on our plantation without violence, but to hit him in front of *them*? You *know* how important it is to keep a certain level of firmness with them. They've got weak minds that can easily become influenced and drawn into confusion." Mr. Waynewright sounded frantic and said all that so fast that he almost lost his breath.

He quickly inhaled and was about to begin again, but James seized the opportunity to finally get a word in.

"Yes, but Father, Loch threatened to lash her. It ain't right, she's expecting. Or *was* I should say."

His father waved his arm in the air. "Well that is certainly no reason to *hit* Mr. Loch. I demand an—"

Mrs. Waynewright who came in with a tray with wine glasses and a decanter full of golden white wine interrupted him.

James' father waved his hand again, this time at his wife who offered him a glass.

"Later, Elisabeth," he said irritably.

"James, I agree it ain't right to threaten to lash a pregnant girl, but again, why didn't you just speak to him? I thought I left the plantation in good hands when I was gone. I did not think that there would be such childish drama, and you panicking and sending for me. Not only have you undermined the overseer's authority in front of almost *all* of our field hands, but also very possibly might have ruined our reputation and standing among our neighbors. I demand that you apologize to Mr. Loch. Thank God that you didn't kill him. People *can* die you know, if the nose bone goes straight up into the brain."

James felt like rolling his eyes, but knew the better of it. "I'm certainly not that strong, Father. He insulted me and accused me of being the father of the baby."

James heard a gasp from his mother.

"Oh, dear lord, you ain't having relations with them are you?" She had become noticeably pale.

James' father cleared his throat, looking rather stunned, "James, explain yourself this instant. Is this true?"

"That Mr. Loch suggested it? Or do you really think I've done that?"

James paused, collecting himself and resisting the urge to get up and leave the room. "That's why I hit him; for suggesting it. He thought I had feelings for her, and advised that I would soon get used to breeding slaves and not be so attached. I handled it very well up until then. When he accused me of being weak for having warm feelings for an Auntie carrying *my* baby, I lost my temper."

Mr. Waynewright's eyes widened, "That is certainly not what Will told me. He said that Johnnie got you because Mr. Loch threatened to lash Martha for not being able to work. He said that she was doubled over with pain but that Mr. Loch thought she made it up."

"Yes, that is correct Father, but none of the field hands heard us talk. Mr. Loch told me that he had been hired to get a rise in production and one way of doing this was to let them work up until it was time to birth. I know that Mother had told her not to work since Friday, so he has disobeyed a direct order from you, Father, and then he insulted me. He would never have suggested something like that to you, if you had dealt with it."

Mr. Waynewright was clearly disturbed; this part of the story was not what he had been expecting.

"Hmmm, well, that is probably so, but you will have to apologize nonetheless. We have to pray that this does not cause disorderly behavior among our negroes. James, keep in mind that not all people think like us. There *are* those that do lash, *and* those who have relations with them. It's not Mr. Loch's fault. He only talks about what he has seen on other plantations, where things might be done differently. I would say that most of our own neighbors have a similar philosophy to us, but on some plantations, they are treated horribly. They are abused and mistreated in the most unchristian way. It's no wonder that there are abolitionists in the north when they hear about such things. They don't know that most of us treat our servants as family and care for them. It is our Christian responsibility to take care of those who cannot fend for themselves." Mr. Waynewright was bright red in the face and was breathing heavily.

"Yes, we have only sold two, and we made a point of selling them to our neighbors so that they can still visit kin," Mrs. Waynewright interjected, "I saw Nancy just yesterday when she was visiting with her son here. She told me she is a house negro now. She sounded mighty proud." Mrs. Waynewright smiled knowingly, and continued, "James, listen to your father. You must understand that Mr. Loch isn't used to our way of doing things." She turned to her husband and said, "Wilbur, it may be sound to have another little friendly talk and teach him some of your Christian convictions," she fixed her eyes on him and he nodded.

"Enough of this now, we'll have some wine."

Chapter 03

James apologized to Mr. Loch; his nose and mouth were bruised badly but nothing was broken. Mr. Loch forgave him, or at least said that he did.

Things ran smoothly after that and Mr. Waynewright and Mr. Loch had many spirited discussions of how one should treat negroes. They never could agree, but Mr. Loch never threatened to use the lash again.

On one such evening, James and his father were sitting on the porch after dinner and upon seeing Mr. Loch he was invited up for a nightcap.

"I'll be delighted, thank you, sir." Mr. Loch quickly climbed the steps and sat down in one of the rocking chairs. He tipped his head at James and then looked to Mr. Waynewright. "Where is Mrs. Waynewright on a lovely night such as this?"

James didn't think it was his business to ask, but his father didn't seem to take offense and answered pleasantly.

"She retired early this evening. She was up early as Mary wasn't feeling well. She is on the mend, but ran a fever last night and she wanted to look in on her."

To James' indignation, Mr. Loch shook his head, "I must say that you coddle them too much. I apologize for speaking so frankly without permission but..."

"Go on." Mr. Waynewright sat up a little straighter, sucked deeply on his pipe as he looked at Mr. Loch.

"Well, if you don't mind my sayin' so, they may seem like dumb creatures to you, and yes they are in a sense, but you'd be surprised what they can come up with when they think no one is lookin'. If they ain't kept in their place it can be very dangerous. I've seen it myself. It wasn't long ago 'round these parts where a bunch o' them had planned a takeover of their Master's plantation, can you imagine, had collected guns and everything since years back, planning it all and hiding it. I say, never underestimate them. They may be the weaker race, but it don't mean they ain't capable of rebellion. " Mr. Loch looked pleased with himself as he leaned back in his rocker. He fiddled with his breast pocket and pulled out tobacco and his pipe. Mr. Waynewright remained silent for several minutes. James glanced at them both. He didn't like what Mr. Loch was saying, and he knew his father didn't either. Mr. Waynewright took his time before he answered.

"I daresay that what you are talking about stems from unhappy negroes that ain't well cared for. If you take care of them properly and treat them kindly, they will be happy, healthy and loyal. As Christians, it is our responsibility to do so."

Mr. Loch nodded thoughtfully and rocked back and forth in his chair. He was still fingering his pipe but didn't light it yet. James noticed that he had a lot of mud on his boots. It irked him and he tried not to look at it as pieces of the mud slowly flaked off as he worked the chair backwards and forwards.

"Absolutely, Mr. Waynewright, with that comes the necessity to keep them in line so they don't get things into their thick heads that they ain't able to handle, like freedom; those wicked abolitionists that are spreading rumors of freedom. The Negro isn't equipped to live on its own."

"Well *that* I do agree with," Mr. Waynewright interrupted. "Normally they know their own limitations and are happy to be taken care of, but then these radicals come and tell them that they are almost like us. It's cruel."

"I say, don't you agree, young Waynewright?" Mr. Loch grinned at James who smiled back politely but took this as his chance to get away from the conversation. Even though he agreed with where the conversation was going, he really didn't like Mr. Loch and he didn't feel like participating. He quickly excused himself and went into the kitchen to grab some cheese for a late snack before bed.

Auntie Ellen and Hettie had left for the night and as he wandered through the empty house, he pondered what had been occupying his mind lately.

He fancied studying medicine. He would open a clinic somewhere. He couldn't think of where just yet, but he didn't want it to be too close to the plantation or Old Woodbank, their little town. He knew for sure that he did not want to stay on the plantation and take over from his father as was expected of him. He thought country life was boring and dull and he did not want to stay here for the rest of his life. Ever since he was a child he had been interested in the visits from Doctor Robinson who came to see to their negroes. He would never forget the day when Pap had broken his ankle when he helped a horse out of the ditch behind the tobacco fields. The horse had somehow been tangled in his reins, panicked and bolted, only to get stuck on her knees in ditch muck. When Pap had untangled her he had to hurry out of the ditch but his foot got stuck under a fallen tree and he fell in such a way that the bone just above the ankle broke.

The way Doctor Robinson had set the bone and put a splint around it to support it had impressed him immensely.

James had not told anyone other than Will about his plans, not told anyone else that he had applied to the College of Physicians and Surgeons in New York. He would not only have the chance to make something out of himself. He would see the world and go to the theatre, museums, restaurants and converse with people from Europe and maybe even India.

When James got his letter from the college just a few days later he must have called out without realizing it, because he heard Auntie Ellen yell out that there was something the matter with Massa Jr.

His mother came down from the upstairs bedrooms as fast as she could, almost tripping on her large skirts. James came inside, rereading the letter as he walked.

"What is it, James? Did you have bad news through the mail? Who would write instead of calling on you?"

James laughed, "Mother, it's The College of Physicians and Surgeons. I'm moving to New York!"

Auntie Ellen tried to hold back a shriek, but it slipped out and she covered her mouth with her hands to stifle it.

"Auntie Ellen, get a hold of yourself," Mrs. Waynewright said sharply, "James what are you saying? Why in the world are they writing to *you?*"

"I applied. I'm planning to study medicine, Mother, and I want to do it in New York," James said grinning.

His mother stared at him with disbelief, "*Medicine*, who will take care of your father's plantation?"

"Mother, that is a long time off. By the time I'm needed to oversee things here, I will be retired from medicine. You and Father ain't old. Besides, a medical degree would certainly be beneficial then, wouldn't it?" he said, hoping that some other solution would manifest itself at that time so that he never would have to move back to the plantation, at least not permanently.

Mrs. Waynewright tried to smile, but was not very successful at it. "Well, you have to speak to your father about this, but I'm not sure it's wise. This is certainly a surprise. I'm not sure what he will think of it. If you insist...well, just don't be influenced by those Yankees up there," she said breathlessly, trying to make a joke of it even though she couldn't bear the thought of her son traveling so far.

James snorted. "I'll be the one who will tell *them* a thing or two."

Neither James nor his mother noticed how Auntie Ellen had run off and was already down at the tobacco fields telling everyone that the only person who would protect them from the overseer when the Master was away was planning on leaving.

James didn't understand how scared everyone was until two days later when he and Will took their walk to check on the fields as they did every Saturday night after dinner.

"Massa Jr., between you and me, because we known each other since we played as children, you saw what happen yourself when he threaten Johnnie's wife. Everyone is terrified of him. He may stick to your rules now, but we can all see that that he won't if you is gone and your father is away. He's just biding his time for the day when you and Massa Waynewright are gone on the same day. He say he forgives you but he is angry that he was shamed in front of us and he wants revenge. Johnnie and his wife are terrified of him, terrified that he will take revenge on Johnnie for getting you and being the cause for you hitting him and him fainting in front of us."

"Will, we will have to figure something out. In fact, I don't like him either.

Anyway, I will think of something. I have all summer before I leave. Maybe we could fire him. I could tell father that I don't like him and that I feel too uncomfortable after what happened."

"Your father ain't never gonna fire him, especially not since you are leavin'.'"

James looked surprised, "You're right Will." He let his eyes gaze at the tobacco fields before he continued and said without conviction, "We'll think of something'."

James did think about it. He even thought of telling his father that that the workers were not safe or well taken care of by the overseer. He was not sure how to express this without betraying Will's confidence so he kept postponing it, and then it slipped his mind.

James and his father were occupied with plans for the future. Instead of telling James that he ought to study in Virginia, Mr. Waynewright saw it as an opportunity to have direct contact with their buyers and exporters in New York and thought it a grand idea. He agreed with James that he ought to have time to spread his wings before it was his time to take over the plantation.

When he and his father were not contemplating the future, James was thoroughly busy with parties, dances and long rides out into the countryside. He went to picnics with friends, lazing around all day in the sun.

He and Will still did their rounds on Saturday nights, but Will never mentioned what they had discussed again. Time passed quickly, as it always does especially in the summer, and then came the day when James had to go. All the Waynewright slaves came one by one to say their goodbyes and James steeled himself so he would not cry, especially when Auntie Ellen gave him three beautifully embroidered handkerchiefs for his pocket that she had made herself. She cried when she gave them to him and told him that life would not be the same without him and that she hoped that he wouldn't stay away for too long.

Chapter 04

James' first impression of New York was the smell and the sounds; it was overpowering and distracting. It was sunny with clear skies but there was a curious haze in the air, as if it was foggy. The sounds were coming from all around him; loud banging and whooshing sounds from the wheels of the many carriages rushing by, and loud voices that sounded angry, or upset. He remained standing with his trunks, collecting himself for several minutes before he was able to call for a hackney that would take him to his hotel where he would spend his first couple weeks. In spite of it all, he smiled to himself as he whistled and looked out into the crowded street. He had never done this before. It felt awkward and exhilarating at the same time, frightening as well. How would he know if the driver was honest and didn't try to overcharge him? He had never been driven anywhere by a white man before. He didn't have a long time to ponder this dilemma as a dilapidated hackney with black paint chipping off of it stopped just in front of him.

"Whester?" said the hackman sitting on the bench in front, looking expectantly at James.

"Pardon?"

"Whester?" he said again.

"Pardon, I'm terribly sorry, sir. I don't quite follow you."

"Ahhww blasted," the hackman cracked his whip in the air as he took off without bothering to explain.

He must have been here to pick up a Mr. Whester, James thought, and was just about to whistle for another hackney, when a new one, this one a little less dilapidated, stopped in front of him and, the driver asked the same thing, "Whester?"

"No, sir, I'm not him, but I'm goin' to the New York Hotel on Broadway...I..."

"Him who?" said the hackman with a laugh. He made a motion with his left shoulder for James to get in, but did not offer to help with the trunks. James shrugged, confused, but didn't have the energy to comment on why he asked for Mr. Whester as well, or why he became puzzled when James politely told him that he wasn't the man in question.

James cursed himself for packing so much. He should have brought Will with him. He had considered it but was worried that Will would feel too lonely with only the free negroes to talk to and had decided against it. Besides, he did not want Will to be exposed to the Northerner's abolitionist ideas. It would be incredibly irresponsible of him to put Will into such temptation. If he decided to run away, he would be without protection on the dangerous streets of New York. James' mother had told him stories of negroes who had thought that they wanted freedom but were not able to handle the responsibility. Many had wandered up and down the streets all alone without a single white person taking pity on them or helping them. Some of them surely wanted to get back home to the safety of the plantation but couldn't even write for help. James shuddered at the thought, heaved the trunk up in the back of the hackney, and got in.

Chapter 05

The next morning James decided to walk over to Crosby Street and look at the College. It was a beautiful day, pleasantly warm, and he felt well rested and full of excitement. The streets were full of all kinds of people: pretty ladies wearing beautiful dresses and flourishing parasols, free negroes—he assumed anyway—carrying heavy bundles. He was very interested in seeing how they seemed to be faring and as far as he could see, they didn't look worse for wear. Some were rather skinny though, and not as muscular and handsome as on his father's plantation.

As James walked down the street he heard yet another hackman ask if someone waiting was Mr. Whester. James saw a heavyset man struggle to get into the hackney. Very odd he thought. *Who is this Whester fellow?*

He shrugged and kept walking. It was amazing that so many people could fit on these streets and somehow everything flowed without any mishaps or brawls. Just as he was about to cross the street he heard a familiar sounding voice. Surprised, he turned around, but saw no one he recognized. Instead, he saw a man gingerly helping an elderly lady get up from a bench right outside the entrance to a bakery.

"There, ma'am, your husband will be right along now. I'll wait here with you." The woman shook her head, but the man laughed, "No, I insist."

She smiled and took the man's arm and squeezed it, and then James saw an elderly man hurry toward them. James walked off to the side and didn't hear their exchange, but when the younger fellow walked away James caught up with him.

"Pardon me, sir, but I couldn't help noticing that you are from the same parts as me. Virginia if I'm not mistaken?"

"Oh indeed I am, sir," he said and bowed his head. "Mr. Gilbert is what those who are obliged to do so call me."

James smiled at the familiarity of the language and manner.

"Mr. Waynewright is my name. I just arrived here yesterday and everything is quite exhilarating."

"Indeed, indeed. I have been here for over a year now. It is a wondrous place, I agree, but these people can be a bit unsophisticated. Did you see how that elderly woman was left all alone?"

"I must admit that I understood from your conversation that she was. I couldn't help overhearing."

"Eavesdroppin', eh?" Mr. Gilbert said with a crooked smile. "Where are you headed?"

"Well, I'm walking around taking in the sights and I'm planning to go to The College of Physicians and Surgeons to take a look around. I'm beginning my studies there in a couple of weeks. They are moving soon though, all the way to 23rd Street, a brand new building constructed just for medicine."

"You don't say. May I ask why you don't study in the South? I imagine it's quite unusual; you may well be the only Southerner there."

"We shall see. I want to see the world. I'm quite tired of life on the plantation. I find it dull and unsatisfying," James said, marveling at his own forwardness with someone he did not know at all.

Mr. Gilbert was silent for a minute and then he touched James' shoulder. "My advice is to not mention the plantation in these parts. You don't know who might overhear it. Why don't you and I have some refreshments? There is a very nice establishment not far from Crosby. It'd be my treat to welcome you to New York." Without waiting for an answer, Mr. Gilbert got the attention of a hackney. This one looked brand new, its paint glistening deep black in the sun.

"Whester?" asked the driver, but Mr. Gilbert did not reply. He just held the door open for James and told the hackman to head to Duane Street.

"Who is that fellow, and why do they all ask about him?" James asked when Mr. Gilbert sat down opposite him.

"What fellow?"

"Whester, they all ask about him? Who is he?"

Mr. Gilbert looked confused, "I'm sorry; I don't know what you mean."

"Every hackman asks if you are Mr. Whester, only they're not as polite to even address as Mr. I had two of them ask me if I was him yesterday, and our own hackman here," James gestured upward with his hand, "he asked for him as well."

To James indignation, Mr. Gilbert burst out laughing. He laughed and laughed, holding on to his sides as if they hurt. "Oh, dear sir. Oh dear, you really had me there for a second, but I can see how a newcomer could think that. Mr. Whester, oh indeed!" He laughed even more and James began to wonder if he had a lunatic on his hands and chastised himself for willingly following the first person he had spoken to since he came to New York City.

Finally Mr. Gilbert calmed down and explained what was so funny, "Mr. Waynewright, no one is asking for a Mr. Whester. They are saying, 'Where to, sir.' Only they say it so fast with their New York speech that they sometimes get the order of the words mixed up and it's more like this, 'where sir to', and yes, real fast it sounds like whester."

James sat dumbfounded and then he too began to laugh. "Oh, *that* certainly explains it. It has been irritating me since I arrived. I simply couldn't get it out of my mind, and kept wonderin' who this man was."

Gilbert grinned, "It took me a while too, to get used to their way of pronouncing things, but never did I make that mistake."

After a delightful meal of shepherd's pie, they smoked cigars and drank whiskey. James felt free, relaxed, and very grown up sitting there alone and having a proper conversation with someone that didn't see him as young Mr. Waynewright.

James lowered his voice and said, "Mr. Gilbert, I have to ask...you mentioned that I shouldn't talk about this, but I must bring it up. These abolitionists... as a Southerner from Virginia yourself, isn't it unfair that they think of us as monsters, even though they have never themselves met any negroes? Well, they may have met them, but I have not seen a white man talk with a negro yet. Though of course I'm brand new in town, but in the South you see it all the time."

Mr. Gilbert cleared his throat, "You have observed correctly in the short time you have been here. It is indeed a curious question. I myself have a large tobacco plantation with over one hundred of them. I can never tell anyone that, but I feel, based upon what you said earlier, that I'm able to speak freely with you. People hear only the bad stories of how someone is mistreating a negro with the whip, or some other unspeakable ways of punishing them that I for one have never heard of. First, it's ridiculous because how could we get any work done if we beat them all to smithereens? Second, they forget that if the African had not been brought here he would still be savage, living naked in a hut practicing his heathen ways. Here, he becomes Christianized, wearing clothes, speaking English and is taken care of by his owners. I rarely speak of this because it makes me so angry how these northern people speak of things that they know nothin' about." He sighed and waved for the waiter to bring them more whiskey.

"I'm sorry that I brought it up, Mr. Gilbert. It was not my intention to upset you."

"No, no, don't take it that way. I do have a need to talk about it with a likeminded person who understands how it really is. Something to keep in mind as well is that people who have never been in much contact with negroes do not understand that they ain't equal to us whites. The Negro race isn't capable to live freely. They are like children or women. It's very possible that they will one day be able to be free, but not now, not yet."

"Well, although I'm a lot younger than you, Mr. Gilbert, I tend to agree. Frankly, I think it is unfair of these abolitionists to put ideas into their poor heads. This could only make them unhappy with their station in life, which is sanctioned by the Bible and Christ the Lord himself for that matter." James swallowed another gulp of the warming whiskey and felt pleased with what he had said.

"That is just so," said Mr. Gilbert, "I have left my plantation almost completely in the hands of my servants. My wife prefers that term. Only the overseer and my wife are there to see to it. Not one of my servants has run away in my absence. Not a one, if I had been such a cruel, lash waving slaver wouldn't they have taken the chance and left after I did?"

"You'd think so," James said. He suddenly remembered how he still needed to talk to his father about Johnnie's problem. He must write to him immediately. He was silent for a bit as he thought about it. Mr. Gilbert looked thoughtful as well and for a rather long time they both sat there smoking and drinking in silence.

Then Mr. Gilbert interrupted and said, "Have you heard of Plymouth Church in Brooklyn?"

"Can't say I have, no."

Mr. Gilbert shook his head, visibly angry but strangely amused at the same time.

"You will be in for a treat. I will take you there one Sunday and you can watch for yourself the spectacle of these people as they listen to Henry Ward Beecher, Harriet Beecher Stowe's brother, no less. You *do* know who *she* is don't you?"

"No, sir cannot say I have heard of her either."

Mr. Gilbert's face reddened and he suddenly stood up and started to walk around the restaurant, waving his finger in front of him. He forgot all about speaking quietly.

"Oh, that awful Harriet, she...she... there ain't a day that goes by that I don't see some fellow or lady on the street with her blasted book in their hands. She has written a novel about a negro named Tom who is sold from the plantation where he lives. *All* the plantation owners are evil and beat and murder their servants in this awful book."

"Really, no, I have not heard of it. When did you read it?" James mumbled uncomfortably.

Mr. Gilbert shrugged angrily. "Oh, I have not read the cursed book, no need to, I know what it says...and it's giving those *abolitionists...*" he said, emphasizing the word abolitionists with a disgusted tone in his voice, "...fuel for thought. They don't understand that *we* are the ones who supply them with all their sugar, cotton and tobacco. Would they want to go down there and work in the hot sun by themselves?"

James stared at him and by now felt extremely embarrassed. Mr. Gilbert was far from discreet and he could tell that every single person in the restaurant was looking at them. He looked angry as he stood and held on to one of the chairs so hard his knuckles whitened.

Suddenly James heard chairs pulled out from a table somewhere behind him and he heard a man's loud voice say, "*We* certainly will *not* use sugar, cotton or tobacco for as long as slaves are forced to produce it."

James turned around and saw a nicely dressed man and woman angrily walk away from their table, their food untouched. The woman appeared as though she was crying and looked at them with horror in her eyes. The man turned to the waiter and said, "Our apologies, sir, but we cannot eat in the presence of people who *own* other people. We feel quite nauseous."

James sat still, not sure where to look as the couple hurried past their table.

Out of the corner of his eye he saw a man with checkered dark pants and a yellow shawl collared vest shake his head at the couple, "Well, those men are right. Who else would supply us with what we need up here?" the man said, as if to himself, and shrugged.

Mr. Gilbert took no notice and sat down looking deflated. "I've done it again. I have such a temper... with the whiskey...I...have quite made a fool of myself and an embarrassment, I do apologize, Mr. Waynewright."

James swallowed hard and nodded; he didn't know what he ought to say. He had never experienced anything like this before. He didn't even know what to think. To save himself, he quickly changed the subject. "What were you saying before about Plymouth Church?"

"Yes, yes, I'm sorry. I got a bit distracted there," Mr. Gilbert lowered his voice to a mere whisper and leaned closer to James, "Plymouth Church is in Brooklyn and the preacher, who is the brother of the author of this awful book, preaches every Sunday about the evils of slavery," he said in all seriousness but with a twinkle in his eye now.

"It is quite interesting to listen to them. The women cry and carry on. I've even seen some men cry. What you saw here today was nothin'."

"You have actually seen this?" James asked a little confused.

"Oh yes I have. In fact, I brought a friend of mine visiting from the South a while back. It has become quite the thing to do. My wife has been pestering me to take her, but I hesitate because I know it will upset her."

"Can't they tell where you're from? Is it really wise to..."

Mr. Gilbert who chuckled and interrupted James, "No, most of them will not notice. They are used to all kinds of people coming to hear their preacher. The church has thousands of people each Sunday."

"Thousands, surely you jest?"

Mr. Gilbert pulled out his pocket watch and shook his head when he noted the time, "Not at all, not at all, most of them of course abolitionist, but it also draws the curious and southerners such as myself who want to know what people say about us." Mr. Gilbert looked at his watch again, "I do apologize, Mr. Waynewright, but I must be going now."

Mr. Gilbert waved to the waiter and slowly rose from his chair, simultaneously pulling out a card from his vest pocket and handing it to James. "Here, please call on me anytime you'd like. It has been a pleasure to meet you. If you'd like to go to Plymouth on Sunday, just send a footman with your card, and I'll meet you there."

James took the card, thanked him for the meal, and then they both left. It felt a little abrupt, but both were deep in thought after what had happened.

James walked to the college and looked around a bit but his heart was not in it so he decided to go back to the hotel. He felt confused and out of place. The excitement of being in this large famous city suddenly felt like a trap. He had been very curious about the abolitionists but had not realized that there were so many and that they would embarrass people in public. He had felt exposed and attacked.

The way that woman had looked at him on the way out. As if he had been dirty. James came from a distinguished family and had never been treated with anything other than the utmost respect by everyone he had met.

As James walked into the hotel he took a deep breath trying not to think of what just happened. He ordered a pot of tea and asked for it to be delivered to his room. Waiting for it, he stood by the window looking out at the busy street below. He could see no less than four horse-drawn omnibuses going by at a steady pace. The street was full of people going in many directions as well. He noticed three gentlemen carrying a huge trunk, two on each end and the third one in the back, looking as if he was holding on to some sort of belt that was wrapped around it. It looked extremely heavy. Sweat was pouring off them, making their shirts darken and stick to their backs. They looked irritated and exhausted. *They should have had a negro or two to carry it for them*, James thought. He wondered if they would have if slavery was legal here, or if those men were for abolition as well. He pulled the curtain aside to let in some light and decided to sit down and write that letter to his father after all. If nothing else, the incident at the restaurant and his conversation with Mr. Gilbert led him to think about Johnnie.

The tea arrived and James sat down at the little mahogany desk that the hotel kindly provided when he had told them that he was to be a student at the College of Physicians and Surgeons and started writing.

Dear Father,

I have safely arrived in this enormous city. I can barely express how large it is, because no matter how I would try, you and mother still wouldn't be able to comprehend it. There is no end in sight in whichever direction you look, except if you look to the East or to the West, and then you sometimes see the river and what is on the other side, but not always. There are buildings, people, horses, omnibuses and hackneys everywhere. They talk funny, too. I made quite the fool of myself not understanding what the hackmen were asking of me.

To come straight to the point, I want to write to you about a sensitive matter.

It came to my attention that the field hands are very nervous being alone with Mr. Loch when you travel since I'm no longer there. I had meant to speak to you over the summer but I never found the appropriate time to do so. I know you think Mr. Loch is a good overseer, but I cannot help but feel that he is overly strict. Please consider this and the possibility of hiring someone else who will follow our principles.

How is mother? I hope she is in good health. Please give her my affection.

With affection, James

James decided not to go into any specifics but still wanted to tell his father how he felt about Mr. Loch. *It was so simple; I should have done this a long time ago*, he thought as he refilled his teacup. He sat back and sipped the warm liquid, feeling relieved.

Chapter 06

James began his studies. It was challenging in a much different way than his earlier studies and he quickly became engrossed. Most evenings he spent at his desk in the hotel room going over lessons and thick medical books. He had not expected that there would be *so* much to learn about the human body. He felt overwhelmed at times, but if he took the time to take notes and reread what he found difficult he was able to understand.

His experience in the restaurant had made him hesitant to speak of himself. Not knowing what his classmates would think, he told people that he was from Virginia and that his family lived on a small farm. No one questioned it.

The weeks passed quickly and although he remembered the invitation to go to Plymouth Church, he didn't seriously entertain the thought. He anticipated that he would be too exposed. Lord knew how thousands of crazy abolitionists would make him feel if just two of them made him feel uncomfortable for days.

Then one Saturday when the rain was beating down on the windows and he was lying on his bed with a book and a thick wool blanket to keep him warm in the damp air, there was a knock on the door and the hotel porter handed him a note that read:

Mr. Waynewright,

My wife and I wish to have the pleasure of your company as we visit Plymouth Church tomorrow. We will pick you up promptly at 9.00 tomorrow morning unless we hear contrary from you.

G

James remained standing by the door with the note in his hand. Mr. Gilbert had signed it G only. *He is a very unusual man*, James thought. He tried to remember when he had told Mr. Gilbert where he was staying, he obviously must have but he couldn't remember.

James was not sure what to do. He didn't even think he still had his card. He rummaged around in his pockets and in his drawers but couldn't find it. He remembered that he had used it as a bookmark at one point, but that he had swapped it for a real bookmark beautifully carved of thin wood. He must have put it somewhere when he replaced it, maybe it had fallen on the floor and then it had been swept out when they cleaned his room.

Having no way of contacting him without his address, there was nothing to do but to prepare himself to go with them.

The next morning he dressed in his suit and hat and went downstairs. Glancing at himself in the large mirror in the lobby, he felt that he looked proper enough. He had chosen a grey hat, not a stovepipe. This one was smaller and he felt that he looked more distinctive in it. He owned a stovepipe as well, but it felt odd on his head, and he had only used it once. With a deep breath, he took one last look at himself. His dark brown hair and pale skin contrasted well with the grey he thought. He lifted his hat and smoothed his hair a bit, brushed a hair off his shoulder and went outside.

He found Mr. Gilbert already standing by a parked hackney waiving enthusiastically. The door was open and he saw his wife's slim gloved hand waving as well.

James hurried towards them, hoping they wouldn't notice how nervous he was and focused on the details of Mrs. Gilbert's dress to still his mind a bit. The dress was beautiful, with salmon colored folds that billowed around her legs and on the seat. She had blonde hair that curled and bounced up and down as she laughed and waved.

"May I present my wife Mrs. Gilbert to you, Mr. Waynewright?"

"Certainly," James said and smiled, kissing her hand before he stepped inside.

"I'm very pleased to meet you," he said as Mrs. Gilbert's eyes danced with delight.

Mr. Gilbert sat down next to his wife and unbuttoned his jacket.

Mrs. Gilbert touched her husband's arm. "I cannot believe we are actually going to Brooklyn. It sounds dangerous, what with all these radical abolitionists."

My thought precisely, James thought but said, "When did you arrive, Mrs. Gilbert?"

"Last week. John's business partner and his sweet wife escorted me all the way here."

Mr. Gilbert nodded at his wife and said, "My name is John, as Briana just said. Do you mind if we use our given names, since you have seen me embarrass myself on the whiskey and all?"

"You did not!" Briana scolded looking horrified.

James laughed, feeling a little more comfortable, but not forgetting that they were on their way to see several thousand abolitionists at once. Every time he thought of it, he marveled at the fact that one single church could hold so many people. "My name is James, and I'm the one who made a fool out of myself. Did you tell Briana...Briana is a lovely name, by the way. John, did you tell her about Mr. Whester?"

Briana started to laugh and James noted the pretty dimples in her cheeks. "Indeed he did, indeed. I cannot blame you. I can't understand what people here are saying either. The first time I came here I didn't dare to speak to anyone because when I went to the shops I had no idea what they were talking about. I had my dear Nellie with me, and she couldn't understand anything either, though she tried mightily each time."

"Nellie is Briana's Aunty. She was given to her as a gift when she was only five years old, and she wouldn't marry me unless Nellie could come. She lives in a room right next to our bedroom. Briana cannot sleep well if she isn't available all hours of the night," John said and rolled his eyes, but he laughed and kissed Briana's hand.

"Not far now. We should be by the ferry soon, I think," he said and looked out the window.

Not long after, the hackney stopped.

Briana took his arm and squeezed it as James helped her out on to the cobblestones. Leaning close she whispered in his ear, "Don't be nervous, we will just have to pretend that we are from here. If we are quiet, they cannot tell that we are Southerners and will never suspect that we do not agree with their horrid political views." She smiled and without waiting for a reply, let go of his arm and went to John's waiting elbow.

They caught the Catherine Ferry at Catherine slip just a few minutes before departure. They were not able to get to a window or to the bow, but had to stand in the middle of the aft in a crowd of people. One man was carrying both a basket with live chickens and a large parcel packed to the limit with smelly fish.

Briana looked as though she was going to get sick and leaned against John as she held her handkerchief over her face. James wished he could do the same, but he didn't want to appear namby pamby and just fingered his handkerchief in his pocket wishing he could use it.

John looked at him and grinned, "City smells gettin' to you? You should see it during the week when the markets are open. We'll be arriving soon, and then we'll take an invigorating walk to the church."

James nodded, feeling embarrassed that he had been so obvious.

James took a good look at the church when they arrived. It didn't exactly look like a church as he had expected. It was a grand building, but he had thought it might have a tower or something of the sort. It did not, but it did have a stately, impressive look.

The street was full of people; it was as if all of New York had decided to come to Hicks Street that day. People didn't fit on the sidewalk but walked on the street, making it completely impossible for the hackmen to leave, or arrive for that matter. He could see a whole line of them further down the street and throngs of people getting off to walk the remainder of the way. It was complete mayhem, James had never seen so many people in one place at the same time.

John took his wife's arm and smiled encouragingly at James, "Come along now, we better get on line here."

James looked ahead and realized that they were in fact standing in some kind of queue on the sidewalk and it was filling up continuously as they stood there. He kept looking straight ahead feeling very uncomfortable. It seemed incredible that all these people were against everything that he and his family stood for. They all looked so *normal*. Still, they held these odd and ignorant views. *Who had taught them to think like that?* James wondered. Many of them seemed very excited. Some were talking animatedly with the other people standing in line, some were shouting to people across the street. He heard somebody tell someone else that he really hoped that Pastor Beecher would get going today and maybe even auction one away from the terrible, despicable South. James couldn't figure out what he meant by it. *Do they mean buying a slave? Aren't they against that?* He thought feeling confused. The queue moved along and sooner than he had expected they were inside the church. It was magnificent. The pews were half circles and there was no center aisle. An interesting look James thought.

James was walking a little ahead of John and Briana and was just about to sit down when he felt a hand on his shoulder, "Did you buy this seat, sir?" someone asked, and when he looked up he saw a tall, extremely thin man staring at him. "I...I'm..." He started but John interrupted and said in a flawless New York accent, "I apologize, my good sir. My friend Mr. Anderson here is not familiar with the customs of this church, do forgive him." John smiled and took the astonished James by the elbow and led him to a pew two rows further back.

"Why Mr. Anderson, and your accent," James whispered.

John replied with a conspiratorial wink, "Never give your real name in this company. You never know who people might know," he said. John looked around the church and then continued, whispering very close to James' ear so low that he could barely hear him, "They sell them, if can you believe it, they sell certain seats to members of the congregation and all the money goes to helping runaways or to actually buy them from us and then set them free."

James tried to keep his face neutral but it was hard when he heard such outrageous information.

He just could not understand it. He could not figure out how these people didn't understand that the planters' whole livelihood depended on their slaves and that they went against their own countrymen by doing things like that.

James felt like a traitor. He could see his parents disapproving looks as if they were right there in the church with him. He felt extremely uncomfortable and wanted to leave, but didn't know how he could do that without exposing both himself and the Gilberts, so he remained.

James had not realized how loud it had been inside the church until everyone became silent as Pastor Beecher strode in front of the assembled crowd and stopped at the podium. He looked confidently at the congregation and just stood there for a moment. He was rather handsome, a little heavy perhaps, but with calm eyes and hair that was so long it touched his shoulders. After starting with a benediction, he began preaching about Christ and the subject of love. As Pastor Beecher spoke, James found that he became more and more relaxed; enjoying what Beecher was saying so much that he almost forgot where he was.

The congregants were given a hymnal that curiously had both music and words on the same page. When the choir began, James again was surprised as the choirmaster sang one line and then the whole congregation repeated it. This was repeated line by line. James felt shivers running up and down his spine as the full church, probably close to 2000 people, sang. It sounded incredibly beautiful, and he felt his eyes moisten. He glanced around and saw several women with tears streaming down their faces as they sang.

James had never experienced anything like that and when the singing stopped, he sat stock still, completely mesmerized.

The Pastor smiled and appeared to look James straight in the eye, then he suddenly stomped his foot onto the floor and in a much louder voice than what he'd been using before he exclaimed, "It has come to my attention that there is a young couple here who is in need of your help. They have struggled for several weeks hiding in the woods, slowly but securely getting north to us, escaping their cruel master who sees fit to own other people."

James came to from his mesmerized trance and at once felt wide awake.

He felt John's hand touch his arm in warning and heard Briana gasp.

"The slave catchers and others who sympathize with the horrid fugitive slave act almost caught these good people yesterday when they went out to get themselves something to eat," Pastor Beecher said and gestured at someone with his hands.

To James' astonishment two mulattos walked in and planted themselves right next to the Pastor. This time John's hand grasped James' arm so hard it almost hurt. He got the message and remained silent even though he wanted to run out of the church and inform the authorities of these criminal activities happening right in front of his eyes.

The woman looked scared and tried to stand behind Beecher. Her man was of a slightly darker complexion than she was. She looked almost white, with long and silky light brown hair. James couldn't deny that she was incredibly beautiful.

"I want you all to give generously to this lovely couple and help them along their way to Canada," Beecher thundered on, simultaneously pointing to someone handing out collection baskets.

James felt his heart take a couple of extra leaps: *Do I have to give money to* ***THIS?*** He thought. *I will not do it, it's insane. They could have been my father's property. I should follow them and send them back to their owners.*

James discretely eyed the baskets as they made their way down the aisles. Most people gave something, some weeping openly as they did so. Even men were weeping just as John had told him they might. Some were reciting prayers quite loudly to themselves as they dropped coins into the baskets. There were some who gently shook their heads and didn't contribute and to James' relief it didn't cause a commotion. Maybe people assumed that they were not financially able to help, he thought, and felt a little more relaxed.

By the time the basket reached their row, it was full to the brim and there was even jewelry in it. Every single person in their row gave something. James looked at Briana and John as the basket slowly approached them. Briana's eyes were full of tears and John's eyes looked hard. He gently shook his head and the basket was passed along to someone in the row in front of them without passing in front of James.

He exhaled inaudibly with relief.

James was so full of conflicting emotions that he didn't notice what happened to the runaways on stage. Suddenly everyone stood up and started to file out of the church. James followed numbly, feeling dazed.

People took their time. They were talking with each other as they stood in the aisles waiting for the crowds to clear, just as they had on the way in. There was a cacophony of voices everywhere. "Oh those dear, dear people imagine having to hide in the woods among snakes and bears," he heard one woman say as another agreed and added, "Not only was it dangerous but it must have been so cold and dark. It's a disgrace that people treat their fellow humans like this."

Treat someone like that; no one forced them to be out in the woods. If they had stayed where they belonged, they would have been safe and warm, James thought to himself. Just then a young man pushed past him as he sobbed uncontrollably into his own elbow. That broke the spell and suddenly James laughed aloud. John grinned at him and took his arm in his and finally they got out into the sunshine.

"James, let's find a place to eat, we can take the ferry later. Let's walk for a while. There is a tavern about ten minutes from here. Some fresh air would do us good don't you agree, dear Mrs.?" he said and briefly touched his wife's cheek.

They remained silent until they were sitting down at a table in a small but very cozy restaurant on a street corner that was open even though it was Sunday. It was a simple place. There were no tablecloths on the tables. The chairs were made of dark wood that had never seen a paintbrush. Each table had its own little lantern that made it feel warm and welcoming. A young waiter brought them coffee, rolls still warm from the oven and a small pot of butter. The pot had a piece chipped off of its rounded edge.

Briana spoke first, her hand shaking when she put her cup down on the saucer as if she was cold. "I don't know what to say, I really don't, but John we must never, ever go to that horrid place ever again. To sit and watch when they openly hide and aid the property of other people..."

"Their own countrymen, too," James interrupted.

"Yes, you are right. They are traitors to their own race, it's terrible. Not only that, they do not seem to understand how helpless these creatures are. You could clearly see how scared and timid they were up there at the podium. Can't they see that negroes ain't able to live on their own? Encouraging runaways in this way will only hurt them, not help them." Briana's eyes brimmed with tears but she continued, disregarding the handkerchief that John held out for her. "Imagine my Nellie lured away like this and being put on display in front of thousands of people."

Well, it must be better than the auction block... James felt his neck getting hot. He cleared his throat and tried to focus on the bun he was chewing. He couldn't explain where the thought came from. His family had never sold a slave on the auction block, but they *had* bought them. Suddenly he remembered the slave markets they had been to. He remembered seeing the slaves standing there as they were being poked and prodded and remembered how they bought a woman who screamed and cried as she was separated from her man and young son that Father could not buy. James suddenly felt cold and stopped chewing as the memory flooded his consciousness. He had not thought of this in years. How could his father have left her family behind? She had died after a couple of years. He recalled that now. They found her outside in the dead of winter, frozen to death.

"James, are you alright?" He looked up and realized that both Briana and John were staring at him. "You look pale," Briana said and touched his hand.

James nodded and tried to smile, "I apologize. I was reminded of how we found one of our negroes frozen to death on our property."

"Oh, James, how dreadful! That is exactly what I was trying to say. It's not safe for them. They are so vulnerable when it comes to certain things. It proves my point precisely."

"Indeed." *No, it does not. What is happening with me?*

Chapter 07

James' mind was full of conflicting emotions. The beautiful singing haunted him, as did the look of the mulatto woman's face as she hid behind the preacher. The sudden memory of the slave his father had bought kept surfacing. He pushed it to the very back of his mind and focused on his schoolwork.

James needed to find his own place to live instead of racking up enormous hotel bills. He had been looking at a couple of apartments and he was thinking of taking one on West 4th. It was smaller, with just a sitting room, a bedroom and a kitchen. The kitchen had a wood burning stove and running cold water. James did not see the point to having a large place just for himself. He had been to some of his classmates' apartments or friends of theirs, and he had realized that he was a lot better off than they were. James had never thought of himself or his family as wealthy. In fact, his friends back home had much larger plantations with hundreds of negroes, huge parks, and enormous mansions. His family's plantation was small by comparison.

One of his newfound friends, Robert Andreason, rented just one tiny room in the basement of a smaller house on 15th street. James didn't want to stand out as the spoiled southerner, so in the end he accepted the offer on West 4th.

Robert helped him move in, not that he needed much. All he had was his trunk and a big satchel for his books. The apartment looked enormous with his few belongings on the floor.

James laughed and looked at Robert. "I ought not to laugh, I ought to cry. I don't even have a bed! Where am I going to sleep? What about coffee or tea? I don't even know how to cook it."

"Oh God help you, you *do* know that you brew coffee and tea, you do *not* cook it. How have you survived this long? Did your Mother do all of that for you?"

"My mother doesn't do anything, our cook and our servants take care of it."

"You don't say?" Robert said. He looked slightly perplexed, but did not comment.

"A bed, a..." James hesitated, "something to *brew* coffee, bedclothes, a pillow...what else?" James pulled on his moustache and looked around the room.

"We should get you a Napier first, and then we will look for a bed."

"A Napier?"

"A Napier is a vacuum machine to brew coffee. I'll show you," Robert said.

"Really, never heard of it, thanks."

By dinner time they were back with bottles of wine, cheese, bread and steaks, a large wooden box containing the Napier, another with a coffee service, a pot, a frying pan, a couple of knives and four plates with matching bowls and a small set of silverware.

They carried it between them, James with the wine bottles in the pockets of his coat and balancing the food on top of the stacked boxes.

"That wasn't easy," Robert sighed and put the boxes down on the floor in the kitchen, "but well worth it. I wouldn't want to go out again."

"Only we have no wineglasses or an opener. Can you drink wine out of coffee cups?"

"Not a problem. Use a knife to push the cork into the bottle, that usually works," Robert said and sat himself on the floor, "hope we won't be too drunk when they deliver the bed."

James laughed and sat down on the floor and began to push the cork in. It was hard, but it slowly went down to finally pop with a dull sound into the bottle. "We will see for sure. I really need some wine. Drunk or not the deliverymen will have to deal with us. Here, have a cup."

Robert grinned, but then sat quietly and looked at him for a long time. He appeared thoughtful and slowly sipped his wine before he spoke.

"James, I will have to ask you, I have not found the appropriate time to do so before, but I'm immensely curious about a particular subject."

James felt his heartbeat quicken knowing what was to come. He tried to think of something that would be plausible, but the question came too soon.

"Since you live in the South, have you ever come in contact with slaves? Perhaps you even know of people who own them. What is your opinion on this matter? Have you ever seen anyone who has been whipped? Oh, and how accurate is *Uncle Tom's Cabin*?"

"Many questions at once, that," James said, again trying to find breathing room so he could think of what to say.

"I apologize; let me rephrase, what about the first question then?" Robert took another sip and pulled himself back so that he could lean on the wall under the window. "I'm just curious about this. I mean no offense to you being a southerner, but I assume that you may meet both folk who are slave owners and the wretched slaves themselves."

James sighed, feeling insecure. He had two choices; he could tell Robert the truth and use this as an opportunity to explain that the abolitionists were spreading false propaganda. On the other hand, he could go with the convenient half lie that he had told at their college and say that they lived on a small farm. Assuming that Robert hadn't figured out that a small farmer most likely would not be able to afford to send his son for studies in New York, let alone set him up in an apartment.

James hesitated, thinking of the visit to Plymouth church and the horrified customers in the restaurant that day when he first arrived. His thoughts also went to his family and friends back home that loved their Aunties and Uncles and took care of them when they were sick. When they were too old to keep working, they let them live out their lives on their plantation, like Uncle Jerome who passed on just last year. He was around ninety, though they were not sure of his age. He couldn't let this pass by and not explain to Robert how it really was.

He took a deep breath and took one steady look at Robert and decided to risk it for the sake of his family, "Robert, to tell you the truth, the South isn't as they say. A lot of people here in New York have heard too much gossip and propaganda from the abolitionists. My own family owns servants," James said, carefully choosing the word servant and pausing to take a sip of wine before he continued, "I can tell you right off that we ain't monsters who whip our people, but take care of them and treat them like family."

Robert's eyes widened. He didn't say anything for several minutes. For a while, it seemed to James as if Robert was about to get up and leave.

James didn't know what to say either so he clumsily got up off the floor and went into the kitchen to get the cheeses and the bread. He stopped for a second, leaning on the wooden counter to catch his breath, wondering what he had done. It was too late now and there was nothing else to do but to go sit on the floor next to his friend and hope for the best. Just then, there was a knock on the door.

"Must be your bed now," Robert said looking more than relieved that the awkward moment had passed. James swallowed hard as he opened the door for a muscular man who immediately turned his head and whistled down the stairs. They heard a clamoring further down as they brought the bed up.

Two men appeared carrying the bed frame. One of them had a large parcel on his back containing the new linens, pillows and blanket. Then lastly, two very young men who looked entirely too young to be able to carry the heavy mattress but somehow did, came up the stairs. One of them grinned happily as if it was all for fun.

James handed a couple of small coins to the heavyset man, and the men disappeared one by one out the door.

The awkwardness still hung in the air. James noticed that Robert had taken the chance to finish his first cup of wine and was pouring a second one, whereas James had only had a sip of his. For some reason this angered him and he sat down and said, "So I assume you are never going to have wine with me again, so we might as well make the most of it, don't you think?" James took a deep sip of the wine and stared at Robert.

"Why would you say that?" Robert looked taken aback. "I have not been to your parts of the country. I'm genuinely interested in talking about this. I didn't say whether or not I'm for slavery or against it, and I do beg your pardon if I have made you uncomfortable as it was never my intention."

James felt his face flush and he quickly took another sip of his wine hoping it would calm him.

"Hmm, well, I... there is much to be discussed about this and I don't mind talking about it, it's just that I have had a couple of experiences with people who have been so incredibly misinformed about us that I get a bit defensive. If you are really interested to hear a planter's side of things, I'd be happy to talk about it."

Robert leaned over to refill James' cup that by now was almost empty.

"I am interested. Please tell me what misunderstanding is circulating."

"Well, as I said, for one thing we do not whip our people." *Except for Mr. Loch, but I needn't tell Robert about him.* "Most people I have encountered here in the North are very compassionate people and tend to be well meaning, and I do admire that. What they don't realize though is that the African race isn't as capable as the white race. If we hadn't brought them here, they would still be living naked in huts like savages. We teach them the Bible, clothe and feed them their whole life. It's not just a one-way bargain. They get a lot out of it, too. They wouldn't be able to live on their own in the long run. It would be cruel to set them free."

Robert sat silently for a while before he answered,"I can understand your sentiment, but are you absolutely sure that they do not have the same capabilities as us? How do you really know that?"

"Well for one, when they were brought here from Africa they did not live in cities filled with libraries and universities such as these. They lived as animals more or less. Our servants are very warm, strong, loving and kind. They are extremely well suited for farm work, for they handle the sun and heat very well, but truly if you would ever meet them you would see that they wouldn't be able to do all these things that we whites do. They just cannot. We do not expect women to walk around town unattended, or expect them to be mathematicians, lawyers or doctors. Nobody questions this. It's the same with the negroes. If they ain't capable, it's our *responsibility* to take care of them, school them in the message of the Bible and so on, just as we do with our women. Truly, the abolitionists do not know what they are doing. It would be a catastrophe to suddenly free everyone and let them fend for themselves. I know they think that they are helping, and possibly, we should have left them alone in Africa, but by now it's too late you know. Now we have to do the best we can with what our ancestors did, whether it was good or not."

Robert nodded slowly. "I do see your sentiment, though I must say that I see our responsibility as something that ought to be different. I believe quite strongly that we *do* have a responsibility to take care of them, but I think we ought to educate and teach them trades so that they *can* live on their own. Besides you mentioned women, Dr. Blackwell is a woman, Dr. *Elisabeth* Blackwell."

James touched his chin, moved his fingers across his stubble as he slowly shook his head and ignored Roberts comment about the lady doctor.

"I understand what you are saying, but the question is if they are able to handle everything that it entails for them to live freely, it's not just learning a trade. Living in the world on their own and making business decisions requires certain mathematical skills, reading a good newspaper requires a certain level of education and understanding. A person has to know what is happening around them to be able to live safely. I truly do not believe that their brain is able to comprehend all of this."

"Are you really sure though, James? Have you taught any of your, as you call them, *servants,* to read and write? Maybe it's a myth. They may very well be as smart as we are...women, too."

James laughed, "May I quote Dr. Samuel Morris Morton to you? I assume you *have* heard of him? If not, let me tell you that he was a brilliant scholar educated at the university in Edinburgh and he did research on brain size. He *proved* that the Negro is the least intelligent of all the four races. In fact, he lists Europeans as the smartest," James held back a smile at his own comment and said, "then in successive order, Orientals, Indians and then the Negro. It's proven. My father has scholarly work in his library from scientists inspired by this man. It aggravates me that these abolitionists do not have all the facts. It really does, I can't help it."

James finished his second cup of wine and poured yet another. He could feel the alcohol making its way through his body. He hadn't eaten anything since breakfast. He felt elated and proud of himself, suddenly glad that he had accepted the challenge and defended his family.

"Here, Robert, please. We should eat I'm feeling inebriated. Have some bread. We should go cook the steaks, too." He pulled off a large chunk of the bread for himself and handed the rest to Robert. He cut up the cheese in thick slices and stuffed his mouth with both bread and cheese, almost choking on it. He put the bread down, trying to chew a little slower, watching Robert as he broke off smaller pieces from the cheese slices arranging them in a little circle on his plate. Ignoring the suggestion about the steaks Robert said, "I'm aware of neither the study you are referring to, nor a study that would dispute this, but it seems to me that even if they are less intelligent, how does it justify owning them, selling them and letting them work without pay? I simply don't see the connection."

James didn't know what to say at first. For a second he felt defeated and confused, but then he found himself. "I can understand how you can ask that, but here I think that the Southern and Northern sensibilities switch places in a sense. By saying that we shouldn't own them, we conveniently remove our own responsibility towards them in lieu of compassion."

Robert shook his head, "No, James, we're not. I see it differently. I think that planters are hiding the sin of slavery behind the notion that the Negro isn't able. I'm not sure I believe it, no matter what... what was his name? Dr. Mott?"

"Doctor Morton."

James fell silent. For some reason he couldn't find a convincing way of explaining it to him. He had never had to do this before, never had to defend the very livelihood of his family to anyone. His way of life had never been challenged nor had it ever been something he felt the need to defend. Finally he shrugged and said, "We may have to agree to disagree here, Robert."

Robert stared at him for a moment before he answered, “Sure, it’s late anyway. I should get going and you should see how that new bed of yours feels.” Robert used the windowsill to pull himself up from the floor. They shook hands and Robert seemed friendly enough, smiling as he left. Still, James got a sour taste in his mouth. He sat down on the floor again and poured the last drops of wine into his cup; what remained covered the bottom of it. His thoughts went back over their conversation and although he felt that he had done the right thing and had debated well, there was a small nagging feeling somewhere in the back of his mind that it might be possible that Robert was not wrong.

Chapter 08

Time marched on, and soon James had finished his first year.

One day he went for an excursion uptown to the forest to see for himself the area that everyone was talking about. There was talk that it would be turned into a public forest, some called it park, but forest sounded much more accurate to James' ears since it was an enormous tract of land, very swampy he had heard, which was why no one would build there. It was to be a place where one could take carriage rides, get fresh air and an alternative for the poor so that they would do something other than drinking in the saloons on their free time. Seneca Village was there for the negroes and the Irish lived there too someplace. They would have to move out and find another place to live according to the park enthusiasts. James took his very first omnibus ride and settled himself right in front. There was a row of seats on each side facing each other. Two horses were effortlessly pulling the bus, their rumps were bouncing with every step, as if they were happy to move along. The air was fresh and clear and he could see all the way up the street. Several new buildings were being built. He saw men on ladders high above the ground and he heard them whistle and shout to each other as they hoisted buckets up and down.

As he got further north, more and more farmland appeared. He could smell the manure in the air and if he looked east and slightly north he could see cows and sheep grazing in the distance.

He must have sighed loudly because a gentleman with a black stovepipe in the row in front of him gestured with his walking stick and said, "Reminds you of home does it?"

James smiled at his comment even before he turned towards him, noting that a beautiful young lady in an equally beautiful blue walking dress accompanied him. She looked at him without a hint of shyness.

"It does indeed. My family has a small farm in Virginia," he said going with the standard half lie to be safe.

"Oh, then it's good to be heading out of the worst of it."

"Yes. I'm headed up to that central area in the woods that they are talking so much about, where they say there will be a park. I'm curious to see it."

"We are going there ourselves. We would be delighted to accompany you. I wouldn't venture too deep in the woods, though. Many negroes live there and there may be runaways as well. It may not be too safe."

The young woman looked a little uncomfortable and glanced out the window silently, but then she looked up and said, "They have their homes there, several churches and their own council. It's not right to displace them if this park is really to be as they say."

James swallowed discreetly. He was glad that he hadn't given anything away but had gone with his official line of living on a small farm.

The gentleman almost shoved his hand in her face as he waved his left arm about in irritation. "Well, well Chrissy, I'm sure that they'll find somewhere to go, you shouldn't concern yourself so much with these things. You'll overtire yourself, dear."

"Yes, Papa," she said obediently, but she looked down into her lap and angrily pulled at her gloves as if she was going to take them off.

"My daughter here has a lot of modern ideas, but at least she is not as..."

Chrissy looked at him angrily, grabbed his arm and stood up in the middle of the moving bus. "Papa, no need to talk of it; we should get off here!"

Her father looked startled and peered out the window but then agreed with a look of relief.

"You are right darling, and here we are." Turning to James he said, "Do you see the pines and those thick oaks? There it is." He walked past James and followed his daughter.

The driver gave James an irritated look and waved his right arm, pointing to the door.

"Get out, get out, we must move along!" he yelled and James hurried off the omnibus. Below stood the gentleman with his hand outstretched all ready to introduce himself.

"I beg your pardon, sir. I have introduced neither my daughter nor myself. My name is Mr. Greenfield and this is my youngest daughter."

"Mr. Greenfield. Good to make your acquaintance, sir," James said and took a deep breath of the lovely fresh air and bowed slightly as he kissed her hand.

"Miss Greenfield, I am delighted. I am Mr. Waynewright." He hesitated before he continued, "Are you certain that it is ok if I accompany you? I do not wish to intrude."

"Nonsense, don't you say Chrissy? Mr. Waynewright is more than welcome, don't you say?" he repeated.

Miss Greenfield smiled at James and he noticed that she was a lot younger than he had first thought. She was very beautiful but couldn't be much more than fifteen years old. She had straight blonde hair that looked very smooth flowing from her blue hat. Her eyes were light brown, possibly hazel, but he couldn't tell and didn't want to be rude and stare at her long enough to discern. Instead, he finally took a good look at the area that Mr. Greenfield had pointed to.

It looked beautiful from where he stood, lush and green, rather impenetrable, and he wondered if it had been wise to come here on foot. Perhaps he should have rented a horse.

He shielded his eyes from the sun with his hand and tried to see a little more clearly. It looked as though there was some kind of path to the left.

Mr. Greenfield and his daughter were already walking ahead arm in arm and they looked completely at ease in spite of the tension they had displayed on the bus.

As they came closer, he found that it was a small dirt road and not a path, which made him feel a little more comfortable as it appeared that he at least wasn't walking right into the wilderness. They walked under a canopy of thick trees and cooling shade. It was truly a beautiful place. The air smelled moist and there was a scent he couldn't quite place.

"Do you smell that, Miss. Greenfield? It's a...I can't really say, a sweet, but at the same time tangy, smell?"

She began to sniff the air, her nostrils forming lovely arches as she took in the scent. James wished she was just a little older, she was so pretty and he suddenly felt lonely and wished for some female company. Not that he had ever had it, but at least he had the sisters of friends back at home to flirt with.

"I think it's a flower, or maybe wild raspberries?"

"Rather a flower I would think, Miss Greenfield. Raspberries would be too early in the season. They are common towards the end of the summer," James said politely.

"Oh, you are so knowledgeable. You're from a farm you said?"

"Yes and I have had plenty of raspberries from our own bushes, my...um, we had them made into jam, and it's quite marvelous on toast."

He remembered Auntie Ellen having to call on the female field hands to come help her with picking from the bushes behind the kitchen. He remembered them singing and laughing out there and Auntie Ellen always saving a mug full of raspberries for him to eat fresh. One time he and his friend Peter had been out riding and he had just handed the horses off to Pap when Auntie Ellen came running down the path with his mug. He had been thirsty from the ride and they tasted so sweet but tart at the same time. His mouth watered at the thought.

Auntie Ellen had laughed at him and gone in for a glass of water. *Are they unhappy there with us? Don't we take good care of them?* He wondered.

"We would have loved to taste your raspberries, Mr. Waynewright!" Mr. Greenfield exclaimed. "Now, let us walk around a little more before we head back."

James laughed and nodded, letting go of his mixed emotions.

They followed the dirt road for quite a bit and then walked around in a little glen with a small stream. They could hear someone chopping wood somewhere nearby and James wondered if it was in the negro village or if someone was clearing brush for the park already.

Mr. Greenfield seemed very content and had been walking silently for a while. James felt his eyes on him as he spoke with Ms. Greenfield, then as they approached the edge of the park Mr. Greenfield gently touched James shoulder and said, "It has been a real pleasure meeting you Mr. Waynewright. My wife and I would be delighted if you would join us for dinner tonight."

"Thank you sir, but I couldn't possibly intrude any more than I have. I've already occupied half of your afternoon." James said, not sure what to do about such generosity from someone he barely knew.

"Nonsense the pleasure is ours. I *insist* that you come home with us and have supper, even though we don't have raspberries." Mr. Greenfield laughed at his own joke and winked at his daughter.

"Oh, thank you, but I wouldn't..." James began but Mr. Greenfield interrupted him with a chuckle,

"Didn't I just say I insist? You simply *must* meet my wife and older daughter."

Later, as they arrived at the home of Mr. Greenfield, a heavyset white woman came and took their coats, breathing hard as she walked down the hall. James wondered if people in the North only hired white servants or if they ever paid negroes to do it. He assumed some did; if they were going to fend for themselves somebody would have to give them money.

Mr. Greenfield pointed to a couch in a corner. "Please have a seat, Mr. Waynewright. Can I get you a drink? A glass of wine perhaps? Scotch?"

"Scotch would be lovely and glass of water on the side if you do not mind, sir."

"Of course." He sat down next to James, picked up a little bell on the coffee table, and rang it. Soon the heavyset woman appeared and curtsied just at the outside of the door.

"Mrs. McNeary, Scotch for both of us and two tall glasses of water."

"Right away, sir," she said with the Irish lilt that James had begun to become familiar with; she curtsied again and left.

James looked on with surprise. Mr. Greenfield seemed brusque. At home they always said please and thank you to set a good example.

Mr. Greenfield cleared his throat and said, "So how does New York treat you. Even though you miss home, how do you find us northerners?"

"I have grown to like it. I like the closeness to restaurants and shops and meeting different people. I have to admit that I had never been to a restaurant until I came here. On the farm, we eat off the land and never have I had occasion to eat in town." *Actually Auntie Ellen and Mary give us a lot better service everyday than what I have ever had at a restaurant here. I wonder what he would say if I told him that?*

James felt as if he were living a double life. He had tried to drop at least some of his southern accent and he felt that he was becoming more and more a part of the large city. He never felt comfortable talking about his views on slavery or how he lived back at home. After the conversation with Robert all those months ago, he didn't want to get caught in the trap of having to explain himself again. Although he and Robert still talked, it felt as if that conversation and that knowledge would always lie between them like a festering sore spot. James had heard that some New Yorkers had similar views to his own. Once he happened to sit on a bench on campus right next to three men having a heated discussion about it, but he didn't dare to join in. He had eavesdropped instead, pretending to be deeply engaged in his book. Another time someone handed him flyers with abolitionist propaganda on the street and it seemed that the majority would disapprove if they knew where he came from.

"You don't say, Mr. Waynewright. Think of the things we take for granted here. I hope a home cooked meal will suit you fine tonight."

"I'm sure I will. I can feel an appetite coming on from our adventure."

Mr. Greenfield was about to answer, but they heard women's shoes and the swish of a dress across the floor and they both looked up.

James got up ready to greet either Mrs. Greenfield or Miss Greenfield, but whom he saw caused him to draw an involuntary breath. A woman with similar blue eyes and nose but with darker, curlier hair instead of straight appeared. She too seemed very direct at first impression. She walked straight toward him and without waiting for an introduction, she held out her hand for him to kiss. "You must be the guest who can grow raspberries that Chrissy has spoken of since she returned," she looked him straight in the eye and smiled. She had a strong gaze, as if she was looking into his soul to see who he was. James felt nervous and very affected by her as soon as he saw her. She wasn't gorgeous; some may have even called her plain in spite of the striking contrast of dark hair and blue eyes, but there was something to her directness and gaze that made James feel like he wanted to kiss her.

"That would be me! I'm pleased to meet you, Miss Greenfield?"

She laughed, "Yes, Miss Greenfield the older one, yes indeed. Please come into the dining room. Mrs. McNeary just called for dinner."

"Thank y—" James started but was distracted by the younger Miss Greenfield as she less than gracefully hurried by and waved at them with another woman behind her, Mrs. Greenfield he assumed.

The older woman looked elegant and poised. Her hair was dark like her older daughter, but smooth and straight, and her eyes were dark brown. She walked into the parlor looking expectantly at her husband who introduced James. Mrs. Greenfield smiled pleasantly but had a calm air without the intensity of her daughters about her.

Feeling a little more relaxed after his scotch and having quenched his thirst with water, James was able to take in the surroundings. He noted beautiful glass doors with inlayed gold squares that were left open wide for them to enter the dining room. A large table was set with a white tablecloth and crystal glasses that shimmered in the candlelight from the large candelabra. An enticing smell filled the room when Mrs. McNeary appeared with a tray containing a steaming bowl of something that looked like a stew.

James sat down and Mrs. McNeary gave him a napkin for his lap. He was surprised that they didn't have a cook or younger woman to serve them. Mrs. McNeary seemed to do everything.

The older Miss Greenfield sat down opposite him. "Miss Greenfield, I'm delighted to have you across from me so that I may get to know you," James said.

"I as well, Mr. Waynewright, I..." Just then, the sound of a door clapper echoed through the house and she immediately stood up. "Oh, they did come after all! McNeary, please get the door and then set the table for two more." She swiftly walked after her, touching her father's shoulder on the way out.

James heard excited exclamations from the other room and then he heard a woman say, "Katherine, thank you so much for inviting us to supper yet again. We are always so happy to converse with you and Chrissy."

He heard the sound of a man's deep voice, "We brought a cake to go with the coffee, she baked it."

"Oh, Mrs. McCune, you are too kind." James heard skirts and footsteps moving across the floor as the voices came closer. "Do come in, we have a guest here. Papa invited him. They met on the omnibus on the way to see the woods that will become a park all the way north."

"We have heard about it," James heard the woman reply, a little subdued, and then they appeared.

Luckily, James didn't have anything in his mouth at that time because he would have choked.

"Mr. Waynewright, may I introduce you to Doctor and Mrs. McCune Smith."

James having already began to stand up to prepare himself for the introduction almost sat down again. It made the chair wobble and it fell behind him with a loud bang.

"Oh dear," Chrissy exclaimed, "first time you have ever met a Negro doctor, Mr. Waynewright?" she teased, not bothering to hide the obvious.

"Well I *am* the first one, so I can understand your confusion," Dr. McCune Smith said looking straight at James as he walked around the table and reached for James' hand. He shook it with complete confidence. "Pleased to make your acquaintance, Mr. Waynewright, this is my wife as Katherine already mentioned," he said and gently touched her arm.

She held out her hand expecting James to kiss it and James had no choice but to take it and do so.

James tried to smile, mumbled an apology, bent down to pick up the chair, and sat down. Mrs. Greenfield kissed the woman on the cheek and Mr. Greenfield heartily patted the man on the back. James felt confused. On the bus, he had had the impression that Mr. Greenfield disliked his youngest daughter's concern for the negroes up there in the woods. *Might it have been a joke, sarcasm perhaps? How can he be a doctor? That certainly cannot be possible. How could he have studied medicine, all those years of schooling?* James sat silent with the thoughts spinning around his head. His mouth was dry and he saw his own hand shake as he began to reach for his wineglass before he stopped himself, remembering that no one had lifted the first glass yet.

Then to make matters worse, the negro doctor sat down right next to him and said, "So Katherine was telling me that you were up in the wooded area. It's beautiful isn't it? I've been there several times myself, treating patients in Seneca when I'm not at my own practice here in the city."

This is too much. He has a practice in the city, he calls a white person by her given name, and ***she*** *calls them Dr. and Mrs. McCune Smith...it's perverse. I don't know what to say. How can this be?*

James cleared his throat, "Yes, it was very beautiful indeed," after that, he couldn't get another word across his lips. The doctor's wife looked at him as if she knew exactly what he was thinking. She touched his arm and said, "James was educated in Glasgow, first Negro American to study regularly to be a doctor just as a white man," she beamed and looked expectantly at him.

His name is James! That too of all things, my father will laugh when I tell him.

"You don't say?" James said. He could hear his voice quiver but hoped that they couldn't hear it. "I just finished my first year of studying medicine myself."

"I don't envy you, Mr. Waynewright. It is overwhelming in the beginning, but you will make it," Dr. McCune Smith said.

Well, obviously, if you did it, the rest of it must be easy, James thought, but felt odd and confused.

James remained silent and Dr. McCune Smith turned to join in the conversation with Miss. Greenfield. James felt relieved to be left alone for a few minutes so that he could collect himself.

Somehow, as the evening continued he was able to relax more and more. By the time the cake and coffee were served, he was even having a relaxed conversation with the doctor.

"What you have to remember when you see patients is to be calm and explain tings thoroughly. Many are nervous and if they don't listen well they might not take the medicine you prescribed properly. I had a patient in the early years of my practice that came back after a month very, very ill. She was an older woman, used to more superstitious ways of healing,"Dr. McCune paused and shook his head before he continued, "I had told her to put the medicine in some water before she ingested it. Well she didn't hear the last part, took the whole vial and dumped it in the river, said a spell too she said, cause it wouldn't hurt to use both the old ways and the new."

James stared at him, “Who would have anticipated that?”

“Indeed, since that day, I have learned to ask each patient to repeat and describe what I said, so no such misunderstandings happen again.” He chuckled,“It ended well, she took the new medicine and she became well… and I, I learned a valuable lesson. It is of course usually not this extreme of a misunderstanding; it may be as simple as with what frequency they should take their medicine. Just make sure that the patient really hears you and understands what you mean. ”

“Thank you,” James said, realizing that he enjoyed the company. After the initial shock, it no longer felt odd to speak to him as an equal.

A couple of hours later, James left with the older Miss Greenfield’s calling card in his pocket as well as that of Mr. Greenfield and Dr. McCune Smith.

He felt conflicted and decided to walk home. It was not very far, only a couple of blocks. As he passed a saloon he decided that after an evening like that he needed another drink to calm himself. He walked in and ordered a double scotch.

The next morning he would barely remember how he got home.

Chapter 09

The next couple of weeks were strange for James; it was as if the city had changed somehow. He seemed to see negroes at every corner, heard them talking everywhere. One time he stood in line at a hardware store to buy a pair of pliers to fix a hinge on a kitchen cabinet. Two were standing right outside the hardware store having a heated discussion regarding an article in the New York Daily Times about the horrible Yellow Fever that had swept through Virginia last year that he had read himself that very morning. It was not close to Woodbank, but it was still something he kept close attention to. People in line seemed annoyed and several people made snide remarks about 'those loud negroes', why didn't they all get on that boat to Liberia." None seemed particularly concerned about the fever, just that the negroes were loud.

James stood silently listening to what they were arguing about. He had never met a negro who could read before he met Dr. McCune Smith. In fact, Johnnie had said himself on numerous occasions that though he wished he could read the Bible he knew that it would be too hard for him to learn. "I'm just a negro, it ain't suited for me," he used to say.

The weeks went by and soon it was July and James had not gone back to Virginia all year. He kept finding excuses to stay and reasons not to go. It was too hot; he wanted to go to the beach with his classmates. He couldn't voice the real reason even to himself. The fact was that he couldn't go home and look their servants in the face and have Auntie Ellen dote on him and feed him his favorite food after he had sat down at dinner with a negro doctor who had been studying in Glasgow.

In August he arrived at a garden party at Gramercy. To his surprise, he saw Miss Greenfield as soon as he came out into the shady garden after walking through the house and past the busy kitchen adjacent to the garden. She stood by herself under the shade of an apple tree with a glass of champagne in her hand. Her hair was bound loosely under a wide summer hat and several strands escaped down her back. She was wearing a beautiful dark green dress as if she wanted to match the lush green of the garden.

Without thinking, James walked straight to her, took her hand, and kissed it.

"Good day, Miss Greenfield. What a wonderful surprise to see you again. I never got the chance to thank your Father for inviting me to supper. Will you please extend my regards to him?"

"Oh, Mr. Waynewright I do remember you," she said and smiled so warmly that James felt something grow soft within him and he grinned back at her helplessly.

For a moment they were both silent and he watched her carefully sip from her glass. She looked amused but didn't say anything.

Finally, James asked her if she too knew Mr. Rickman who had invited him to the party.

"No, I'm a good friend of his sister. I cannot say that I have much in common with Mr. Rickman," she lowered her voice, "he is rather conservative and we are not always on the same foot when it comes to abolition. His sister insisted that I come, so how could I say no?" She exhaled as she motioned towards a server who walked around with a tray with glasses of bubbling champagne. "Would you care to have a glass with me?"

James gratefully took a glass off the tray and lifted it towards her, but wished he could find an excuse to leave her. He felt awkward after her comment and expected her to pester him with questions about the south, just as Robert had done, but instead she began asking him questions about New York and his impressions of it and its people.

“I’m always curious to hear what people think of us. Having grown up here I have nothing to compare it to, other than the Catskills which I assume is full of New Yorkers.”

“The Catskills, what is that?”

She laughed and gently touched his arm, “Oh you haven’t heard of it? I will have to insist that you come with us next Sunday then, even if it’s unladylike of me to ask a man myself.” She stopped talking and laughed, taking another sip of her champagne. “The Catskills is a mountain range north of here. We are leaving on Sunday morning and we’ll be staying for the rest of the summer.”

James laughed, “Don’t worry, Miss Greenfield. I don’t find you unladylike at all. The Catskills sounds beautiful.” *I’m sure she only meant that it in jest; she couldn’t possibly have been serious. I can’t spend time with them and their abolitionist ideas anyway. They would insult my family.*

Mr. Rickman came sauntering over to them with a glass of scotch in his hand, already looking rather tipsy. “Adam,” James exclaimed, “what a lovely party you have invited me to. We have a friend in common as well.”

“Ahh, Katherine...well I’m glad you have made her acquaintance,” he said with a smile that didn’t look altogether genuine. Miss Greenfield excused herself and disappeared into a group of people at the other end of the garden. Adam shrugged and wrapped his arm around him. “James, let me get you something stronger. Come in with me, will you?”

Adam pulled James with him through the throngs of people that had filled the garden in the short time that James had been conversing with Miss Greenfield. He had been so absorbed with their conversation that he hadn’t seen how beautiful the garden was. Well-pruned apple trees gave ample shade and narrow flowerbeds filled with forget-me-nots and a small white flower that James couldn’t name flowed along the hedge.

“You have a very beautiful place here, Adam.”

"Thank you, my parents were among the first residents; well, me too, but I was just a wee lad then. I only remember a lot of boxes, trunks and chaos," he winked at James and pulled him into the kitchen. It took a minute for his eyes to adjust, but he followed Adam as he continued up a flight of stairs and then he opened a door to a spacious living room with beautiful tall pane windows and a high ceiling.

"A scotch, James? Have a seat, old friend," he said and motioned towards an armchair while pouring the drink without waiting for a reply.

"I thought I ought to save you from Katherine's radical ideas before she puts poison in your glass, knowing your family owns a plantation."

James stared at him and took the glass. "How did you know?"

Adam smiled, "It doesn't take a genius to figure it out, James, what with your vague mentions of a small farm in Virginia and having your own apartment. No one from a small farm would study medicine at our College and live in their own apartment. No one does unless they come from money. Besides, my father is one of the buyers of your fine tobacco. I knew immediately when you introduced yourself as a Waynewright."

James felt his face flush and he quickly drank the liquor down. It warmed nicely in his throat. "I don't know what to say, Adam. I had no idea. I must say that it's nice to be able to talk to someone who doesn't think I'm a monster!"

Adam laughed, "Monster, hardly; the abolitionists are crazy and they don't know what they are talking about. I would love to see them work in the fields all day without a parasol for their lovely white skin. The negroes are strong and well suited for their work. There is nothing wrong with that. That does not mean that we shouldn't take good care of them and help them have a good life. I certainly do not agree with harsh treatment of them. In fact, my father has people visit each of the plantations he does business with and report to him. I must say that your plantation is one of the better ones."

"Your father has informants spying on our homes?" James' pulse accelerated as he stared at him.

"Relax, James. It's a compliment. We are not spying. It's simply someone with our interests in mind who visits all our associates every year to look at the crop. I'm sure you have met him. He is also an overseer that has upped business revenue at several places in your area. Mr. Loch is his name.

Mr. Loch! Oh dear God! This cannot be happening. James' thoughts started spinning out of control. If Mr. Loch was so concerned over the treatment of field hands, why was he so harsh? Yet it made sense, reporting on the very plantation he worked on, he must very much want to see a profit, as he was most likely getting a hefty sum from his associates in New York. *What a two faced son of a bitch!* James thought with distaste.

Adam was much too drunk by now to notice James' reaction. Instead he leaned back on the love seat yawned and said, "All those niggers should be thanking us. They live with never any care in the world. They have an easy life, no responsibilities other than work. They get everything else taken care of; housing, retirement, doctors taking care of them for free, so what is the fuss about?"

"Indeed," James said feeling relieved that he'd escaped talking about Mr. Loch but he couldn't shake the foul taste in his mouth and the feeling of being spied upon.

James stood up slowly and made an excuse to Adam who just mumbled something and looked as if he was about to fall asleep.

James felt conflicted as he made his way back to the garden. He had been so relieved in the short moment upstairs when Adam told him that he had known who he was all along. Quickly he had felt at home again; at home with his own feelings and the knowledge that there was nothing wrong with slavery, until Adam mentioned Mr. Loch and he was catapulted back into the confusion he had felt the last couple of months.

He found an empty white wicker chair under one of the apple trees and sat down. The memories of when he hit Mr. Loch in the face and Johnnie's fear came over him. For some reason another memory surfaced, something he hadn't thought of in a long time. He must have been about five or six. He had been sitting on the porch with Auntie Ellen and suddenly he saw two negroes run past them in the field in front of them. They ran fast and he heard Auntie Ellen mumble, 'Run along North now, where no whip shall ever touch you...' He had seen that the shirt of one of the runners was stained with blood. Then they were gone.

Shaken from his memory he bent down and rested his elbows on his knees.

"Are you all right?" He looked up and saw Miss Greenfield standing there with her blue eyes full of concern. He felt odd, as if he was confused after taking too long of an afternoon nap, and had to muster all his strength not to sound like it before he answered, "I think I might have caught something as I feel quite out of sorts. I think perhaps I should leave."

Miss Greenfield nodded and stepped aside when James got out of his chair. "I apologize that I feel poorly," he said, then quickly kissed her hand and left the party.

Chapter 10

In spite of what Adam Rickman had told him, after a couple of days of anguishing over it and ruminating on it, and considering writing to his father about what he had said, James decided that Adam must have been too drunk for him to take seriously, especially since he fell asleep just scant moments after their conversation.

He still felt uncomfortable when he thought of his family and their workers. He felt confused when he thought of the doctor and his wife whom he had met at the Greenfields'. He tried to tell himself that there must be different negroes, some like their own who surely would never be able to learn to read and to live independently and would do better at home on the plantation.

James suppressed most thoughts on the subject. He spent time in the backyard studying his textbooks or Sundays at the beaches of Long Island. Miss Greenfield never sent her card so he assumed that she had not been serious about him visiting them in the Catskills. He was barely able to entertain the thought that Adam may have told her the truth about him after he left. If he had, she didn't say anything. For at the end of the month, he happened upon her walking all alone on the street. Katherine appeared to be in the midst of shopping as she was holding a hatbox under her right arm, several bags in the same hand and a parasol in the other.

"Miss Greenfield," James exclaimed, searching her face for any inkling of what she may know. "What are you doin' here all alone, carrying all these parcels by yourself?"

"Scandalous isn't it," she began, her eyes twinkling merrily, "I'm not much for convention. I do go out on my own now and then if it's a nice day like today and I have no one to escort me. I feel quite trapped sitting inside on a day like this waiting for my father or a cousin to protect my honor."

James laughed, but he gently took her bags and held out his arm. "Then I shall do so, Miss Greenfield. Please allow me the privilege of escorting you home."

"Oh, there is no need, Mr. Waynewright. I shall be just fine, shocking though it may seem." She winked at him, trying to take back her bags.

"Please, Miss Greenfield, I insist. Your father would never forgive me, should he find out I had passed on this opportunity."

She sighed, but smiled happily in spite of herself and leaned backwards to stretch out her back a little. "Why not, thank you, sir."

"Certainly, it's my pleasure. How was your summer? How were the Catskills?"

"Oh dear, I had invited you hadn't I? I'm so sorry, you must think me a terrible person, inviting you and then forgetting...I don't know what to say. Frankly, I have no excuse. It just slipped my mind with all the preparations and all the plans for the summer. I do apologize, Mr. Waynewright."

James walked on relieved that she at least hadn't decided *not* to invite him. "There is no need to apologize for anything. I know how it is. It's easy to forget. Besides, if I remember correctly we were interrupted by Mr. Rickman so it's no wonder."

James noticed the look of displeasure on her face at the mention of Adam's name, but she didn't say anything. *She will hate me if she finds out. Why did I have to insist on taking her all the way home? I could have put her in a hackney, and then I bring up Adam of all people!*

As if he didn't feel nervous already, she turned towards him with a brilliant smile, lightly touched his arm, and said, "Shall we call for a hackney then, Mr. Waynewright?" She motioned toward the corner as one was rushing by. He could feel the warmth of her gloved hand through his shirt. It made something stir within him and he swallowed awkwardly.

He waved and it stopped right away. "Where to, sir?" the driver asked.

James glanced at her as they sat themselves down. He felt that she looked more beautiful each time he saw her. He noticed that she had rather high cheekbones and that they were not completely symmetrical, the left one being just a little higher than the right. Also, her nose pointed upward and the nostrils didn't have the beautiful arch that her sister's did. There was something to the way she looked. Her whole being intrigued him in a way he hadn't experienced before. The fact that she wasn't a classical beauty made her face charming and different. He wanted to lean over and pull her hat off and loosen her curls. He wanted to see them tumble out over her shoulders and pull the collar of her dress down so he could see her neck.

He felt embarrassed at his own thoughts and looked out the window instead to distract himself. *She is an abolitionist,* he told himself. *I shouldn't be here. I should make my excuse and leave as soon as I see her safely at home.*

When they stopped at her house and he helped her out, he heard a familiar voice behind him; there was Mr. and Mrs. Greenfield walking towards them on the sidewalk.

"Mr. Waynewright," they both shouted at the same time. Mr. Greenfield's eyes narrowed and Mrs. Greenfield looked clearly disturbed. She walked up to her daughter and gently took her arm, lowering her voice so as not to make a scene but James heard it clearly, "What *is* this Katherine? What are you and Mr. Waynewright doing alone in a hackney? Have you no sense of your honor? Do tell me you haven't been somewhere with him without Papa's permission?" She lowered her voice even more, but James still heard, "Katherine, we have neighbors and doormen. We don't want talk amongst them."

James caught Katherine's eye and cleared his throat, "Mr. and Mrs. Greenfield, I must apologize. This is entirely my fault. We happened upon each other and I insisted on escorting her home. I didn't mean any disrespect. I just felt that she shouldn't be alone with so many parcels and boxes. I do apologize."

"I happily obliged," Katherine said loudly, completely unfazed by the whole affair.

Mr. and Mrs. Greenfield still looked taken aback, but Mr. Greenfield found himself quickly. He touched James' shoulder, "Mr. Waynewright, we are delighted at your thoughtfulness. Thank you for bringing our wayward daughter home."

Mrs. Greenfield waved her hand in the air and laughed as if the awkward moment was something she could wave away like a fly, and then she leaned forward and kissed the air next to James' cheek. "You are welcome in our home, Mr. Waynewright. Why don't you stay for dinner, where did you find each other?"

"He found me shopping on Broadway, thinking me scandalous being out without an escort."

James caught Mr. Greenfield's eye, he shook his head conspiratorially, and then nodded happily, "Please do join us, it would be an honor."

James couldn't find it within himself to say no.

Mrs. Greenfield laughed again as they walked up the stairs to the second floor. The Greenfields were an interesting family, James thought. They were very forward, almost brusque, but at the same time obviously concerned with etiquette. He had never met anyone like them before, such a contrast to his own family.

The same routine as his last visit repeated itself. James was invited in to have a glass of scotch with Mr. Greenfield as the women disappeared somewhere. Mrs. McNeary brought them each scotch and a glass of water for James, remembering without prompting.

Mr. Greenfield took a deep sip of his liquor and handed him a box of cigars that he'd grabbed from the coffee table. James took one gratefully. It had been a while since he smoked; he hadn't yet acquired the habit, in spite of the family business.

Mr. Greenfield struck a match on the mantle and leaned over to light James' cigar before he lit his own. He leaned back and after taking a noisy puff he said; "I realize that many boycott it now. Katherine very much disapproves but I can't forgo it completely."

James felt embarrassed as it dawned on him that he should have declined. He didn't know what to say. Mr. Greenfield must have sensed his discomfort and changed the subject with a slight raise of his eyebrows.

"James... may I call you James? I had the most interesting experience yesterday afternoon. I went to take a look at the designs for the Cooper Union Building, have you heard of it?"

"No, I haven't."

Mr. Greenfield puffed noisily on his cigar. He picked up his glass, spun it in his hand, and said, "Well, it's rather surprising and exciting. Peter Cooper, the designer and mastermind of this building," he paused and took a large sip before he continued, "has built a cylindrical shaft for a passenger lift. Can you believe it? He thinks someone will come up with something that will safely pull people up and down without using stairs." He shook his head. "I actually saw the shaft. I don't know what this man is thinking. Imagine being pulled up and down by something deep in a hole in the wall." Mr. Greenfield looked quite horrified at the thought. "No, I will take stairs even if they make buildings as tall as seven floors."

James laughed. "How would he get something like that to work? Buildings with so many floors. What a thought, can you imagine the view?" James said and took another warming sip of his scotch, thinking that he would have to go take a look at that building himself before he could believe it.

Mr. Greenfield shook his head, "I don't know. Apparently he is convinced that there is someone who will figure it out. Why don't you go into the dining room? Take your scotch and have a seat. I'm going to speak to my wife for a moment."

James had only just sat down in the dining room when Miss Greenfield showed up looking even lovelier than before in a different dress, this one dark green with silky puffed sleeves.

She sat down right next to him and lifted her own glass of scotch. James couldn't help but stare at her. He had never seen a woman drink scotch before and he didn't quite know what to say.

Katherine laughed aloud, "Shocking isn't it? I shop all alone *and* I drink scotch, just like a man."

James laughed too, "I do admit I'm a bit surprised. I have not met a lady quite as interesting as you before." Surprised at his own frankness he took her hand in his and looked her straight in the eye, "I'm very intrigued by you. I would like to ask your father's permission and come calling on you again more formally."

Oh, you idiot, she is an abolitionist. I can't do this. She hates my family, she will hate me. Miss Greenfield looked at him with dancing eyes and replied, "I would be delighted."

"May I call you Katherine?"

"Of course, James."

He grinned helplessly, but just then, Mrs. and Mr. Greenfield joined them so James quickly composed himself. Mrs. McNeary appeared right away with a tray full of thinly sliced roast beef, vegetables and gravy.

Whether it was sane or not, James ended the evening with a talk with Mr. Greenfield asking if he may call on his daughter. He told himself that he would sort it out somehow, that he could avoid telling her the truth, even that she never needed to know.

Chapter 11

James began his second year of studies and he didn't have a lot of time to go calling, but on a Saturday in early October he finally had the opportunity. Yet again, he sat in the little library next to the dining room at the Greenfields. This time Katherine sat opposite him. Mrs. McNeary put out a plate of fruit and tall glasses of lemonade; then she discretely left the room and went to sit in the dining room, leaving the door ajar. He could hear her move things around, but he wasn't sure what she was doing. Surely, she had been told to perform this task at this time to make sure that Katherine's honor was not compromised.

Katherine eyes lifted slightly as she glanced at Mrs. McNeary, then she leaned forward and helped herself, filling her plate with grapes and slivers of cut apple. "My parents are conventional. Sometime I wish I was a man so that I could live on my own."

James tried not to look stunned, but she watched him with a gleam in her eye and finally he laughed, "You truly are an unusual woman, Katherine. I don't think I have ever heard a lady say that before."

She smiled, but the gleam in her eye was gone and she said, quite seriously, "I don't think it is as unusual as you might think, James. Think about it. You can go about as you please. You can travel to New York and study, go calling on me, and visit the shops and pubs all on your own. We women cannot. I have to have an escort with me to make sure that I'm not mistaken for someone's servant, or worse. You yourself witnessed the dismay of my parents the other day when I had gone shopping on my own. Wouldn't you have wished for freedom if you hadn't had it?"

"I most likely would," James said honestly.

"Every time I think of my own limitations, I'm reminded of my brothers or sisters who have it much worse; the poor slaves who are *owned*." She pronounced the word owned with disgust in her voice. "Their owners whip them, sell their children. When the owners die, they are considered property that will be distributed among the surviving relatives as if they are nothing more than pottery. Or worse, they are auctioned off when the rest of the estate is sold if the widow isn't able to sustain the plantation on her own!"

Katherine's face flushed a deep red and her blue eyes looked almost black. "They are sold to whoever pays the highest price with no regard for family relations at *all*. Husbands and wives are separated, children torn from their mother's bosoms and...and..." she paused for a moment and looked as though she would burst into tears, but she collected herself and continued in a calmer tone. "I saw Sojourner Truth herself speak at the Ohio Women's Rights Convention in Akron. *She,* a woman speaking in front of all those people, men and women alike. She spoke of having ploughed fields, chopped wood and how her baby was sold away from her. She said that if *she* could do all that work, we women should have all the rights a man has. I—"

"Sojourner Truth is a negro?" James interrupted having a hard time picturing a negro woman speaking at a convention. *It cannot be true*, he thought and he would have laughed aloud if it wasn't for Katherine's obvious passion.

"Yes, she is. She was a slave who was freed by her master and has devoted her life to abolition and women's rights. Bless her heart! I traveled there with my mother; I was very young then, but I have not forgotten that day. We spent the whole spring of '51 in Ohio. My father has family there and he had some family affairs...well, that is of no matter. I'm glad we were there, because had my mother not taken me, I don't know if my eyes would have been opened to the plight of the enslaved."

James wasn't sure how to respond.

He mumbled something inaudible as a reply and that seemed to satisfy her. She was silent for a time, eating a couple of grapes and drinking a little of her lemonade.

"I apologize, James, if I have been too forward with you," she said and blushed.

"Don't worry, Katherine," he replied, taking a sip of his lemonade. It tasted excellent; tart and sweet at the same time. "This is quite delicious."

"Thank you! I'll be sure to tell Mrs. McNeary."

James smiled and raised his glass. The uncomfortable moment had vanished, and he realized with relief that the best way to handle slave conversations was to just listen. He didn't have to say anything at all about his family.

On the way home James tried to collect his thoughts and think logically about the situation. He could understand what Katherine was thinking, but she had only heard the worst stories from all these abolitionists. They never spoke of the happy singing negroes who loved the work in the fields and who were well taken care of by their owners. If Katherine had come to visit his family she would be surprised. She would see well fed workers resting with their families in the evening sun as their children played at their feet.

He felt hurt that she could have such a slanted picture of life in the South and he decided that no matter how infatuated he was, he would not go calling on her again.

Years later, James would look back on this day and be sure that God himself had arranged for him to get a letter from home on the very day that he went calling on Katherine; but on this very day it felt as though the Devil was teasing him.

James' landlady was paying to get the mail delivered and James saw the mailman walk away from their door, having waited to no avail for someone to open the door.

James caught up with him just as he was about to open the gate and leave.

"Mrs. Harris isn't home today, I'll take it," James said pleasantly, the mailman quickly handed over the mail, nodded and hurried down the block.

There were three letters, two for his landlady that he put on the little table in the hallway and one for him from his father.

Happy to have news from home, he wanted to savor it so he went into the kitchen to made himself some coffee first, waiting impatiently for the Napier to finish the process. Then sat himself down in his recliner by the window and opened the letter.

Waynewright Plantation Sept 24th 1856

Dear James,

I hope this letter finds you well and in good health.

I'm afraid that I have some bad news to tell you and I advise you to sit down before you continue.

James took an involuntary intake of breath and put his cup on the windowsill.

I wish I could tell you in a gentler way, but it is hard to do so in a letter so I'm just going to go ahead and tell you.

Your mother and I were woken up at first light yesterday morning by little Matilda knocking frantically on our bedroom window. How such a young little pickaninny could climb up so high and reach the window I don't know, but both your mother and I thank God that she managed it, for God knows what else could have happened?

Little Matilda was crying and wouldn't say anything. Your mother thought that someone had a miscarriage and readied herself to go but Matilda pointed at me showing me without words that she wanted me to come. I'm glad that your mother did not insist on going with me.

By now James' mouth was dry and his hands felt ice cold. He took a sip of coffee and let the letter sit on his crossed knee.

After getting myself dressed, I picked Matilda up and hurried all the way down to the quarters, but just before we got down, she jumped out of my arms and ran to the woods instead. She didn't get far; Will appeared and yelled for Matilda to run to her mom.

Will nodded at me and without a word he turned and pointed into the forest. I followed him.

Johnnie was hanging there, upside down, tied by his feet. I will NEVER forget the look of it! How could anyone be so cruel? His wife and daughter sat tied to a tree so they were forced to watch. It's just a baby, but still not even a baby should have to watch this!

This was done in the dead of night, but the screaming woke everyone up and they all saw it from their cabin windows.

They were afraid to leave, afraid to help him, but finally they sent little Matilda running for help, hoping that Mr. Loch and his drunken companions, whoever they were we will most likely never know, would not notice a small pickaninny sneak outside.

They were gone by the time I got there, must have heard me come down.

Johnnie was alive when we took him down, but he was dead by the next morning.

There is nothing more to say, Loch is gone. We are having a council with the planters tomorrow.

By God I wished I had listened to you.

Papa

James faintly noticed the coffee cup crashing to the floor as he ran out to the vomit in the water closet.

Chapter 12

He had to go home; there was no question of doing anything else.

The couple of days it took to get to Virginia he spent in a state of confusion and overwhelming emotion; at the same time strangely detached. He was not able to focus on either his thoughts or the medical books he had brought with him to pass the time. He felt responsible; that was the real reason for why he traveled all the way home. If he had not hit Loch, and if he had only told his father what Will told him before he left, how Johnnie and Martha were terrified of Loch, had he only told him, this would not have happened. Part of him felt that he couldn't face anyone at home but another part of him felt that if he did not go home he couldn't live with himself.

The last leg of the journey was especially hard as the hired coach hurried past their neighbors and he saw their workers in the fields. It seemed to him that their heads were hanging low and they didn't seem as happy as usual. *They must know,* he thought. *Someone must have been running around to all the plantations with the horrific news of what had taken place at my home.*

Both Mother and Father were sitting on the porch as if they had known exactly when he would arrive.

James took a deep breath as the driver got his bag down. He looked for Will or Pap, expecting one of them to help with his luggage, but when neither of them approached, he carried the heavy bag to the porch as his parents watched.

His father got up and pulled him into an embrace without a word. Over his shoulder James reached for his mother's hand. She stifled a sob.

"Where is everyone? I didn't see anyone of ours in the fields either."

His Father's voice sounded hoarse when he answered. "We told them to take a day or two off. There's no sense in their workin' now. The weather is good and the harvest is in. Only Auntie Ellen is cooking, and Uncle Pap and Will are tending to the animals."

"She is crying constantly," Mother volunteered.

James nodded and mumbled that he would go see her and his parents stepped aside without a word.

Auntie Ellen was scrubbing a pot when he came in. Her backside looked even skinnier than usual, and bent as if she had aged 20 years in the year or so James had been gone.

She slowly turned and looked him straight in the eye. Instead of her usual jolly embrace, she only stretched her hand to him. Her gaze was full of despair and pain.

Katherine is right! They all are right. How did I not see that?

Chapter 13

"Massa Jr. You needn't be interrupting your schoolin' for this," Auntie Ellen whispered and sat down on one of the many stools in the kitchen, still holding his hand.

"Yes I do," James' voice was so full of emotion that what he said was almost inaudible. "How are his wife and the baby?"

Tears began to course down her wrinkly old face, but she only shook her head.

Bastard, bloody bastard, why didn't I write to Papa when Adam told me that he was spying on us? WHY? It's my fault. I'm glad I hit him... Nausea overcame him and he sank down next to Auntie Ellen, leaning on his haunches. He didn't vomit, though.

It's my fault, if I hadn't hit him, he would never have done it. Will warned me about this. They should have run away! Why didn't they?

Again the memory of him and Auntie Ellen sitting on the porch that summer evening came over him and he heard her voice almost as if she said it again: *Run away North now, where no whip shall ever touch you!*

He looked up to see if Auntie Ellen had spoken but she sat silent with her hands in her lap, tears slipping past her closed eyelids.

James couldn't bring himself to go back to the porch. Instead, he sat down in front of the fireplace with his father's pipe and smoked it silently. He stared into the fire and wondered absently if Will had chopped the wood. It was still early in the day but it was chilly and he was grateful that it was lit.

James could barely voice it to himself, but he had known. He had known from that day when they went to Plymouth Church in Brooklyn and he had felt the emotion when the congregation was singing; saw the beautiful woman and her husband up on the stage and when he saw the piles of money thrown into the collection baskets. He had known then that his family was wrong. He had known that what they were doing in the South was cruel and unjust; he had known it all along. That's why he had been so interested in Katherine. He wanted someone on his side. He needed her.

He hadn't noticed that he had known until today.

He must have fallen asleep because when he came to it was dark outside and his father sat in the recliner with his newspaper and his mother was embroidering next to him.

She smiled, "You have been sleeping sitting on the couch for two hours, but it's no wonder with such a long and trying journey. Auntie Ellen left but she prepared a meal for us. If you are hungry I will set it up in the small dining room."

"I am a little hungry. I would love some of Auntie Ellen's cooking," he said but felt his heart contract at the thought of her standing there cooking and crying at the same time.

"How did all this come about? Did you notice anything amiss before he did his awful, awful slaughtering?" James asked when they finished their meal. None of them could speak about it as they ate and had carefully skirted around the subject speaking only of New York and his studies.

His father looked pained, stricken really, and remained quiet for several moments.

"I wish to God that I had, but I didn't notice anything at all. In fact I thought that he had finally seen reason and agreed with our philosophy after all those discussions last summer. I wish to God that I had taken your letter seriously, James. The letter you sent me once you went to New York in which you told me that Loch was too harsh...if I had only fired him right away after he insulted you and went against my orders. Instead I got mad at you." He paused clenching his teeth so hard that James could hear it and then he exclaimed, "That horrible, horrible man! How *dare* he treat someone that way? How? He should be—"

"It's my fault, Papa," James interrupted his father, his voice so low it was almost a whisper, but they heard. "I spoke to Will and he told me that they were all terrified of Loch. He told me that they were afraid that he would take revenge on Johnnie for making him feel humiliated in front of all of them. He said that since it was Johnnie who ran and got me to help his wife and then...then when I hit him it made him lose authority in front of them. Will said he felt it would only be a matter of time before Loch took revenge."

James' mother put her hands in front of her face and sobbed.

James' father barely glanced at her and was silent for several minutes before he spoke up again.

"No, James, it ain't your fault. You were young and foolish, Loch is older and should have taken it for what it was and not become so terribly put out by it. I think that he just needed an excuse so that he could do what he did. It's my fault. *I* should have dismissed him immediately. We are Christians. It is our responsibility to take care of those who cannot take care of themselves."

James' mother clumsily got out of her chair and hurried out of the dining room sobbing violently behind her hands.

"I'll go after her," James' father said.

James remained seated. His father's familiar words of responsibility echoed in his ears. *I had dinner with a negro physician. A physician!* James thought, and for the first time his father's words that he always took pride in seemed false.

He glanced at the Grandfather clock and seeing that it was only seven thirty, he decided to go down the quarters and speak with Will.

He silently walked through the kitchen that was adjoining the small dining room and as quietly as he could he opened the kitchen door and snuck out in the dark cold October air.

He knocked on the door of the cabin Will shared with his mother Ellen and his sisters Hettie and Mary.

He heard them move around in there and then Will's familiar voice, "Who's there?"

"It's me...Junior!"

"Hold on a moment."

James heard shuffling as if someone was pushing something heavy across the floor and then the door opened a crack and Will's familiar face appeared, "Come in, hurry please, Massa Jr."

As soon as he came inside Will closed the door and began to push a chest of drawers in front of the door to barricade it. James swallowed when he realized that they must be scared that Mr. Loch was coming back.

James didn't know what he ought to say, but he managed to clear his throat and mumble something about making sure they were doing all right. He heard steps behind him and Hettie and Mary came up and gently touched his shoulder. "God bless you, Massa Jr. God bless your kindness, we're so scared we ain't sleepin', we take turns keepin' watch. Mama is sleepin' now so that she can get up and take her turn." Hettie gestured toward the bed in the corner where Auntie Ellen lay under a pile of blankets.

"I'm so sorry, did I wake her?"

"Oh no, Massa Jr. She ain't awake."

James looked at Hettie and Mary and shook his head. "I'm so very sorry... I know not what to say."

"No need, no need, we know," Mary tried to smile but it looked more like a grimace and James just nodded and then turned to Will.

"I'd like to speak to you outside if I may?"

Hettie laughed, "Such fancy talk you have learned in New York.

Once outside and hearing the door safely barricaded from the inside, James looked at Will, "It's cold here, let's walk up and sit in the barn."

Will didn't say anything but followed him and they walked in silence all the way through the fields and up the little dirt road that was used as a short cut.

As soon as they came inside James took Will's hands in his and looked right into his eyes. "Will, I am *so* very, very sorry. I'm *so* sorry. It's my fault, I shouldn't have hit him. You were right; you were right all along... that *bastard*, bloody bastard."

Will didn't say anything just slowly pulled himself out of James' grip and sat down on a hay bale outside one of the stalls. The horse inside it stuck his head out and started to nibble on his head. Will didn't laugh, just shoved the head away and moved out of its way.

"No, Massa Jr., Please don't blame yourself none. It ain't your fault; you only showed you care. You gotta do what your destiny calls you to do; you was meant to go to New York."

James didn't answer him, instead, he asked where he thought that Loch had gone.

"No one knows. Massa says that they are trying to catch him. Dawson said he was harsh with theirs too, that he whipped a woman so she lose her baby."

"Whipping... at Dawson's plantation? Why didn't they fire him? No one here whips anybody. That's something they do in Kentucky and other places."

Will looked down at his feet and didn't reply.

The memory of when he sat with Auntie Ellen on the porch and saw the two negroes running and the blood on the back of one of them flashed through James' mind.

Then Will started speaking,

“We woke up by the noise. He scream so loud that I can still hear it. Martha she screamed, too. I think she scream louder than him. It’s not your fault…it’s our fault. We should have sent Matilda right away, but we never thought he would do it for that long. We knows it happens and we thought we just had to deal with it. Mama has taken care of folk who ha…” Will choked up for a second before continuing,

“I mean, we know it happen… and folk survives it, but it went on and on, he wouldn’t stop. He had some other men with him, none I had ever seen, they was drunk and kept eggin’ him on. Martha fainted and then Johnnie stopped screamin,’ that’s when we sent her runnin’.”

Chapter 14

They never found Mr. Loch, or his companions. James, his father and Mr. Wilson rode around for three days looking for them at all the plantations and in the towns, but no one had seen nor heard of him. They even had Will and Rob ride out on their own to speak to everyone on the neighboring plantations to see if they had heard anything, but nobody had.
They had been out this morning too, without result. "I'm so sorry, boys," Mr. Waynewright said when Rob and Will got off their horses in front of the house. He took back their passes, shook his head and sighed audibly.

"If you ever remember anything of importance that someone has told you and you want to go back and ask again, then you just come anytime and get these again, you hear? We don't approve of such horrible treatment here. We want him to answer for it as much as you do, boys, you hear?"

"Yes, Massa, we know it, sir," Rob answered. Will didn't say anything but looked him right in the eye.

"I'll send Matilda to call the stable hand. You two go in the kitchen to get yourself something to eat now. Auntie Ellen is making pies."

James swallowed hard and looked at his father after Will and Rob went inside.

"Papa, I need to tell you something. Can we stay out here on the porch?"

"Sure thing, son," he said and whistled for Matilda who came running out of the house smiling and hopping happily with a young child's ability to be happy in the midst of trauma.

"Run and get Uncle Pap to come get the horses. I'll give you a sweet!"

"Yes, Massa, I be obly," she answered, meaning obliged but she was too small to pronounce it properly.

When they were alone James turned to his father again. "Papa, I happened to run into someone in New York that you ought to know about. I should have told you. I should have written about it, but I...well, I have no excuse. I ran into Mr. Adam Rickman, he is the son of Mr. Rickman who buys tobacco from us. Sound familiar?"

"It does indeed, and mighty good customer he is," he said puffing deeply on his pipe.

"Well yes, but were you aware that they have hired Mr. Loch to go round and work all the plantations and report back to him on our quality, and apparently also to ensure that we treat our negroes properly. Can you imagine?" James said and got out of his chair and spit his chewing tobacco over the porch railing. "I'm sure he wants us to get the harvest yield up. The better and the more of the product we put out, the more they can sell to Europe, the heftier his bonus," James said in disgust.

Mr. Waynewright's face darkened, and he clenched his teeth, "Are you sure about this?"

"Yes I am, Papa. I am." James told him the whole story of how Adam brought him upstairs at the party and their conversation.

"I was goin' to tell you Papa."

"How the hell could you keep this from me? How the bloody hell!" Mr. Waynewright got up so fast that the rocking chair bumped the wall loudly.

"You see where it got us? Having expensive negroes slaughtered in the most inhumane way and his woman traumatized beyond work."

James cringed, "I know, Father, how do you think I feel? It is my fault entirely, every bit of it."

"Hrmnp...well...next time you get such a nice little tidbit of information you write to me immediately, James," he said, sounding a little calmer and he sat down in the rocking chair again and sucked on his pipe.

"You have enough tobacco up there, James?"

"Well, I'm not smoking or chewin' much in New York. I haven't quite acquired the habit yet, only now and then if I get the opportunity."

"I should send you some to give as gifts."

"Thank you Father." *Excellent idea, splendid really. I'll bring a box to the Greenfields, personally delivered from our very own plantation.*

James stood up ready to leave the porch, but Mr. Waynewright held him back.

"When you get back to New York in a couple of days, you go speak to Rickman and tell him that we ain't doin' business with him anymore, you hear? You tell him that we have told all of our neighbors as well. Tell him that they won't be sellin' anything to him anymore. We don't deal with spies or cruelty here."

"Yes Father," James replied dutifully.

He had been dreading it and had avoided it the whole week, but he had to go visit Martha. He didn't want to, but he was leaving the next morning and it was the right thing to do.

He felt almost nauseous walking down the narrow dirt path to the quarters. He wondered if she would blame him. She must know that it was because of him that her man was dead. Even though he had done what he did to protect her, now she must truly wish he hadn't hit Mr. Loch.

Martha sat on the ground next to her cabin. She had been clawing the dirt so much that her nails were almost completely gone and her fingers full of caked blood mixed with dirt. When James gently touched her shoulder, she looked at him with eyes that didn't appear to see him at all.

"No use, Massa Jr.," he heard and looked up to see Hettie stand there shaking her head. "The doctor has been here, he said ain't nothin' we can do; it has to take is own sweet time."

"Ain't sweet at all," James lamented, and for the first time he felt his eyes brim with hot tears.

Chapter 15

It was as if the very color of the sunlight looked different, as if the whole world had changed overnight. Their new overseer looked cruel and harsh as he walked around among the barns checking on the work. He carried a walking stick, and even though James knew that he would never use it for violence, it still had the potential and threat to be used as such. Everyone working in the curing barns and at their other tasks looked bent over and tired.

Suddenly the light in their eyes that he used to think was happiness seemed to have been replaced by a feverish shine caused by the need to hide from him who they really were.

The beauty of Will's muscles moving as he worked had used to make James so proud. Now he averted his eyes, knowing that he ought not to look at another man that way.

James couldn't say goodbye to his parents; instead he wrote a letter saying that he couldn't sleep because he suddenly felt nervous about missing the train to the steamer and he left in the middle of the night. He woke Pap and asked him to come with him and take the horse back, telling himself that it would be the last time he would ever ask a negro to do something for him without paying him. James looked into Pap's eyes and tried to somehow convey his feelings, but Pap didn't notice. He just bent his head and said, "'Ave a good trip, Massa Jr."

James waited alone, staring out into the chill air until the train finally arrived several hours later.

The first Sunday home, James went back to Plymouth Church. This time he placed several coins into the donation basket.

He went every Sunday after that and the Congregation started to notice him with friendly smiles and nods as he came in and sat by himself.

One Sunday an older man and his wife came up to him after the service. He was rather tall and skinny, in fact, his black suit was too short on him and his large hands and wrists were completely exposed. His wife was tall and slim too, but was wearing a well-fitting grey dress and a dark green shawl thrown over her shoulders.

"My name is Ericson and this is my wife. We have seen you here several weeks now and we wanted to introduce ourselves."

"Mr. and Mrs. Ericson, I'm pleased to meet you. I'm James Waynewright."

"Oh, a Southerner I hear. It is so very nice to have a Southerner with sympathies for our cause here in our church. Where are you from?" Mrs. Ericson said in a melodious voice and he immediately recognized her as one of the women who sang so beautifully during their services.

"I'm from Virginia, Ma'am."

"Oh that is a beautiful state. Such a shame that it has the stain of slavery on it let us pray to God that we can one day end it."

"Indeed," James said smiling, inwardly not even surprised anymore that he agreed with her.

"Mr. Waynewright, how would you like to meet some other congregants and have some refreshments? We usually sit a while in the Parish Hall and talk. We would be delighted to have you join us."

"Certainly, thank you very much. I would be delighted." *I shouldn't have said yes, what if they find out who I am? What should I say?*

"Come here, Mr. Waynewright," Mrs. Ericson took him by his arm and led him out of the chapel and down a long corridor, then down some steps and finally into a large room with several tables set up and a sparkling fire in the fireplace. She went straight up to one of the tables where a young negro woman with a baby on her arm sat. James assumed she was the woman they had collected for today but she had not appeared on the podium. She might have been too scared or nervous about bringing her baby for everyone to see.

"Normally we don't introduce newcomers to people that we help quite so quickly," Mrs. Ericson whispered and leaned close to James, "but we have seen how much money you have been donating every Sunday and we can see that you are surely a man of our compassions."

"Thank you, Ma'am. I appreciate your confidence." *If you only knew.*

"Here, sit please," Mrs. Ericson said gesturing to the table with the young woman. She touched the baby's chubby little hand and cooed at it. "This gentleman is new to our congregation, Miss Emma. He is from your parts down in Virginia."

Miss Emma glanced at him with a slightly suspicious look but said good day politely.

"Miss Emma and her little son here are staying with us to rest up a couple of days before she heads to Canada. She had always dreamed about living here in New York but since the horrid Fugitive Slave Act she is realizing the good sense of going even farther North. She hadn't eaten for over a week, just drank water from springs and streams when our contact got her at the station a couple of days back," Mrs. Ericson said as she shook her head for effect.

James didn't say anything. He had heard his father speak of a railroad that some negroes were said to travel on at nighttime, but he had thought it had been one of those rumors that floated around and one of the stories that they used to entertain themselves with in the evenings.

Mr. Ericson sat down next to James and without asking poured James a cup of coffee from a kettle on the table and one for himself.

"Oh dear, I'm so sorry. I quite forgot!" Mrs. Ericson said and resolutely pulled the kettle out of her husband's hand and put it on the table, then placing in his cup two spoons of sugar.

Mr. Ericson laughed. "Don't worry yourself, my dear. I'm quite capable to pour it even though I'm a man." Emma laughed as well and James noted that she had pretty dimples in her cheeks.

"Two, please," James said when Mrs. Ericson looked at him with the sugar spoon in her hand.

"Where exactly are you from, Miss Emma?" James asked, the word Miss seeming strange and out of place as he addressed her.

She didn't answer immediately. Instead, she glanced at Mr. Ericson with a fearful look in her eyes.

"It's all right, Miss Emma," he said and James wondered why they trusted him like this. He had only been coming to church for about a month and surely it was foolish to assume this much only on the account of how much money he donated.

"I escaped from a plantation far from here, very far, North Carolina."

Mrs. Ericson shook her head and smacked her lips in a disapproving fashion.

"It is an outrage that a young mother should have to travel so far on foot with a wee little babe, an outrage, but such bravery. I don't know if I would have had the courage."

"You came *all* the way on foot?" James asked incredulously.

"Why sir, yes...most of it was, but some nice people on the railroad drove me bits too in their carriages." Miss Emma glanced at Mrs. Ericson who smiled back warmly.

Not knowing if he would give himself away or not, James decided to ask, "I'm hesitant to admit my ignorance, but could you enlighten me on this railroad please. I don't know enough about it."

"No need to feel ignorant, Mr. Waynewright. It's meant to be secret and not meant to be known to all," Mr. Ericson said and picked up a cigar and lit it as he spoke.

"It is an ingenious system that we have in place. There are courageous people throughout our country that open up their homes at night to people escaping the horrors of slavery. The people come at night, stay and have a meal and then sleep there during the day. The next night they move on, either on foot or sometimes they are taken to the next station as we call it, hidden in feed trunks or under blankets in the backs of carriages."

"How do they know who will help them?"

"The helpers put a candle in their windows, or hang a quilt on their line," Miss Emma said proudly and touched Mrs. Ericson's arm.

"A quilt?"

"Not just any quilt, Mr. Waynewright, but a quilt with sewn messages of where to go!" Mrs. Ericson added.

This is outrageous, right under our noses, James thought.

Mr. Ericson took a deep draw on his cigar and looked at James a while before he spoke.

"If you are able to donate more, we collect money for our station masters and for the conductors. We send money to someone who knows Tubman so she can take it down there."

"She?" James asked. He had heard of Tubman a while back, the way he remembered it, it was an abolitionist from up North who came and snatched the negroes away from them. He always assumed it was a man.

"Praise Jesus for sending us Moses!" Miss Emma exclaimed with shining eyes.

"You have a lot to learn, Mr. Waynewright. Tubman is indeed a woman, an escaped slave herself. Indeed she is, bless her brave soul. Going back down south over and over again to help those still trapped." Mrs. Ericson smiled at James who swallowed hard.

A woman? The slave snatcher is a ***woman, a*** *former slave! Who the hell is she?* James thought. He felt an odd sensation in his stomach and his heart was thumping harder than usual. He had felt so convinced before. The knowledge placed before him made it starkly clear that there were people who conspired against his own family and his friends in Virginia. Suddenly he didn't feel so sure anymore and he felt as if he would weep.

He pulled out his pocket watch hoping that they wouldn't see his hands shake and then he made an excuse that he had lost track of time and he got up to leave.

The Ericson's and Emma looked surprised and he hoped that he hadn't given himself away by hurrying out. He didn't know what else to do to hide his conflicting emotions.

Just as he put his hand on the door, it opened and Pastor Beecher came in. He would have bumped into him if James had not jumped sideways.

"I beg your pardon," Pastor Beecher said and laid a hand on his shoulder, "I do apologize. Are you alright son?" If it was divine intervention, coincidence or the warm look in the Pastor's eyes, James would never know, but something made him clear his throat and ask if he may have a word with him.

"Why of course. Come with me."

The Pastor led him down the long corridor that James had taken with Mrs. Ericson before and then they went into a little office behind the chapel. There was a small table and four chairs. A bowl of red apples and a small candle stick with a white candle on the table. Pastor Beecher motioned for him to sit down and then he lit the candle and sat down on the opposite side of James.

"We have not been properly introduced, but I have seen you here for about a month or so; you are most welcome to our congregation." Pastor Beecher smiled warmly and held out his hand and James felt torn again and so full of emotion that he was barely able to speak. He could hear how shaky his voice sounded when he told him his name.

"Are you quite alright, Mr. Waynewright?" Pastor Beecher looked at him calmly without judgment.

James looked back for a moment and then he told him the truth of who he was. If Pastor Beecher was shocked, he didn't show it.

"If I understand you correctly you are beginning to see the error in the ways of the South. One of the parishioners has mentioned how generously you have been donating each Sunday."

"Yes, sir, yes, Pastor. I have since come to the conclusion that it is...I cannot... I cannot I...feel...it's hard to describe how I feel, I don't know exactly, I cannot believe that I didn't see before," he stammered knowing that he didn't make much sense.

"It is as if a veil of delusion has been ripped from your eyes," Pastor Beecher stated calmly.

James swallowed hard and looked up to the ceiling to stop the tears threatening to well up again.

"May I ask how you came to realize this, Mr. Waynewright?

James took a deep breath to collect himself and looked Pastor Beecher in the eye for a moment before he spoke, "I'm not really sure when I began to see things differently, but there was an incident on our plantation with an overseer who was much too harsh on one of our...one of the, the workers in the field who was pregnant."

James paused for a moment and then he told Pastor Beecher everything, including how he had come to know Katherine and once had dinner with Dr. McCune Smith.

"Oh, Dr. McCune," Pastor Beecher interrupted, "very nice man he is. I apologize. Go on, please."

"Its fine," James said and then he continued again, his words flowing out of him now as if he couldn't stop. When he stopped talking and a deep sigh escaped his throat, he felt Pastor Beecher's arm on his back. "Take a deep breath. I'm glad you are letting this off your chest."

James swallowed and looked desperately at Pastor Beecher, "How could I not have seen this before? I went home, I met everyone, and when I looked into Auntie Ellen's eyes...she is...she raised me more or less... and I saw the pain there...I...I understood, but now I feel confused. I sat with the Ericson's today and I met...Miss Emma. They told me all about the railroad and...I still think slavery is wrong, but it's my family they are talking about, my own family...my friends and their livelihood. I feel conflicted."

Pastor Beecher opened his mouth and began to say something but James kept going. "I left the plantation in the middle of the night last month. I couldn't look my Mother and Father in the eye anymore. I know that they are wrong. I don't know how to speak to them anymore...but I love them they are my parents...I..."

Pastor Beecher got up from his chair and went to a cupboard behind him, he brought down two glasses that he filled with water from a pitcher standing at a little counter underneath it.

"Here, Mr. Waynewright, have some water," he said and sat down again, taking a large sip himself before he continued.

"I understand that this is conflicting for you. It is not always easy to know which direction is the correct one in a storm. Jesus himself disagreed with his community because he felt that things needed to take another direction."

James swallowed hard, "You are right."

"Mr. Waynewright, I would not recommend you distancing yourself from your own family, but God is calling you to do the right thing, Mr. Waynewright. You do feel this, don't you?"

James took a deep breath. "Yes, I do."

"Good. Keep in mind what God is telling us in Exodus. He makes it clear that slavery is wrong again and again. He sent frogs and swarms of flies to show the Pharaoh that he was wrong to keep the Israelites enslaved. When the Pharaoh refused, he killed the cattle. It is very clear to me that God never approves of owning another human being."

James sat silently and listened. He had learned that they were livestock, good valuable and intelligent livestock, but not fully human. He felt ashamed, but still it was hard for him to completely let go of this notion.

"Mr. Waynewright, I want you to know that you are a very brave man to truly follow Jesus' example and not be afraid of doing what's right. Never forget this. Do not stray from this. It *is* important for you to oppose slavery. I believe that God has *you* in his mind because *you* are from the South. *You* have the power to help, because *you* really know what goes on there, Mr. Waynewright."

"But, Pastor Beecher, how can I do this without offending my family?"

"Son, I cannot tell you how. Our commandments say that we should honor our father and mother, but they do not say that you must agree with them."

James laughed suddenly, and Pastor Beecher grinned, his eyes twinkling. They remained locked in each other's gaze, and then Pastor Beecher stood up.

"There you go son, go in peace now and stay on the narrow path. It's not going to be easy, but God is calling you to do what must be done."

James got up as well and shook his hand. Pastor Beecher looked deep into his eyes, as if he could really see his soul. He nodded approvingly.

Chapter 16

James decided to call on Katherine again.

It was a gray day with heavy clouds threatening to give them rain and he abandoned his plan to ask her father if he may walk with her outside.

Katherine opened the door herself when he knocked, explaining that Mrs. McNeary was occupied and led him into the kitchen.

"I apologize, James, but our rugs are being cleaned, and we cannot sit anywhere but here. I hope that is all right. I will make you a cup of tea and we have biscuits." She pulled out a plate covered with a cloth and sat it on the table. The kitchen was large with a window facing west so that the late afternoon sun shone in on the wooden table. The table had no tablecloth and he could see how well-worn and smooth the wood was. It smelled of spices and baking and reminded him of Auntie Ellen's cooking.

Katherine brought the tea and sat down in front of him, pushing his teacup towards him. "I haven't seen you in a long time, James. I'm a little surprised to see you now."

James cleared his throat, before he spoke. "I have been back in Virginia, a family emergency."

Katherine's hand went to her mouth, "Oh, I'm sorry. What happened?"

"Someone was murdered," he said without thinking.

Her eyes became round, "murder?"

"Yes, I'm afraid so." James realized that this would lead to all sorts of questions he was not willing to share, but it was too late—he had already blurted it out.

Katherine looked close to tears already. "Did the Sheriff catch him? Is he in jail? Did they hang him?"

The Sheriff wouldn't lift his finger for a negro killed. "No he escaped; no one has seen him since," James said without hiding the anger from her.

"Oh that is dreadful, just dreadful! How can...? Who was murdered? Anyone close to you?"

"Yes, very close," James answered, without looking at her. He picked up his tea and took a sip of the hot liquid instead.

"I'm so sorry, how...what happened exactly?"

The image of Martha's bloody and dirty nails flashed before his eyes. "I'm sorry, Katherine. I prefer not to talk about it. Would you mind if we changed the subject? I don't mean to be rude but it is still very painful for me."

"Oh of course, I'm the one who should apologize. I did not mean to pry. I don't know what to say. I'm so dreadfully sorry. Can I do anything? I can ask my father; he may have some ideas."

"I appreciate it, but I don't think there is anything anyone can do."

"I understand. I'm sorry...you had asked to change the subject."

James smiled, "I had hoped to ask if you wanted to come to church with me on Sunday, if you could ask your father. I go to Plymouth Church all the way in Brooklyn, but I think you may love it there."

At first Katherine became silent and for a moment he wondered if she wasn't as against slavery as she had made him think. Then she breathlessly said, "Oh James, you go to Pastor Beecher? I would love nothing more!"

The courtship that had begun reluctantly, at least for James, evolved into a warm mutual feeling of love rooted in their now shared passion for abolition.

By bringing Katherine to church there was no turning back. James had fully embraced the movement and he suppressed all thoughts of his own home life. Whereas in the beginning he had felt as if he was a double agent and a spy, now he felt as if his old life had been a dream or as if *that* part of his life had been what he had been spying on.

Sometimes he wondered what his family would think if they knew, but he told himself that they would understand that he worked to prohibit those who treated their negroes poorly and that they on some level would be on the same side as him. He told himself that there were *different* slaveholders, those who whipped and sold their negroes, and then those who took good care of them like his parents. He no longer approved of what his parents did, but he felt that they could at least find common ground should they find out.

It was what he did to justify his actions in his imaginary conversations with his parents, because he knew he wanted to marry Katherine now. He wondered how he would tell his mother that they could not marry on the plantation because Katherine would refuse to set foot there. He pushed his old life further back. He felt as if he was standing in the middle of a lake. Behind him was a frozen sheet of ice getting thicker and thicker each day protecting him from the murky water of the plantation. Behind the ice sheet was his old self, and so thick was the ice that it was as if it was another person entirely, an unimaginable force would crush the ice and the water would flow in from all directions much sooner than he thought.

Each Sunday, James brought Katherine and Chrissy to church. The two first Sundays their Uncle Peter Greenfield had accompanied them as a chaperone. He was not a religious man, and after seeing that James was honorable he had a long conversation with his brother, explaining that he felt completely comfortable with the young Southern man. Unconventional as it may be, they decided that as long as Chrissy chaperoned it would still be seemly and proper and they let the young women visit Plymouth Church without Uncle Peter.

James, Katherine and Chrissy looked at the family on the podium. The man was large and muscled, his quadriceps prominent under the cloth of his grey pants. His wife looked strong and muscular as well, but her eyes were large and hollow and wouldn't focus on anything; they darted about the room as if she was getting ready to bolt at any minute. They had two small boys with them, and they were both hiding their faces in their mother's skirts. Pastor Beecher touched the father's shoulder and looked out at his audience, his voice bellowing louder than usual. "Imagine trudging through deep snow, more at risk because the slave catchers can see your footsteps, while the rest of us are sitting by the fire celebrating Christ's birth this season. Traveling on our railway in the winter is harsh, but this family here saw no other choice. If it hadn't been for our station masters they could have all frozen to death in the dead of night." He stopped for effect and caught the eye of several of the congregation. "We need to give generously this week. Please spare what you can in the spirit of the Christmas Season and let not our brethren go hungry and unprepared to their new life in the north."

Just as the basket came around and James put his hand in his suit pocket to pull out his donation, he caught the eye of the husband on the podium. Everything became still and a persistent ringing began in James' ears;z his heart began thumping uncontrollably.

He knew that man...and the woman, too. They had come to their plantation each summer for years, his father having rented them so that they would have extra hands for the fieldwork and in the kitchen, the woman had even cooked with Auntie Ellen. He had been in the kitchen with them several times. James held the man's gaze for a split second longer and he knew that he was recognized.

James didn't notice that the basket had passed him by, nor did he notice Katherine and Chrissy's look of surprise and concern.

The ice began to melt, but it did not crack—not just then.

James was silent on the way home, barely noticing Chrissy and Katherine's chatter. He stood looking out over the East River as the ferry slowly pulled them toward Manhattan. It was full of large ice chunks floating along, bumping into each other and the boat. James wondered if the negro man would speak to Pastor Beecher and tell him that he knew who James really was. Silently he thanked God that he had already spoken to Beecher himself.

As the ferry anchored in the harbor and everyone slowly shuffled out, he suddenly noticed what Chrissy and Katherine were saying.

"I do feel strongly about it, Chrissy," Katherine said, "I will speak to Father today. It's cold; Pastor Beecher made it clear that it is extra dangerous in the winter since you can easily track their footsteps. We do have an extra room that is never used for anything other than scraps of stuff and mother's embroidery yarns that she never touches anyway. I have thought of this for a long time. They can stay with us and then move on to Canada closer to the spring.

James swallowed, trying not to panic.

"Well, Father will *never* allow it. Katherine, he thinks you are too radical...Oh I'm sorry, sir." Chrissy apologized to an older gentleman with a walking stick whom she'd accidentally bumped into as they walked across the gangway to solid ground. "Certainly," the gentleman flashed her a smile with surprisingly white and strong teeth.

Not missing a beat, Chrissy continued. "He will talk you out of it; he will think it's too dangerous."

"What could be so dangerous about having guests, Chrissy?"

"Well for one thing, it's illegal. Your father may face jail time or expensive fines should the authorities find out," James said, hoping that she would change her mind, terrified that they would do it and the couple would confide in her who he was.

"That's ridiculous. No one will find out. Even so, we have the right to have whatever guest we want in our house. I have yet to see the police knocking on doors to see who your guests are. I say we go right back on the ferry and speak to Pastor Beecher." Her cheeks were deep crimson and she waved her arms so animatedly in the crowd that people had to give her a wide berth so as not to get slapped by her. "Those little boys were so scared they couldn't get their heads out of their mother's skirts, and she looked *so* tired. We can't have them walk to Canada in this weather."

James gently took her elbow and pulled her out of the crowd, trying not to think about would happen if her father said yes and the family told Katherine and Chrissy who he was.

"Katherine, they will not walk all the way. There are ferries and trains, trains at least, and surely we can help them arrange for carriages for those routes that have no train. I will make a donation." James felt for his wallet inside his jacket as if he was about to pull it out right then and there.

"James, but when they arrive it will be cold and they will have nowhere to go."

Chrissy hugged Katherine and glanced at James, pleading with him with her eyes. "Katherine, James is right. I want to help them too but I really don't think that Father would allow it, and mother would be too nervous."

"Let's walk. No need to discuss this right here," James said as the crowd from the boat filed past them from both directions now as the people who were going to Brooklyn were let on.

Chrissy stopped midstride and turned to him clapping her hands together in excitement, "James, I know what we should do. They should live with *you!* You live on your own. Do you have space for them?"

"Oh that's a splendid idea, James, please say yes!" Katherine's broad smile would convince him of almost anything, but he shook his head. *Of all the negroes we have helped, why do you have to be so adamant about these?* He thought.

"My landlady would never allow it, and she would notice. She complains if she hears me move at all during the night. I don't know of her political views, but we could never take the chance."

Katherine sighed audibly, "I will at least ask father for a donation then," she said. James drew a deep breath of relief and caught Chrissy's eyes as they gleamed merrily, relieved of nothing more than that she won the argument with her older sister.

***

James felt proud as he took Katherine's arm and they walked out of her building on to Waverly Place. They had never walked unescorted before but for the short walk and carriage ride that day when he found her shopping alone. He felt elated by the honor bestowed upon him by her father. It proved that Mr. Greenfield did trust and like him.

Katherine smiled at him, squinting as the sun hit her face when she turned towards him. Gently, he pulled her hat a little to the side so as to shade her gaze. Her eyes relaxed instantly. She squeezed his arm and smiled again but remained uncommonly quiet. They were both nervous and it felt very unusual to be out alone.

Katherine looked towards the park. "Did you know that this was a military parade ground until just a couple of years ago, James? My dad still calls it the Washington Military Parade. He says he used to watch them train here all the time when he was young. He said that there was a cemetery here that they closed just before the military started using it. Can you imagine all the dead resting peacefully and then they start hearing thumping and gunshots on top of their heads? Sometimes I lie awake at night and think about it. I wonder if they are wandering around at night now, scared and confused. Do you think they are, James?"

James looked into her face, but she didn't notice as she was still looking away. She knitted her brows in thought and she looked genuinely concerned. He wanted to take her in his arms and smooth her forehead with his lips, but instead he said, "Yes, but now they can rest again since we have a beautiful park with trees and walkways. Shall we take a stroll and have a look?"

Just as he said that the sky overhead darkened as the sun became obscured by a cloud and Katherine shivered. "It's nicer in the summer, but why not?" She pulled her scarf tighter around her neck and moved a little closer to him. He noted that she genuinely seemed nervous about it, even in the early afternoon like this. She, the scotch drinking abolitionist was scared of ghosts. James felt something tug at his heart.

"Come," he said, and couldn't help but laugh as he pulled her across the cobblestones and into the park. "It's beautiful, I love the dark black branches against the white snow."

He took a deep frosty breath and looked around. The park was still. Only a man with a dog of unnamable breed walked on one of the paths on the east side. There was a lot of snow, but some places were bare and the dark black earth contrasted the snow dramatically.

Katherine shook her head at herself and laughed too, a pearly happy laugh.

I want this woman, I want to marry her, James thought looking at her silently.

She stopped laughing and their eyes met. He pulled her towards him and as she let herself get close to him with complete trust he almost wept. *I need to tell her the truth!*

The thought came clearly and unbidden. All these months he had avoided it. He had pretended to be someone else, but he couldn't help who his parents were, he was his own man.

"I want to kiss you," he whispered, his voice hoarse and full of emotion, "but we should speak first."

Katherine blushed and looked at him with such anticipation that he almost wavered, but he cleared his throat. "Come," he said, "let's walk for a bit more." They continued to walk silently through the park and he couldn't bear to begin, but there was no delaying it any longer and he turned to her and stopped. His pulse rose in his throat, "Katherine, there is something I need to tell you."

"Yes?" She didn't look concerned, if anything she looked excited. He hoped she didn't expect him to propose, but in fact he was, in a way. The question was if he would be able to when he had told her what needed to be said.

"Please, let me explain everything before you make any assumptions, Katherine. I need to tell you something. You will not like it, but it's time you know the truth," he swallowed trying to stay in control of his emotions as he saw the light in her eyes change. "I have not been quite honest with you. My family does not live on a small farm in Virginia. We...they have a large tobacco plantation." He waited to let the thought sink in and at first she looked as if she hadn't heard him or understood what he had said. She didn't say anything so he continued.

"I grew up with slaves, Katherine. They were my friends and part of my family. I didn't realize how wrong it was, and what it really meant for them to be owned by us. I never questioned it. Not until I came here. Not until I met you."

She still didn't say a word, but she had become pale and he felt her hand loosen its grip on his.

"I don't understand, James."

"Yes, you do."

At that, her hand went to her mouth and tears sprang to her eyes, but she didn't run away from him as he had feared she would. He tried to think of something to say, anything at all to soften the blow of what he had just revealed, but he was at a loss for words seeing her tears flow freely now down her cheeks and over the gloved hand still covering her mouth.

He took up her wrist hanging by her side and then the other one and held them firmly but gently between them. "Katherine, please don't cry!"

He had expected her to yell, hit him or run from him, but not this, not her silence and her tears. It was almost too much to bear. They stood in silence for what felt like an eternity but was perhaps only a few moments when finally she spoke. Her voice sounded different, harsh and raised, as if she was speaking to someone else, and in a way she was.

"What are you saying, James? *You* own slaves? How can... I thought you were for abolition?" She pulled her hands away from him. She looked surprised, as if she had held them over the hearth but hadn't noticed until they were already scorched and blistered that she'd been burned.

His heart was racing and he repeatedly had to swallow. He was afraid that she would walk away, but he couldn't speak to explain himself. He just stood there staring at her, noticing that the clouds kept passing, the sun making it sunny at one moment and darker the next.

Not until she turned to leave did he find the courage and his voice.

"Katherine, please let me explain."

She shook her head and kept walking, and he followed her almost running to keep up.

"Can you please let me explain; you have not heard my side of the story yet. You don't know what I'm going to say."

She turned then and looked at him, "Yes I do, James. I know exactly what people like you say. You take *such* care of your sweet property and they are *so* happy with you. They're like your own family. Yes I know, but it's wrong, James. You cannot own *people.*"

He was taken aback, hearing what he used to think and tell other people sounded tainted and ugly when she said it. He heard now how he used to sound.

"I will listen. I will listen to what you say, but then I would like you to leave and never speak to me again. I will speak to Pastor Beecher. I will tell him that he has a traitor in his midst."

"He knows already. I told him."

Katherine's mouth opened and closed and she stared at him in disbelief, "I beg your pardon? When did you tell him this?"

"About a month or so ago… fairly close to two months when I come to think of it."

"But you have come to church every Sunday? Why? I don't understand?"

"You should not draw such conclusions, things ain't always what they seem," James said loudly, his voice losing its civil tone. "*I* don't own any. Have you seen one about me?"

"James, you said…"

"I know what I said, but people change Katherine. I'm *not* my parents."

For a moment he thought she would stay and hear him out, but she just shook her head and quickly left the park.

She lifted up her skirt and hurried across the street to avoid a hackney. The horse was so startled that he almost reared up on his hind legs. James saw the hackman pull back on the reins and yell out. The horse snorted so loud that James could hear it from where he stood and he could see the breath form a cloud around his head. Katherine took no notice, she hurried on and then he lost sight of her.

He remained standing there for a long time staring at the spot where he had last seen her.

Chapter 17

It was hard to concentrate on his studies that night. He sat at his desk with a glass of wine to try to calm himself down and focus, but his thoughts kept going through the events in the park over and over again. Each time he remembered more details; the way her tears had fallen down her cheeks and the pain evident in her eyes. That he chose to tell her the moment when she probably had thought that he would propose must have struck her as incredibly cruel, he now thought. He sighed and got out of his chair. He stretched his back in several directions. He felt stiff and cold; he ought to put some more logs in the hearth and in the woodstove in his bedroom before he went to sleep.

He would have another glass of wine and eat some cheese and meat left over from yesterday. The medical books would have to wait until tomorrow.

He went to the kitchen, found a plate and got what he wanted out of the icebox. He grabbed the wine bottle and the food and walked back to the living room. It was warmer than the kitchen that was barely heated at all unless he cooked on the tiny stove.

Finally he grabbed a blanket and curled up in one of his comfortable chairs with the wine and his plate.

He decided to think of it logically. It was understandable that Katherine had left as she did; he had shocked her and surprised her in such a way that it was only to be expected that she would run. He was not surprised. Still he had hoped for another outcome, one where she would be as proud of him as Pastor Beecher had been.

What if she had really had the same thought as him, that they would spend their life together as man and wife, that she had received his intentions to mean that he intended a future together? She must have, as did her father. No father would let his daughter go to church with a man for several weeks, if he didn't think that man had honorable intentions. Not that she had left a church on her own to join his; she had told him that her family didn't go to church that often.

She would never say yes now. He poured another glass and drank it down fast, forgetting about his food. Instead, he abruptly got up and went outside.

After a half hour he knocked on Robert's door.

Robert was wearing thick flannel pajamas and a nightcap.

James laughed, "Oh, did I catch you in bed. Do you really wear a hat for bed?"

"James, you are drunk! What are you doing here at this hour? It's ten o'clock at night, man. Yes, it's cold in here. I can't afford to use too much wood," He held up his left foot and pointed to it, "I use two pairs of socks, too."

James stared at him thinking of how cold he had just been in his apartment and how he had added more wood. It would be warm and cozy when he came back home.

"This won't do, I'll go get you some more. Is there a place that is still open?"

Robert shrugged, "Possibly Thompson's Country store down the street. They are open late sometimes, but it really is not necessary..."

James was down the stairs before Robert could say any more. He didn't feel that he was as drunk as Robert seemed to think he was. In fact, he wanted more wine and something to eat. He was ravenous, just now remembering the food on his plate at home. The street was dark except for a dim light in a shed-like building on the corner. It was indeed Thompson's Country Store; it was written clearly with thick bold black letters on a wooden sign above the door. *Country Store, in such a large city!* James laughed to himself and went in.

Thompson was an elderly man with leathery, weather-bitten skin, a blue wool hat and a thick coat although he was inside. Everyone was cold on this night it seemed.

James got his wood, and asked for bread, a bottle of wine, and lastly a hunk of butter in case Robert didn't have any. Thompson helped him to add the wares on top of the pile of wood and held the door open for him.

A few minutes later, he was back at Robert's door. James had expected him to change but he was still wearing pajamas and his nightcap.

James walked past him and went straight to the fireplace and added three logs to the embers then piled the rest on the almost empty log basket.

Robert cleared his throat and came up behind him to sit down on his bed as he motioned to the recliner chair for James to sit. The bed and chair was all that fit in the room; there was not even space for a desk, just that, a bed, the fireplace and the chair. There was no table or anything else. There was a tiny window next to the door.

"James, thank you for getting the wood. I appreciate it."

"Don't think of it. It's my pleasure. You are my friend and it's cold."

"Thank you," Robert said simply then he eyed the bread and the butter and took a knife out of a little box that he pulled out from under his bed. He proceeded to pull out two wineglasses as well. "Sorry they aren't that clean. If you want to go out and rinse them under the pump in the backyard, you can. I usually just wipe 'em off with a towel."

James shook his head. He tried not to think about how dirty the glasses must be and how seldom they got washed. He just shrugged. He had worse troubles than dirty wineglasses at the moment.

He pulled off a hunk of bread and ate it slowly without butter and then he told Robert everything.

Robert chuckled and poured himself and James more wine.

"I'm sorry to look so joyous, James, but I'm very, very happy to hear that you have come to an understanding of the plight of the negroes. I didn't want to say anything when we spoke last. I didn't want to embarrass you, but I have never liked it. I *am* sorry about Katherine, but she may come around, you know. Just give her time."

James swallowed, feeling ashamed and uncomfortable about Robert's admission.

"How could she? What are we going to do, marry in Plymouth Church or at the Plantation in a large southern wedding; all the guests driven by their negroes and the negroes serving at the wedding ball? It will be dandy. All of Katherine's friends and my friends will get along splendidly."

"Marry here; marry at another church, or at Plymouth. Your family will not know that it has such an active abolitionist congregation."

James looked embarrassed and took a large sip of his wine. He felt rather inebriated now, but he didn't care. "They might know, actually. *I* didn't know, but I met a fellow southerner who took me there before I had changed my...before I had learned...you know," James stammered a little but Robert listened patiently.

"We went there to see what you northerners occupy your time with. My friends thought it hilarious, and said that they have taken other southern visitors there. It is common I hear. Who knows if any of my family or neighbors have heard? They would never speak to me if they knew I go for other reasons than entertainment."

"People go to Plymouth for entertainment? I don't understand."

"They think it's fascinating and funny to see how many people are so stupid and believe that negroes should be free." James felt his cheeks go hot. He remembered that day and how they were laughing in the hackney on the way to the ferry. It seemed as if it had been years and years ago.

Robert shook his head, "Damn, who would have thought?"

"I know, but I'm sure that I don't need to worry about what to do. Katherine hates me. She as much as said that she would never talk to me again." *If I by some miracle do marry her, then what will my parents say, and everyone else? They will laugh at me. I'm an embarrassment. Robert thinks we are all idiots, and so does my family. I'm a failure wherever I go.* James put his head in his hands and leaned forward in the chair. Everything was spinning. He felt Robert's hand on his shoulder. He hadn't heard him get up but all of a sudden he sat next to the chair on the floor.

"James, it will be fine. I'm sorry if I said something to offend you. I'm sure you will sort things out."

James couldn't answer. He saw some snot dribble down in between his knees, and he tried to sniffle but it landed on the floor. He sat up embarrassed.

"Robert, I'm very drunk. I'm sorry."

"No need to apologize. You can stay here. I will sleep on the floor."

"No, I'll go home."

"Nonsense."

James felt Robert pull him toward the bed. The next day he could not remember actually getting into it, but he was in it the next morning with a splitting headache to boot and Robert snoring on the floor

Chapter 18

Several weeks passed and James managed to focus on his studies at least somewhat. When he didn't study he spent almost all his time with Robert, either at a saloon or staying at school and studying together. The College had been at 23rd Street for over a year now since the move from Crosby Street. It was spacious and much more conducive for studying than at home.

James had entertained the idea of calling on Katherine to try to explain again, but he never worked up the courage.

He was taken completely by surprise when he came home one afternoon and found Katherine standing downstairs all alone. She looked nervous but she smiled slightly when he opened the little gate that led into the front garden of his landlady's house.

"Katherine," he said simply, not sure what else he should say.

"May I speak with you, James?"

He only nodded and walked past her to open the door with his key, trying not to get too close, but he still brushed her skirts with his side.

He held the door and gestured up the stairs. "It's on the second floor."

He tried not to look at her bottom as she walked up ahead of him.

Once inside she stood awkwardly by the wall and didn't take off her gloves.

James felt angry all of a sudden and clenched his teeth. She had left him standing in the park and now she appeared unannounced, not having even left her calling card with his landlady so that he would be expecting her. He waited for her to speak.

"James," she said finally, "I felt, I felt that I ought to speak with you. I am unclear on many things and I may have reacted a bit strongly, but I feel lied to."

He was going to ask her to come inside and sit, but he didn't. He let her stay where she was. "I tried to explain, but you saw fit to run out of the park and almost get yourself killed by a horse!'

She blushed, but didn't respond.

"Katherine, why don't you look around? See if you see a little side room behind the kitchen where my house negro lives. Look downstairs in the backyard, you never know, I might have a shed down there for one as well."

"James, stop! I know you don't have any, but how do you want me to feel? Your whole family...and you saying that you grew up on a plantation, it's against everything I stand for and have been against for years."

"So why are you here then, Katherine?"

She didn't answer, but her look told him everything he needed to know. He took one step towards her and put his hand behind her neck and pulled her towards him.

She smelled lightly of perfume and sweat. It was intoxicating. He put his lips close to hers and was going to kiss her, but at the last moment he moved his face and kissed her cheek. He felt her arms go around his waist and he hugged her close, feeling her strong heartbeat against his chest. After a while he had to move away or he would embarrass himself.

"Katherine, would you like a scotch?"

She laughed, "I would love one, James. Thank you"

He laughed too and hurried into the kitchen hoping that going in there and getting the glasses ready would solve his dilemma.

When he came back it was less obvious, but Katherine still stood by the wall. "Oh, I'm sorry, Katherine. Please have a seat, do make yourself comfortable. I apologize, it's not very grand."

She pulled her gloves off as she sat on the sofa where he usually sat and he sat down at the other end as he handed her the glass.

She flushed and took a sip. “James, I have been thinking about what you said, and that you have changed, that you hadn’t realized how it was for your slaves until you came here.” She went quiet and he tried to breathe calmly while he waited for her to continue.

“I…did you really tell Pastor Beecher?”

“Yes, I did. You can ask him yourself.”

“No, my mother won’t let me and Chrissy go all the way to Brooklyn without you.”

“Well isn’t that something. You didn’t tell them then, I take it?”

“No.”

James felt upset again. He swallowed the scotch in one gulp and looked at her.

“Katherine, I don’t think you have any right to come here and ask me if what I told you was true or not. Really, Katherine, haven’t I showed you already where I stand on this issue? You really think that I would go against my whole family and everyone I know from back home because I have some kind of dishonorable intention with you. Have you thought about how *I* feel? How do you think it feels to figure out that your very own family is doing something horrific and immoral? That people you have grown up with and have been loved by since you were a little babe ain’t happy but want out of there with all their hearts!”

He abruptly got up and grabbed his glass to go back to the kitchen to fill it up again. He felt so angry that he wasn’t looking where he was going and he bumped into the doorsill with his left shoulder and arm. It hurt and he would have yelled out in pain if she hadn’t been there. He heard her gasp.

James had a small mirror on the kitchen counter that was leaning against the wall behind it, and he peered into it, looking at his face. His blue eyes looked cold, he thought, and his cheeks looked blotchy and red. He took a deep breath to calm himself and poured another scotch. He stood there for a while, but became fearful that Katherine had left while he was in the kitchen, but she was still there, sitting at the edge of her seat with her hands clasped on her lap. She looked as though she had been crying. She had finished her scotch, but he didn't ask if she wanted another.

He wished he knew what she was thinking. Her brow was furrowed and her lips moved slightly over her closed mouth, but she remained quiet for a long time.

Finally, she raised her gaze and looked at him,

"James, will you forgive me. I have never looked at it from your point of view. You must be feeling wounded. Please, James."

He swallowed hard.

"I accept your apology," he said quietly and tried to keep his voice level. He saw her take a sudden deep breath as if she had been holding it for too long.

"I should apologize, too, for not telling you right away. For lying and sayin' that I come from a small little farm. I lied to your father and sister, too. It's unacceptable."

"I forgive you, but please tell me you do have raspberry bushes?"

He saw her eyes twinkle and he laughed, "That part *was* true! We do have them, right behind the house as I said."

Katherine laughed again and he just sat there looking at her. She was so beautiful.

Finally he got out of his chair and went and knelt down in front of her. He took her hands in his and squeezed them a little. "Katherine, I realize that this may not necessarily make you feel better, but I want you to know that my family isn't cruel and we do take care of everyone. No one has tried to run and..." *only one person was whipped to death! His wife has lost her mind. Other than that they are SO happy!*

“And what, were you about to say?” Her voice sounded sweet and he wanted to tell her, but how could he tell a woman such horror? “No, I forgot. I don’t know.” He pulled himself up and taking her face between his hands he kissed her right on the lips.

She didn’t resist and they kept kissing for several minutes until James pulled back.

“I’m not much of a gentleman, I should have asked you to marry me *before* I kissed you. Will you...marry me?”

“Oh yes!”

“I will speak to your father and ask him for your hand,” James grinned helplessly.

***

Before James had a chance to call on her father, the ice behind him finally cracked and everything came flooding in.

A letter arrived.

Dawson Plantation March 15th 1857

Dear James,

I am writing to you with the most unfortunate news.

Your parents died last night in a tragic accident. They were at a dinner party at Burnham’s Plantation. It was very hot inside and your parents and four other guests decided to go out for some fresh air in spite of the cold. They walked all the way up to the third floor veranda get a better look at the full moon that was setting beautifully yesterday. The railing had rotted over the winter and it didn’t hold. Your parents were leaning on it and they fell right through, and landed on the hard ground. Your mother died instantly and your father one hour or so later.

I am so very, sorry. My deepest condolences to you from me, my wife and our children.

We will of course look after your plantation and everything else until you get here, but please make haste and return as soon as you can.

Mr. Eric Dawson

PART II

Chapter 01

James did not have to say a word. The look on Mr. Greenfield's face made it perfectly clear that he understood that something horrible must have happened.

"James, you come in here and sit down, come," Mr. Greenfield took him by the arm and led him into the living room couch, gently pushing on his shoulders to make him sit down.

"Mrs. McNeary, get us a blanket and a glass of water will you. No, make that tea, with brandy in it," he hollered over his shoulder as Mrs. McNeary's concerned face appeared in the doorway.

James would never forget how kind Mr. Greenfield was that day.

"You just relax, James. Tell me when you are ready. My wife and Katherine will be here shortly. Chrissy isn't here. She is with her cousins."

James wasn't able to say anything. He just sat there. He felt extremely cold and he couldn't think clearly. For some reason he kept thinking of how he had left his anatomy books spread out on his bed; it felt wrong and he kept thinking that he should have closed them, as inane as that thought was at a time like this.

His mouth felt dry and he could hear his pulse in his ears.

As if from far away he saw Mrs. McNeary come in with a blanket thrown over her arm and a steaming teacup and saucer on a tray. “Dear Lord, what has happened to Mr. Waynewright? Has he come from an accident?”

Mr. Greenfield shook his head and gestured a question without a word. He took the cup from the tray and handed it to James, “Here, drink this.”

The teacup rattled so much on its saucer that Mrs. McNeary took it back, letting James drink from the cup alone. She carefully wrapped the blanket around his back.

He slowly sipped the tea and brandy and was finally able to muster up the strength to pull the letter out of his pocket and hand it to Mr. Greenfield. It didn’t cross his mind that Mr. Greenfield may still not know everything, forgetting that he had neither asked him for Katherine’s hand nor apologized for not having been truthful.

Without a word he read it, and then he neatly folded it and gave it back to James.

“My sincere condolences, sir, I’m so sorry.”

James tried to nod, but he just stared at him.

Just then they heard the front door open. Mr. Greenfield got up immediately and went to the vestibule. James heard muffled voices. “Katherine, James is here, his parents...they...” He heard her run and behind her Mr. Greenfield’s voice again. “His parents live on a plantation.”

Katherine fell into James’ arms and he held on to her and sniffed the scent of her hair.

He still couldn’t get a word out of his mouth and they sat like that for a long time. If her parents thought it improper, they were kind enough to let it be, discretely staying in the adjoining room with the door just slightly ajar.

It had darkened in the room when Mrs. Greenfield came in with a platter with more tea and sandwiches for both him and Katherine.

"James, I don't know what to say. I'm very, very sorry for your loss. You are welcome to stay in our guestroom tonight. Mrs. McNeary will make it up for you. Eat this and go to bed, try to get some sleep. We will talk tomorrow and we will help you in any way we can."

"You are very kind." His words sounded strange to his own ears, very hoarse, as if he had been crying but he hadn't shed a single tear.

Katherine looked relieved that he said something and smiled at him.

"James, dear, please tell me what I can do."

"I want you... I want you to come with me tomorrow. I cannot go down there alone. Please, I need you by my side. I cannot do it alone."

She went pale and let out a little gasp, but he was in too shocked a frame of mind to understand the implications of what he had asked of her.

Later Mrs. McNeary showed James to the guestroom. Katherine and her parents sat in the parlor talking until late. Katherine told them everything. She explained to her parents that James had intended to speak to her father this very week, to ask for her hand and to apologize for not being honest about his background. She told them that they loved each other and that James had proposed already.

Mr. Greenfield made it clear that it was out of the question for her to go with James, not even if Chrissy and Uncle Peter came. No father would ever send his daughter to another state with a man she was not married to, even if they were engaged and no matter the circumstances. James was obviously not thinking clearly.

Katherine kept saying that if she married him she would own slaves. She had never considered a scenario like this in the very short time since James had proposed. She had had many mixed feelings and worried what his parents would think of her. It had not crossed her mind that she may have to live on the plantation. James had said that he wanted to stay in New York and urged her not to think too much about their family business. She realized now that she had been naïve. James, being the only child, the only son, it was inevitable that he one day would have to move there and take over, as that was his birthright.

She didn't know how she would ever be able to set foot on his plantation.

The next morning, James woke up and found the whole family sitting at the dining table eating breakfast. Seeing them all together and Chrissy's sorrowful eyes as she saw him for the first time since it happened, finally brought the tears to his eyes and he turned on his heels and went back to the guestroom. He sobbed with his head in the pillow to try to muffle the sounds, but he was unable to stop for several minutes.

When he had pulled himself together, Katherine was alone. Wordlessly, she pushed a cup of coffee towards him.

"Are you all right?" she asked.

"No. No, I am not."

They sat silently together for a long time and then James began to speak.

"I will have to interrupt my studies. I will have to stop altogether. The plantation is mine now."

He didn't notice that she cringed.

"I've been up thinkin' most of the night, thinkin' of what we should do." He sighed and took her hand in between his, "Katherine, I had hoped that we could have a large wedding with all of our family present, and the right thing to do may be to postpone the wedding for a year."

"Yes, one full year of mourning is what you are supposed to do, or it would not be seemly," Katherine replied quietly.

"I know, it would, but I have been thinkin', Katherine, would you consider marrying me today?"

"Today?" she looked at him incredulously.

"I know it's not what you have dreamt of, of course, but due to my circumstances do you think that you may consider doing so? I cannot bear to go home on my own, I can't, I have no one. No family to help me and no one who feels as I do."

"You have friends, you most certainly have friends, and the...neg...the servants, you said that they were your friends. What will become of them?"

He sighed deeply and looked her in the eye. He felt the tears gathering in his eyes and he tried not to blink or they would drip. "If I don't go down there, I'd be forced to sell and they would surely be sold along with the tobacco crop and the animals. For a time people would help, but they have their own plantations, I might hire someone, but it would not hold in the long run."

Katherine looked horrified but didn't answer; instead she got up and started pacing back and forth.

"If I marry you, I will be a *slave owner.* I can't say I ever sensed that of my future," she said, her voice sounding like ice.

"Your husband will be," he said quietly, not sure if she had heard. If she had, she kept pacing and didn't respond.

Finally she sat down, "James," she said fiercely, "if we marry today, who would do it and how could we convince a pastor to do it on such a whim? No matter the circumstances, it *is* a little outrageous. Don't you think? Do you really expect me to just up and go on a moment's notice and leave my family just like that?"

He swallowed hard; he clenched his teeth, just as his father used to. "Katherine, please. I understand I'm asking a lot, but there are things...there are things that I haven't told you. I cannot bear to go back there alone. Please, Katherine, I'm begging you. My parents died. I have to go now, as soon as possible. I don't even know if they can hold the bodies above ground before I come down."

"I was thinkin' that we could ask Pastor Beecher. We could leave right now and ...he would understand...he...Oh God." He leaned forward, feeling dizzy suddenly and he let his head rest on his arms. He felt weak; there was nothing else he could say to get her to agree. He should have left yesterday, right away, but he had had this faint hope that she would join him.

"All right, James. I will do it, I will, but you must promise me something."

At first he thought he misheard and kept his head on his arms, but then he slowly turned towards her so he could see her face and he knew that he hadn't. "Oh, Katherine, you will really do it? Thank you, thank you." He reached for her and pulled her close. "Katherine, my darlin' Katherine."

She smiled but firmly took his hand. "James, you must promise me that when things are settled down there you will set them all free, every one, do you hear me? I cannot marry you unless this is a clear understanding between us."

He didn't answer at first. He just hugged her close and sat there trying not to cry. "I will do whatever you want if you come with me, my dear wife."

Chapter 02

Mr. and Mrs. Greenfield did not readily agree. Katherine was honest about the reservations she had but convinced her parents that she loved James and did want to marry him with all her heart, despite the circumstances. James silently thanked God that he had already proposed to Katherine and that her father was a modern man who respected that, even though it was unconventional that James had not asked him for his daughter's hand in marriage before he proposed.

Katherine's mother was concerned that everyone would think that Katherine was pregnant, but how could they say no? James *had* proposed, Katherine had said *yes*. Mrs. Greenfield liked James and had hoped that they would marry since the day James asked her husband if he might call on Katherine. Of course the not so small detail of his background changed things tremendously, but her heart ached when she saw how devastated he was. She understood that James would need his wife by his side.

So they dressed in their Sunday best. James borrowed a clean shirt from Mr. Greenfield, it was a little large but it had to do, then they went all the way to Brooklyn praying that the Pastor would be there. It was Saturday. He could be anywhere and if he was there, how would they convince him to say yes?

Pastor Beecher was standing right outside his church cutting excess branches off a tree when they arrived and he agreed a lot easier than they had expected.

After his condolences and inquiries of how James was managing he said, "We do many unorthodox things in our church. If this will help you and prevents your negroes from being sold and their families split up, if you as you say are planning on freeing them, how could I in good conscience say no?"

They were married right then and there. It was very emotional; Pastor Beecher was gentle and compassionate and made the vows sound different somehow with just the tone of his voice. James looked at Katherine with tears in his eyes and when she said I do, she cried.

A quick wedding lunch and they were on their way. James packed a small satchel. The Greenfields promised to take care of everything else and have his belongings sent to him.

Katherine packed a small trunk, her mother promising to have her belongings sent as well. Then they were off.

Chapter 03

James was too emotional to notice Katherine's round eyes and pale face as their hired carriage passed their neighbors' plantations with their negroes working in the fields. He didn't see her sit rigid, leaning forward in her seat and the tears falling down her cheeks, or her hands clasped so hard that her knuckles were white.

As they approached the main house, they heard the kitchen door slam and saw Auntie Ellen, Mary and Hettie hurry towards them.

Auntie Ellen looked even skinnier and more bent than she had a few short months ago.

"Massa Jr. Thank the lord you come home." Auntie Ellen hugged him close. Hettie touched his cheek and said, "Massa Jr., dear Massa Jr. We gonna help you, anything you need, we're here for you. We're all so terribly sorry and we're all so heartbroken," she burst into tears, hiding her face in her hands. Auntie Ellen put her arm around her daughter without a word.

"Thank you, Hettie," James mumbled struggling not to cry himself.

"Who is with you, Massa Jr.?" Auntie Ellen asked and peered at Katherine, her wrinkles creasing around her eyes.

"I'm sorry. Everyone, this is my wife. This is Mrs. Waynewright. You will like her, I'm sure of it;" *A lot more than you know.*

Katherine stood on the side by their two small trunks that the driver had taken down before he left. She was surprised at the closeness and genuine affection displayed by them. She felt confused. It didn't make sense. She certainly had not expected this at all. Every day during their journey when James had been silently grieving she had played out scenario after scenario in her head. She pictured negroes already sold off and the neighbor greeting them telling them that he had split up the families. She had expected fearful negroes running about nervously wringing their hands. She had even pictured James ordering them around and she had been terrified that she had married a monster, but she was not sure how to absorb what took place in front of her.

"A wife? You got married, Massa Jr.? Congratulations!" Suddenly they surrounded her and James laughed for the first time since the tragic news.

"Please everyone, make my wife feel comfortable here. She isn't used to plantation life." He squeezed her hand and she laughed, at least somewhat relieved.

The next morning James rose early. His body felt heavy as if the grief literally weighed him down. He had so much to do but all he wanted to do was to lie in bed next to Katherine and hold her. At the same time he almost regretted bringing her here. James had been so sure that he wanted Katherine with him, but in hindsight, it may have been better to wait out the year of mourning.

It would have been a lot easier to deal with everything himself without having her stare with her big sad eyes at everything.

He could just imagine what she was thinking, seeing everyone buzzing around them and then going back to work in the fields and in the house while Katherine sat down with him and ate a nice meal served and cooked by Auntie Ellen and Mary. Last night he had seen how Katherine kept eyeing Auntie Ellen and Mary; thanking them so many times, that Auntie Ellen began to look nervous. Mary even started laughing and said, 'Mrs. Waynewright, no need to be thanking us overly. We're your negroes now.' Katherine got such a pained look in her eyes that she quietly set her fork down and did not eat another morsel, which caused Auntie Ellen to get upset. James heard her bang the pots and pans angrily in the kitchen afterwards when they were sitting on the porch having port.

The warm fragrant scent of home hit James' nostrils as he opened the door and went outside. Slowly he walked to the stable to get a horse so that he could ride over to the graves of his parents. It seemed impossible that he had not been able to be at his own parent's funeral, but they had needed to get into hallowed ground. There was no way that they could have waited. He had simply been too far away.

Pap was already there. He tried to smile when James opened the stable door but it came out more as a grimace. "I'm so sorry, so sorry 'bout Massa and Missus. You goin' to see the burial place, Massa Jr.?"

"I didn't even say goodbye to them. I just left in the night." James went into Sweetface's stall and stroked her dark brown neck under her warm mane. "Yes, I was planning on goin' there. Will you get Sweetface ready?"

"Of course Massa," Pap quickly left to get the saddle and bit and James remained with Sweetface for a moment as he faced the reality that he was now the Master at his own plantation. Then he gave Sweetface another pat and went outside.

The white paint on the barn looked a little chipped; it hadn't been painted in years. James wondered who he should put to paint it. Where would they buy the paint? He really had no idea who did what. He knew Auntie Ellen and Mary in the kitchen, and sometimes Hettie, too, then Pap in the stable. He had assumed that everyone else was out in the field handling the tobacco, but there must be a thousand other little things that needed to be taken care of. He just never paid any attention to it all. He let his eyes gaze to the roof. It looked alright as far as he could see; the shingles looked sturdy still. The morning sun hadn't hit the roof yet, but it was light enough for him to see that there were no cracks or loose tiles.

He startled when the heavy black stable door opened and Pap came out with Sweetface.

"I'm so sorry, Massa. Did we scare you?"

He does not seem scared or unhappy. What if the stories we hear at Plymouth are all lies? Massa. I'm not Massa, Jr. anymore. "It's alright; I was looking over the stable. It looks as though it needs a coat of paint. Who would paint it?"

Pap's face darkened and he said, "Johnnie and Tim usually does the paintin', but now Tim will have to find someone else to work with him. Maybe I could do it, if you wants Massa?"

James nodded, feeling completely overwhelmed, "There is so much to do."

"Not to worry, we'll take care of it. We will do everything you tell us to."

"Yes I know, Pap," James replied. He felt an odd sensation in his stomach.

His family had their own private graveyard on the Plantation property just south of the tobacco fields in a little glen in the forest.

He found the graves with temporary wooden crosses and two little lanterns in front of each. It startled him at first, but then he realized that Dawson must have been waiting until he would pick out a gravestone for them.

His grandfather's gravestone looked as if it had been scrubbed; fresh soil was put around it and someone had weeded.

It seemed surreal; he couldn't believe that the bodies of his parents were underneath his feet. The last time he spoke to them they had all been so upset and his father had been disappointed in him for not letting him know what Adam had told him about Mr. Loch. Now they were gone, from one minute to the next, just like that, because of a lousy rotten beam.

James didn't cry but he remained standing by the gravesite for at least an hour.

It was warm, the bees buzzed about him, and several hummingbirds went from flower to flower on a purple Buddleia bush, but James didn't notice.

When he left he found Sweetface grazing on some thick green grass tuffs a lot deeper into the forest than where he had left her. He hadn't even remembered to tie her up to anything and he didn't remember *not* doing so.

He hurried back and rode all the way to the house without stopping by the stable first. He felt nervous that Katherine would have woken up and said something inappropriate to Auntie Ellen who always showed up early to get the breakfast ready before Mary and Hettie came.

Instead James found Katherine sitting in the rocking chair with a cup of tea on her lap and she smiled and waved happily as he approached.

He tied Sweetface to the hitching post in front, hurried up on the porch, and kissed her cheek. "Good morning, my wife." he said and sat down next to her.

"Good morning, my husband." She smiled and reached for his hand. "Ellen gave me tea and she is baking scones. It smells lovely, reminds me of Mrs. McNeary's cooking."

James smiled, "She is an expert baker. Wait until you try her pies."

Katherine didn't answer. Instead she lowered her voice, "I found her crying in the kitchen this morning. She said she misses your parents, her Massa and his dear wife she called them. She genuinely must have loved them. I hadn't expected that James. I see that things are not as simple as I had thought...but then she said that the plantation is cursed and that she is scared. I don't understand that."

James took a deep breath of relief when she told him that she understood more now. He squeezed her hand.

"Katherine it *isn't* simple. You may see now why I never questioned what we are doing..." He stopped and glanced at the door standing ajar for the airflow, to make sure that Mary, who must surely be there by now, wasn't coming outside. When he didn't see her he continued. "We really do care for them as part of our family, but ironically enough that is what has made me see things differently these last months. The fact that they are completely dependent on us no matter what happens...is not right, Katherine, it really isn't."

He saw relief in her face and she grasped his hand clasping it between hers.

"Katherine, there is something I have been meaning to tell you. It's not pleasant, but you need to know everything. You will hear it from someone else if I don't tell you. I know what Auntie Ellen might have meant about things being cursed, my parent's accident so soon after..."

He looked into her beautiful blue eyes and he knew that things would never be the same again afterwards, but he had no choice, he had to tell her.

"Katherine, do you remember when I came calling on you, and we sat in your kitchen because your carpets where being cleaned, and I told you that there had been a murder in the family?"

Her hand went to her mouth and she nodded.

"It was one of our own field hands. Our overseer murdered him, Katherine. He and some other men hung Johnnie from a tree. Then the overseer whipped him to death while his wife and baby watched."

Katherine didn't say a word; she just stared at him as all color faded from her face. He could see the pulse above the collar of her dress. He was sure she was about to faint, but she didn't. She grasped the armrests of the rocking chair so hard that he could hear the wood crack.

"*Where* is that man?" she said, tears flowing down her cheeks now.

"Mr. Loch," James spat, "the overseer? He is long gone. We have looked for him everywhere, even in New York. Our *dear* friend Adam knows him, too. I found out his family has used Loch for years, spying on the plantations, driving the field hands cruelly to get the revenue up, not knowing that he had a personal stake in it in more than one way."

"You mean Adam Rickman?"

"The very one! We ain't doin' business with him anymore."

Katherine's cheeks had gone from pale to blotchy red and she stood up and went over to the railing. "Oh that man, that man... I knew that there was something not right about his family. We had horrible arguments over slavery and he was always terribly smug about it. I could never put my finger on it. So he owns slaves, too?"

"No, they only bought and sold our tobacco and cotton from others further south. It was a coincidence that we happened to study together, I didn't know he would be in New York. If I had only told my father after their garden party that summer..." James said as if to himself. Then he looked at Katherine again, "Remember you found me in the chair and I said I wasn't feeling too well?"

"Yes, I do?" She looked surprised.

"Adam had told me that he recognized me and my name and knew who I was from the beginning. He smugly, as you said, and drunkenly I might add, told me how they were associated with Loch and how he doubled as an overseer and someone who spied on the plantations so that they would know where the best crop was before they bought..." James cleared his throat and pulled his left hand through his hair before he continued.

"This was before the murder. I haven't told you yet why he murdered him."

Pap had quietly picked up Sweetface without them noticing. Mary had set the table, put the eggs under an egg warmer but the coffee had long since cooled. Auntie Ellen and Mary were already preparing the midday meal while Hettie had cleaned and dusted the second floor before James and Katherine had finished talking or even noticed that they were hungry.

"Do you know what really changed me, Katherine? What really got me to realize that no matter how well loved they are by us, it is still wrong?" James asked when they finally rose to go inside.

Katherine shook her head and looked at him in anticipation.

"It was when I looked into Auntie Ellen's eyes and saw the desperation and utter helplessness within them. When Will told me that they had all stood there watching for a long time, thinkin' that they had to deal with it, that this happens from time to time and that there was nothing they could do. They didn't go for help immediately because they thought they had to take it! It about broke my heart when he said it, and I knew that there is no excuse. *No one* should ever think that they have no right to defend their loved ones from *torture.*" His voice cracked and became hoarse. Katherine touched his hand not bothering to wipe her own tears that flowed freely down her cheeks.

He grabbed her hand and mumbled, "Now you know everything about me, you know that it is my fault that Johnnie is dead. I promise that I don't have any more dark secrets to share with you. Can you forgive me for all these lies? I'm not at all what I seemed to you when we first met and when we began to go to church together."

Katherine smiled. "Yes, you are, even more. You were an abolitionist long before you knew it, James. You defended your family. You didn't know that Loch would murder him. You could not have known."

James pulled her close and they stood thus for several minutes, not caring that anyone might see them. They did not know that Auntie Ellen had heard Katherine speak of abolition when she had been on her way to ask them whether she should clear the untouched food on the table and set it up for the midday meal. She had stood stock still with her hand on the doorknob and a secret smile on her lips, not moving until James and Katherine embraced, then she slowly retreated to the kitchen.

Without a hint of difference in her behavior after what she had heard, Auntie Ellen made more coffee and toast and unfolded white napkins and carefully placed them in Katherine and James' laps.

"Massa Jr.," she said, calling James Jr. without hesitation; she had no plans to stop what she had called him since he was a toddling babe. "Have you shown Mistress her new house properly? Shown her your beautiful art all the way from Paris?" My other Mistress, bless her sweet soul, told me everythin' about it."

James looked surprised, "Mother talked to you about our artwork? I didn't know that."

"Yes, Massa Jr. When you and Massa were out doin' all that stuff you men folk do, me an' the Missus was alone in the house; she tell me many things. We were friends she an' I, not many people know that. Her father own me before an' I move here with her." Auntie Ellen's chin began to quake but she swallowed and managed not to cry.

"Auntie Ellen, I'm terribly sorry for your loss. I am just now beginning to understand how nice James' parents were. I never had the honor of meeting them," Katherine said, surprised that she actually meant it. If someone only two months ago had told her that she would regret not meeting a couple of slave owners, she would have thought that someone had been trying to insult her.

"You are right, Auntie Ellen. I have not showed Katherine anything. I should do so as soon as we finish with our breakfast."

Auntie Ellen looked satisfied and quickly left the dining room.

"So what do you say about a tour?" James said and pulled Katherine close and then they slowly walked around the house arm in arm.

James never paid that much attention to his manor, but it truly was beautiful. His Great Great Grandfather, Sir Chauncey Waynewright, had built the plantation in 1709. According to James' Great Grandfather, Sir Waynewright had been knighted by George II, and had the King's special encouragement to go across to Virginia to get the tobacco production going.

James' father had not believed it. He didn't think that a King would knight someone like his grandfather just for starting a plantation. He thought that Waynewright Senior just made it up to seem important, and back in the 1700's no one questioned you if you came from England calling yourself Sir.

The dining room where they had just eaten breakfast was considered the small dining room. It adjoined the kitchen and was used by the family when there were no guests present. It had dark wood floors and beautiful Turkish rugs. The "little" table as they called it, was dark mahogany and had six chairs around it. The room had a large Grandfather clock in the corner; it was one of the few belongings that had come over from England with James' Great Great Grandfather.

Leaving the smaller dining room led you to a large entranceway, the very first room that guests saw as they came inside. It was empty except for a large ornate fireplace and a large crystal chandelier hanging from the ceiling.

"This room is grand, James. I noticed it when I first arrived. The chandelier looks antique, is it?"

James shrugged, "I really don't know, Katherine. You should ask Auntie Ellen, she probably does."

"I see." Katherine stood silent and touched the ornate mantelpiece. Her forehead was furrowed and she cocked her head to the side, sliding her fingers absently along the smooth surface. "James," she said and turned to him, "so if Auntie Ellen went with your mother when your mother married, then did she leave her family behind?"

James felt ashamed. That question had never even crossed his mind before. All he remembered was his mother telling him that Auntie Ellen had been loyal to her since she was a little girl.

"Hmmrp," James cleared his throat and made a humming sound. "Um, well Auntie Ellen's daughters are here, Mary and Hettie, whom you have met. Mary cooks and Hettie cleans, and her son Will, he works the gardens and with the horses and other animals, and with the tobacco off and on. Auntie Ellen had a man once, their father, but he was a lot older and he died."

"Oh. Why do you call her *Auntie* Ellen?"

"It's a term of endearment. Uncle Pap is our stable hand, but I always call him Pap. My father, though, called him Uncle Pap. They are usually the older negroes who have been with someone a long time; it is a common term."

Katherine didn't answer. "Let's go in here," she said and disappeared into the larger dining room. This one had a table that could seat eighteen, another chandelier in the ceiling and artwork on the walls.

"This was shipped from Paris, probably the one that Auntie Ellen spoke about I believe," James said, moving close to a painting displaying a rather interesting scene; four Roman soldiers were standing guard in front of a massive stone building, a voluptuous woman lay splayed in front of them, her thick red hair spilling on the ground.

"Hmm, I can't see who made it?" James said thoughtfully, touching the frame as he scrutinized it for a signature. "Well, these here are portraits of my Great Grandmother and her sister who lived with them."

He pointed to two portraits, "These I know are made by John Smibert. This lady is my Great Aunt," he said proudly and pointed to the one on the left. A large eyed woman with black hair pulled back sat calmly on a chair looking as though she was in deep thought. She was wearing a green silk gown, exposing both her bosom and bare skin on her lower arms. The other woman was wearing a blue gown that was a little less revealing and she held a baby in her arms. The baby was clad only in a diaper.

"This is my father," James said with a grin, "I'm afraid it's the only likeness we have of him."

"Nothing of your mother?" Katherine asked.

"There is a small one in the bedroom upstairs. I'll show you." James took her by the arm and they continued.

The dining room led through a large archway into a drawing room. Large comfortable couches with shiny mahogany side tables, a large bookshelf lined one wall and next to the fireplace stood two tall beautiful cabinets with the most gorgeous woodwork.

"Oh, James! These are extraordinary, who made these? Is it old? Where did you get them? Are they Chinese perhaps?"

James laughed, "Not at all. Will made them!"

She stared at him in disbelief. "Will? You are joking, are you not?"

"No."

She let her hand slide up and down on the sides of the cabinet, opened the door and looked at the hinge, felt the ornate carvings along the glass window of the cabinet door.

"James, Will should have a studio in New York with staff under him. This is extraordinarily well done. He could sell them all over the country and in Europe. The craftsmanship is beyond anything I have ever seen."

"It is?" James said confounded. The pieces were nice, but he had never thought much about it. Come to think about it, he really had not noticed much at all about their home. He had just taken it all for granted.

"I thought you knew that Uncle Peter has a furniture shop and deals with antiques. I spent a lot of time with him in his shop and I have never seen anything as good as this. It is flawless. When does he have time for this?"

"He usually fidgets at night, sometimes outside by the stable or in the shed." James smiled awkwardly, not sure what to say.

"Fidgets?" she said, raising her eyebrows. "This is not fidgeting, I can assure you. Please, can I talk to him? Uncle Peter would be able to find buyers. Some of them ask for replicas of antiques. I must write to him today. As a matter of fact, can I invite him down here to take a look at these? He would hire Will immediately, I'm sure of it."

You have been here less than a week, and already you are finding ways for them to get work elsewhere. "Of course you can. Why don't we go look for Will now? I expect he is probably seein' to the horses that are grazing. Let's ask Pap to get the horses ready, we'll ride down," James said and started walking back the way they came, relieved that the house tour was over. He didn't want to spend too much time inside looking at his parent's belongings. Every single piece reminded him of them.

"James, I cannot ride, I have never even tried." Katherine caught up with him and she looked embarrassed.

James laughed and kissed her on top of her head. "Do you not? Well then it's time to learn."

Chapter 04

Three days later, James and his neighbor Mr. Eric Dawson sat around the table in the large dining room. Dawson's plantation was the largest in the area with tobacco as well as a dairy, something that had evolved from Mr. Dawson's father Cornelius' obsession with fine cheeses. As a young man, Cornelius Dawson had worked his way up to Captain of a Slave Ship after the War of Independence. When the Abolition of the African Slave Trade Act of 1807 forced him into early retirement, the Old Salt purchased the plantation and put his pick of the last shipment to work on it.

Eric Dawson and his wife had three children, a son Peter, and two daughters, Adeline and Aurora. He and James' father had been friends since they were children together. Dawson had even saved James' father once when they foolishly had played on the ice on their lake one unusually cold winter. It had not been cold enough for the ice to hold two little boys and James' father had fallen right into the cold black water. If it hadn't been for Dawson's quick help, James would not be sitting here now.

James was well aware of all this, but he also knew that Dawson was overly strict and had a temper, something that his mother had pointed out to his father on more than one occasion. James himself had been victim of this temper several times and he used to be scared of him when he was a boy.

James sat silently as Mr. Dawson glanced at his papers one last time and handed them to James.

"Here is the inventory that I took the few weeks I was here before you and Mrs. Waynewright were able to get here."

"Thank you for takin' care of the plantation and for all the arrangements you have dealt with, including the funeral," James said.

"Of course, James, of course. There is no need to thank me." He looked at James for a moment without saying anything. Both of them were lost in thoughts of what had happened.

Then Mr. Dawson swallowed and gestured at the papers that James was now holding.

"I did not look at the house, just the horses, negroes, pigs and cows and the tobacco of course. You have the same amount of slaves since the last inventory, with the death of one and the birth of one; 84. It's a lot."

James resisted the urge to comment as Dawson casually mentioned the death and birth as if it was just an ordinary event.

"Are you planning on keepin' everything if you stay here, all the livestock? If you are plannin' on selling any of your negroes I'd be happy to take one or two, and if you are selling more, Wilson mentioned that he would be interested as well, and the slave outcry in town is..."

James was annoyed at Dawson's gall to assume that he would sell when the soil on his parents' graves was still fresh. It hardened his determination that if his father could handle it all, then so could he. Looking Dawson in the eye, barely able to hide his annoyance he said; "I'm *not* selling." Dawson didn't seem to notice and went on as if nothing had happened.

"Well, I see, so you are plannin' on staying here for a while then and not go back to New York?" He phrased it like a question but he didn't wait for an answer. "If you should feel that it is a lot with the husbandry of the negroes and the rest of the livestock, please consider selling some. Your father started off small and then built himself up."

He wants it for himself, what a bastard. I thought he was my father's friend.

"Respectfully, *Mr.* Dawson, I have no intention to sell, nor scale down that which *my* father has built up from what *his* father started. I do hope you can appreciate that losing my parents is still a fresh wound. While I understand your pragmatism in bringing this up, please let me make my own decisions.

Finally Mr. Dawson picked up on the mood. James could hear his chair scrape on the floor as if he was about to get up, but he remained. He cleared his throat and patted James' hand. "I apologize, James...I'm sorry if I sounded as if I was pushing you. That was not my intention. I just thought that if you *were* moving back to New York and leavin' the plantation in the overseer's hands, it would be easier if...well. I apologize. Since I was your father's closest friend, I just wanted to make sure that his estate was in order so that I could help you. So that you would know that everything is in place and what it's worth. I apologize."

"Thank you, I'm very grateful for all you have done in my absence, but I have returned prepared to rise to the occasion. I am married now. Katherine and I have some big shoes to fill."

"I understand," Dawson said. He looked as if he was about to say something else, but didn't and James left it at that. They remained small talking for just a few minutes and then Dawson rose to leave.

As soon as Dawson was out the door, James went into the small library behind his office where Katherine was sitting. She had a book in her lap but her eyes sparkled with held back tears. It was clear that she had heard every word.

"He spoke of them as if they are oxen or pigs to sell."

James got a hard look in his face. "You should prepare yourself. It will not be the first time they are referred to as such," James sighed. "I don't know how long I can keep this up. I feel like I'm a traitor on both sides. If our friends in New York could see us they'd be horrified. If our neighbors here knew, they...I don't know what they'd do. They might kill me, and on top of that our negroes don't know that I've become an abolitionist.

If anything, the conversation with Dawson made James realize that he ought to familiarize himself with the plantation and do his own inventory.

He spent the whole afternoon and evening looking over everything; the tobacco fields, the barns, the pigpens and the negro quarters.

He visited Martha, too. She was doing better than when he saw her last; at least she didn't sit and claw at the ground. She was resting on her bed. She recognized him immediately and sat up when he walked in.

He pulled a chair out and noticed that it did not scrape the floor at all. Will must have put felt on all the furniture. Katherine was right, he should be doing it full time.

"Are you feeling better, Martha?"

"No, not really, Massa Jr. It just look that way."

James swallowed. "I'm SO sorry, so sorry, Martha. If I hadn't hit Loch, it would never have happened. It's my fault, I'd give anything to go back and redo that day..."

"No."

Martha looked at him with a piercing look in her eye and slowly started talking, her voice was shaky and each word sounded slightly jagged as if it was hard for her to speak, but he heard every word.

"No, Massa Jr. He had his eye out at Johnnie and would have found another reason for it anyway...babe's his, he was jealous of Johnnie."

The room seemed to still, and James could hear his heartbeat roar in his ears. *That's why he accused me of being the father... he knew the baby would be lighter brown.*

"Did...did he have his way...did he?"

She took a deep breath and continued in the same slow and jagged fashion. "Every night...for months... Johnnie couldn't do nothin' about it; he had a hard time with it in the fields...No one could've been happier than us when you hit him," her eyes shone, but she didn't smile.

Overwhelming emotions, relief that he may not be the cause of the torture after all, relief that Martha didn't blame him, relief that she was able to speak, disgust and raging anger that Mr. Loch had raped one of their own for months right in front of her own man who was not allowed to protect her. James started to feel nauseous as if he was about to vomit.

He wanted to ask why they hadn't told his parents, but he didn't want to lay more guilt on her. He took her hand and said, "I promise you, Martha, that things will be very different round here; you will see soon."

Martha looked at him for a minute without saying anything. He remained with her for a few minutes before he made an awkward goodbye and left.

As he stepped out it had begun to darken. The cicadas where playing their nightly concert and the air was full of the perfume of spring, but James didn't notice.

To think that that Mr. Loch had tried to make her work during labor, threatening to lash her with his own babe about to be born, then killing her husband who had tried to protect her and *his* baby. Obviously here it was Johnnie who was more human than Loch, more of a man than Loch. James felt overwhelmingly disgusted as he walked back to the house and looked for Katherine.

He found her by the small dining table with a cup of tea next to her and her head bent in concentration over a letter she was writing. She looked beautiful and it distracted him for one wonderful second.

He touched her shoulder and said, "Katherine, no more! We are tellin' them tonight."

Slowly she put her pen down. She grabbed his hand as he sat down next to her.

"I am... I am utterly at a loss for words, so I will just come out with it. Loch raped her, do you understand?" His voice sounded shrill and hoarse, "It was *his* baby that Johnnie died for. He forced his *own* baby to watch!"

Katherine didn't say a word, but if he hadn't been so upset he would have noticed her face drop and seen her pulse race at her throat.

Finally she spoke. "Shouldn't we be a little more prepared first? If they all leave then how are we going to handle everything? How can they all leave safely, you know how treacherous it is for them to get up North."

"We will have to help them the best we can, then we'll sell and go back to New York."

Katherine nodded, "It can work, but we must be careful."

James got up abruptly causing his to chair fall backwards with a crash. The memory of his chair falling and his awkwardness when he met Doctor McCune Smith as well as his wife flashed before his eyes and suddenly he felt defeated, all the air went out of him and he just stood there his arms hanging by his sides.

"James, dear James, it will be all right. Go to bed now and I will bring you a brandy and some hot milk. Then you will sleep on it and we'll talk to them tomorrow. I think we should consult Pastor Beecher and have him advise us on how to do things right." She patted his cheek.

He tried to smile and pulled her close. "All right, Katherine, I will sleep on it. I'm too angry and upset right now anyway, but I don't want to wait for a letter to reach Beecher and then wait for his response. I'm at least going to speak to Will tomorrow and then we'll see."

Chapter 05

They decided to speak to both Will and Auntie Ellen. When Auntie Ellen showed up at 5:30 to prepare the breakfast they were both waiting for her.

She looked terrified when she saw them sitting on the stools in her kitchen and a high-pitched noise came from her lips before she clamped her hand over her mouth.

James laughed. "No need to worry, Auntie Ellen, everything is fine, but we would like to talk to you and Will. Would you mind getting him? Don't wake anyone else."

"Everyone is up already, Massa Jr."

James felt ridiculous. Dawson was right; he really didn't know anything about his plantation.

"Of course...but please it is important that it is only you and Will who will speak with us. Try to go unnoticed if you can."

Auntie Ellen gave him a quizzical look and left without a word.

James and Katherine nervously grabbed each other's hands and prepared to wait yet again. They sat there silently, each involved in their own thoughts.

Auntie Ellen may be old, but she must have run down to the quarters, because only a few minutes later the small kitchen door opened and Will pushed himself in with Auntie Ellen trailing behind. She didn't even look out of breath.

Will had a look of anticipation and seriousness in his eyes when he wished them good morning.

"You too, Will." James took a deep breath. "Katherine made coffee, please help yourself and come join us in the small dining room."

They both looked surprised. If it was because they were offered coffee or if it was because Katherine had made it he didn't know, but they each took two cups from the negro cupboard and poured a large helping each.

When they came into the dining room, James took a deep breath and looked at the two of them where they stood by the wall and he pointed to the chairs, "Auntie Ellen, Will, please sit down."

Now Auntie Ellen was not able to hide her surprise and exclaimed, "What's this here fuzz? You ain't sellin' us Massa Jr?" Will threw his mother an angry glance but he didn't say anything.

"Quite the contrary, please do sit." James looked at Katherine who reached her hand out to Auntie Ellen and then to Will as she said,

"We have something to tell you, and we ask that you keep this to yourself for a while until we can figure out how to deal with it the best way."

"Yes, Missus," Will said. Auntie Ellen nodded cautiously.

James cleared his throat and took Katherine's hand in his. She squeezed it firmly. He took a deep breath again and started speaking.

"I have changed a lot. I admit that I had never really thought much about my life before I left. I went to New York in the hopes that I would be able to become something else, a doctor..." He stopped and looked at them both for a moment. "My father told me that I better watch out so that I wouldn't be influenced by those northerners and abolitionists up there. I don't think that my father anticipated that I might become one of them." He paused looking at their faces, but he didn't see any reaction in their eyes at all. They kept looking at him with interest, but did not seem to understand the magnitude of what James had just said.

"Do you know what abolition means?" Katherine interrupted.

"No, Ma'am," Auntie Ellen said, maybe a little too quickly. Will didn't say anything and avoided her eyes.

"What abolition means is someone who wants to abolish slavery. Someone who thinks it is wrong to keep other human beings in bondage. When my father warned me of their influence, he most likely did not anticipate that I would be involved with a church in Brooklyn that aides runaway slaves," James said.

The silence was complete.

James was struck by the look on Auntie Ellen's and Will's frozen faces.

They stared at him and Katherine without moving a muscle or even breathing differently. James could hear the sounds of the morning outside the kitchen, the birds chirping loudly to each other from several directions as they too woke up. He heard a bee buzz and a fly hitting the window. Then it was as if the spell was broken and Auntie Ellen's lower lip started to quiver. She grabbed Will's hand and just looked at her son pleading with her eyes for him to speak.

"Hrmn...Massa Jr....I"

"There is no need to call James Massa anymore, Will. Mr. Waynewright or James will do," Katherine interrupted. James could hear the emotion in her voice.

Will looked stunned and stammered something inaudible and then he sat back on his chair and scratched his head, not bothering to try to speak.

Auntie Ellen let go of her son's hand, leaned forward, and spoke to James in the same tone as she had done when he was a boy. "James, if this here is one of your pranks, I'm not humorin' it no more!" James laughed and looked at Katherine, "I'll explain later.

He cleared his throat again.

"This ain't a joke, not at all. I have come to the realization that I cannot own anyone. I do not think it is right anymore. I don't know if I ever did, it's just that I never questioned it. Then I met Katherine and my experience in New York made me see more clearly."

Will's eyes widened slightly, but Auntie Ellen didn't seem to react. James continued. "Then when...when the murder happened and you told me, Will, that you thought you all had to take it..." James became silent, feeling overwhelmed. He swallowed and was able to go on, "I realized that it was unspeakably inhumane, to think that you had no right to protect your friend." He shook his head sadly.

Auntie Ellen abruptly got up and left the room. For the first time in her life she left a room with a white person in it that was in the middle of talking to her without asking for permission. They heard the screen door slam behind her in the kitchen.

"Massa Jr... this is quite the shock. What you plannin' on doin'?" Will asked.

Katherine and James looked at each other. "We have spoken about it a lot the last month or so since my parents died. Before they died I thought more of how to distance myself from them and how to have a wedding where Katherine's abolitionist family and mine would be able to be civil to each other," James said trying to make light of the situation.

Will stared at him without responding.

"What we would like to do," James went on, "is to sign your freedom papers immediately. If you all want to leave, then we will sell. If you don't we will pay you for your work."

Truth be told, they hadn't actually spoken of it in those terms, but it came to James as the obvious solution.

Katherine smiled at James, agreeing with him, and said, "Will, we realize that it is not as easy as it sounds to leave even though you'd have freedom papers. Everyone around here isn't exactly agreeing with us, but we will help you and we will have to figure out how this can be done safely for everyone."

Will opened his mouth to say something but was interrupted by Auntie Ellen coming back. Her eyes looked swollen.

"Sorry I lebt," she said, sounding congested.

Katherine grabbed her hand and squeezed it, "No need to apologize."

Auntie Ellen tried to smile but it became a grimace and tears spilled down her cheeks.

"Mama, sit. It'll be all right, Mama."

She plunked down on the chair next to Will and then she put her head in her hands.

"We got nobhere go," she mumbled and blew her nose in her handkerchief.

James looked at her, taken aback. It hadn't crossed his mind that she would say that.

He didn't know what to say. He glanced at Will who looked back at him with a look James realized he had never seen before this day.

It only lasted for a fraction of a second, but it was there; defiance and a look that said, *See! See what this does to us.*

Shaken, James turned to Auntie Ellen, "I was just tellin' Will that if you don't want to leave you can stay, but we will pay you for your work."

She looked at him silently. She seemed a little more relaxed but her eyes were still full of disbelief.

"Massa Jr.," Will said, still ignoring Katherine's suggestion that he didn't have to call him that. "What is going to happen if almost everyone leaves except for ten and you have to sell? If ten stay and you sell, then we'd have to go too, even though we don't want to."

He could feel Katherine's eyes on him and he looked Will straight in the eye and said, "Don't worry, Will. We will take care of you. If we sell and there are people who want to stay, we will figure something out." James would never know how surprised Will was to hear him say the word *people* instead of negroes.

Auntie Ellen looked relieved, but Will still looked as if he didn't really believe him.

Then Katherine broke in. "Will, I have been meaning to ask you something for a while. In fact I was on my way to, the other day, but I got distracted with riding lessons. Anyway, you say that you don't want to leave, and that is fine, but I have seen your craftsmanship and having a bit of experience with such work I can tell you that I have never seen anything finer." She paused, "My uncle has a furniture store in New York City. I would like him to see your work, if you don't mind it? He would hire you right away. I was telling James that there are many people who'd want replicas of antiques."

" I don't understand, replica?"

"Oh...I'm sorry, Will, it means a copy or likeness. Many people want copies of antique furniture in their homes. My uncle has been looking for someone for months as a matter of fact, because he has a client who wants the same bed as Henry VIIIof England had."

Now Will laughed and said, "You want me to make the bed of a king? You sure this ain't a prank like my mama said?"

"No." She laughed.

Katherine held her hand out to him and then she grabbed Auntie Ellen's, too. James' eyes burned as he watched them. Will locked eyes with James and for a long time he just looked at him.

"Thank you, Mr. Waynewright," he said softly.

Chapter 5.5

It was a moonless night and the journey had gone well, though the man was thirsty. He had not found many streams to either drink from or walk in to hide his scent from the dogs.

Instead he had tied pouches of ground turnip mixed with pepper on his feet.

He had slept under trees and in an old abandoned barn even though that would probably be the first place the slave catchers would look, but he took the risk because it was raining and it was cold and so dark. The moon had already been waning when he left as was the plan and on that rainy night he couldn't see the North Star. He had prayed and hoped that the Catchers would stay indoors by their warm fires on such a night.

*"Let the Morningstar greet me on the praying ground, let the Morningstar greet me on the praying ground...*he prayed over and over again as he continued on his journey.

After many hours he reached the station and knocked on the door of the tiny cabin.

The woman was old and skinny with a face full of wrinkles. She opened the door with a warm smile. "Come in my child, come inside."

The old woman smiled again as she pointed to a large cupboard that had been moved aside. Under it was a hole big enough for a man to squeeze through.

Chapter 06

The next couple of days were ripe with emotion and change.

James wrote to Pastor Beecher asking him for advice and help should any of their friends, as Katherine and he sometimes called the negroes now, choose to move north.

Then he had a talk with the overseer and told him that though he did an excellent job, he had decided that he wanted to work the fields on his own as he learned what it was to own a plantation. Mr. Berns had looked completely stunned, but with a letter of recommendation in hand and two weeks' salary he mumbled something about visiting family in Charlottesville for a bit before he would look for more work, and he was off.

Will and Auntie Ellen went on as before, working as if everything was just the same. But each morning Auntie Ellen flashed them such a smile that there was no mistaking her being happy now that the news had settled in.

James wondered if she and Will had managed not to say anything to Hettie and Mary what with them living in the same cabin and all, but none of them seemed different in any way when they came and cleaned and cooked.

James wrote his accountants both in New York and in Richmond to see how much he owned. He really had no idea, but realized that if he was going to pay everyone, he needed to know what would be reasonable. He felt embarrassed, he had taken so much for granted and ignored his father when he had tried to get him involved in the business.

The undertaking they had just bonded themselves to was enormous. If they all choose to stay then it would be him and Katherine who were in bondage, and would not be able to sell because then their friends would have nowhere to go.

James would have to speak to Will. He didn't know the field hands very well. His father and mother knew every single person on the plantation by name. James barely knew if the field hands belonged to him or not. If he met someone who said that he or she was visiting from another plantation they could walk off and he'd never be the wiser.

He decided to ask Will to tell his sisters and Pap and then they would see with the rest.

Many questions remained; for one, what to tell their neighbors. James could picture Dawson's shock if he told him. He knew what he would have thought himself just a little over a year ago, well almost two. The sensible thing to do would probably be to pretend that they still owned them at least in the beginning. There was no knowing how Dawson or the other neighbors would react. They might even get angry.

Two days later, Katherine and James were relaxing on the front porch in the evening with cool glasses of white wine and cheese when Pap walked up with Will, Hettie and Mary.

By the expression on their faces it was clear that they knew.

Katherine laughed at the sight of their beaming faces, a pearly laugh that made James' heart swell with pride and confidence that everything was as it should be.

Pap came straight up to James, took his hand in a strong grip and looked him straight in the eye for a long moment. "Mr. Waynewright..." Pap helplessly grinned when he called him Mr. for the first time. "I don' rightly know what to say."

"Don't say anything, sit down and have a glass of wine."

Katherine looked over at her husband with an approving look.

Mary and Hettie giggled. "We have never had wine before. Our Massa never allowed it," Mary said and Hettie filled in, "said it'd cause all sorts o' trouble, negroes drinkin'."

Pap looked startled, almost scared for a second but then he glanced at Will who nodded, and then he relaxed and said, "I be obliged to say yes to such'n honor. Thank you, Mr. Waynewright," Pap looked moved. James noticed his eyes tearing up.

Will grabbed the two remaining rocking chairs and motioned for his sisters to sit in them and then he and Pap sat on their haunches leaning against the porch railing.

Mary pulled her chair a little closer to Pap so that she wouldn't be too close to the ghost spot.

At first they all looked at each other, unsure of what to say or what to do until suddenly Katherine stood up exclaiming that she was a horrible hostess and disappeared inside to get more glasses.

Pap looked long and hard at James, "I always knew you was a good man, Mr. Waynewright." He looked as if he was about to say something else but stopped as Katherine came back with another bottle and the glasses. She put them down on the little wicker table and poured a little bit in each glass.

Katherine sipped a little more wine quietly and then she turned to Will, "Have you thought about what we talked about?"

"I have ma'am. I'd like to like to try it if you really think your uncle would be keen on that idea."

"I know he would. I wrote him already...it made me realize something writing him." She looked at each of them, "I think it would be appropriate if I would teach you to read and write."

No one said anything. Both Katherine and James were surprised as they had both talked about it at length and thought they would be happy.

"We will make sure we'll sign all the necessary papers before we begin. When you are free, no one will get in trouble for readin'," James said. He wondered if they were scared, since it was illegal for them to read.

They still looked nervous. He and Katherine glanced at each other and Will looked troubled.

Finally Pap cleared his throat and changed the subject entirely.

"I've been thinkin' on it since yesterday when Will told me and I spoke to Ellen... we're both stayin'.

James smiled, relieved; he had hoped for that.

"Hettie wants to come with me, to help me up North," Will said but was interrupted by Mary who said, "I come after they settle... I can't really believe it... I have always dreamed about it, but I have never thought it'd be true...is Will really gonna make a bed for a king?"

"Unless my uncle has found someone just as good as Will, but I highly doubt it. Knowing him, he'll be on the way down here as soon as he receives the letter, so it could be only a couple of weeks." Katherine paused for a moment and turned to Will. "I've been meaning to ask you how you learned such excellent carpentry?"

Will nodded and hummed a little before he answered, "My father... I helped him from the time since I was no more than a little boy. My father was very exact about measurin' each piece, and sandin' it smooth, then his eyesight went and I did more and more. Old Massa Waynewright gave us all the things we needed, all the wood, tools, fine saws n' all. He let us work out in the shed out back behind the stables."

"That is lovely," Katherine said.

"Where is Auntie Ellen? Didn't she want to join you tonight?" James asked surprised that she stayed down in the cabin by herself. For some reason he hadn't thought of it until now.

"Oh we'd not expected to be invited in to such fine company," Pap said real quickly and James caught Hettie glance at him nervously.

James couldn't put his finger on it, but there was something going on, something in the air that felt tense. Maybe it was just the newness of it all, the new experience of sitting together on a warm spring evening listening to the crickets and cicadas, but James wasn't sure if that was all.

They remained awkwardly silent for a time, their breathing and the slow movement of the rocking chairs the only sound. James decided to light another pipe and as he bent forward to reach for it, there was a loud hoot from an owl. It startled him and he dropped the tobacco on the floor.

As he poked around feeling for it in the dark he heard both Pap and Will stand up.

"We ought to be gettin' on home, it's gettin' late..."

Hettie and Mary got up, leaving their wine untouched on the wicker table.

They thanked them and quickly left the porch, disappearing down the lawn.

As soon as they were out of sight, Katherine looked at him.

"You do understand don't you?"

"What?"

"You really couldn't tell?" When James shook his head she said, "I feel rather stupid to be honest. They must be laughing at us right now."

"Laughin' at us? What are you talkin' about?" James lit the pipe and took a long calming draw. It certainly was shaping up to be an odd evening. First their negroes acting odd and now his wife was mystifying him.

She got up and leaned over the railing and looked across the lawn and wooded area where the quarters were and turned around towards him. "James, I think they already know how to read."

"Of course not. Don't be ridiculous."

"I'm not, James. It was rather obvious, and I'm surprised that you did not see it. As soon as I asked if they wanted to learn, the mood changed. I could see it in their eyes that they weren't comfortable telling us the truth, but they know, I could tell."

"I doubt it, Katherine. I have known them all my life, and I have never seen them read anything at all. In fact, I have seen them pretend to read things upside-down only to quickly put the book or paper back when I came in so that I wouldn't think that they were reading, not knowing that it was obvious that they can't since they didn't even know what side is up!"

"Oh really, that is a clever deception for sure," she laughed. "Don't underestimate them, James. I used to help a lady who taught runaways reading. It was Mrs. McCune actually. She told me that several young women and men had a pretty high reading level that they had been hiding from their owners for years."

James looked doubtful and took another draw on his pipe before he put it down on the ashtray and reached for his wine. "I highly doubt it here, honestly Katherine. As much as I would like them to, I truly don't see it. Will used to tell me himself that he had tried it once but that he realized soon that it was too hard."

"How could Dr. McCune become a physician then, James?" Katherine asked indignantly.

James shrugged. "Probably has a lot of white blood in his veins I'd assume."

Katherine did not respond.

Chapter 07

The next morning, James was on his way to the stable to ask Pap to get the horse ready so that he could ride into town to see if there was any mail at the post office. It was nice to go into town to get supplies as well as talk to the storekeepers and sometimes have a drink in the saloon.

Just as he turned around the corner of the barn, he saw a negro riding up the lane to their home. Curious, but disappointed that something was getting in the way, he yelled out but the rider didn't hear him with the thumping of fast hoofs on the road. James turned back. He could see Katherine waving and smiling on the porch as if it was a long lost friend approaching. He would have to talk to her about this. They may believe what they believed, but she had to learn some restraint or people would start talking.

People already had as James would find out shortly.

"Please, Massa, sir," he said when James caught up with him, "you and your wife..." he paused and bowed to Katherine with a broad smile, probably very happy about the enthusiastic wave he'd been greeted with. "My Massa Dawson invited you for breakfast this mornin', he say it short notice but he really like you and Missus to come."

James glanced at Katherine, and without waiting for an indication of what she wanted to do he nodded. "Tell Mr. Dawson that we will be happy to visit. We'll try to be there shortly."

"I sure will tell him, Massa Waynewright," he said and turned his horse around and was off.

"What do you think this is about, James?" Katherine wondered as soon as he had ridden off. "Isn't it a little strange to invite people on such short notice, not leaving a card or anything first?"

"It is," James said and felt an odd sensation in his stomach, "unless something has happened; but why didn't he come himself then? We will see. Are you ready to go if I get Pap to bring the carriage, unless Matilda is here? Maybe she could go tell him?"

"She is in the kitchen as usual. I'll tell her."

Katherine had become very fond of little Matilda, Jenny and Morris' daughter. She had been coming with Auntie Ellen off and on since she could walk so that her parents could tend the tobacco. Since the first day that Katherine had been there, Matilda ran from the kitchen to wherever Katherine was to try to impress her with her skills for jumping, singing or whatever else the little five-year-old thought important. She was adorably cute; she had thick shiny curls and the largest brown eyes you could imagine.

About an hour later, Pap drove up the private road to the Dawson plantation.

It was a lot grander than theirs was; James smiled when Katherine's jaw almost dropped. The main house was about twice the size of theirs and made of light brown bricks. It had three floors and a fourth with six dormers, two larger buildings on each side of the main house with ornate orangeries in front. Meticulously manicured lawns stretched far beyond the buildings and down to a lake with a large Gazebo on an island. There was a barge moored to a small dock by the beach. James had been to several parties on that island. One summer evening he and Peter had gone skinny dipping there. He remembered Peter's insistence and how much fun they had had when he finally gave in and jumped after him. He had not seen Peter since they got back. He didn't even know if he was home or why he hadn't even called on him to give him his condolences. James had been so overwhelmed with his grief and the responsibilities for the plantation that though he had thought about it, he had not dwelled on it much.

A house negro came down the steps as soon as they stopped in front of the house and without so much as a look in Pap's direction he held his hand out for Katherine, assisting her as she stepped out.

Mr. and Mrs. Dawson greeted them by the entrance. Mrs. Dawson embraced Katherine and immediately pulled her aside as she exclaimed, "Dear Mrs. Waynewright, I'm *so* very pleased to finally meet you. Do come in, let us sit in the parlor a while and I'll have Lilly bring us refreshments. I have heard so much about you, and I've been meaning to call on you, but I knew that you must be tired and have a lot on your hands with a new household and new negroes to deal with. It's not easy, I know, and the pickaninnies, I heard you have one hangin' around in the kitchen day in and day out. It can be quite tiring."

"Oh, I'm pleased to meet you, too. It has not been too trying, to be quite honest. Little Matilda is rather darling actually," Katherine said, wondering how she knew that Matilda spent so much time in her kitchen.

James swallowed nervously as he watched his wife disappear and he heard what Mrs. Dawson was saying. *Please play your part, Katherine.* He begged silently.

Mr. Dawson lightly patted James on the back winking at him at the same time.

"Let our women get to know each other a while. I wanted to talk to you privately anyway which is why I suddenly insisted that we invite you for breakfast. I was going to ride over, but then I thought why not have an impromptu visit here instead. I can be rather spontaneous sometimes," Dawson smiled, but it didn't quite reach his eyes. "Come to the office with me for a minute and then we'll join our wives for a sumptuous breakfast."

James felt uncomfortable as he followed him through the house into the office; several negroes were busy dusting or polishing in the large floor-to-ceiling library adjoining the office. They immediately bowed and curtsied as they walked by; all of them averting their eyes so as not to look at them directly. James got the feeling that they were scared of Dawson.

"Have a seat," Dawson said and pointed to a leather recliner as he reached for a silver cigar box and held it out to James who gratefully took one to have something to do with his hands. He could feel that this conversation was not going to be pleasant.

Slowly Dawson lit their cigars and sat down in front of him, at first just looking at him silently as he puffed deeply.

"Well, James Waynewright, I'm not sure how to say this or where to begin, but I will just come right out and say it. I rode over to your place last night to speak with you about an important matter."

"You did?" James raised his eyebrows in surprise. "We were home the whole evenin', I don't understand?"

"Well, neither do I, as a matter of fact, I'm rather appalled and disappointed." The last word came out loud and sounding angry. Dawson reached out for the ashtray and aggressively snubbed the cigar out. "I thought my dearest friend raised you right, raised you to be an educated and responsible man."

James stared at him incredulously.

"I rode over to talk to you as I said, but I find you fraternizin' with your niggers on your porch and from the look of it you even gave them wine. I saw Katherine come out with a tray." He raised his voice again, "Your wife serving your niggers, for God's sake, James, what are you doin'?"

Dawson looked at him but before James had a chance to respond, he continued.

"I really do not know what to say, James. Is this some sort of Northern bullshit, or what the bloody hell is it? You should at least know that you have to keep them in their place or they will become uppity. It's dangerous! It causes all kinds of trouble, rebellion and runnin', which is what I came to talk to you about yesterday."

He got up from the recliner and pulled out another cigar even though he never smoked the first one. He went over to the bar, an ornate mahogany piece with small cabinet doors with inlaid stained glass. James realized with a start that Dawson had bought it from his father a couple of years ago; he had paid him handsomely for it, too. Will had made it.

Dawson picked up a crystal decanter and poured lemonade for himself, he did not offer James any, and sat down again.

James sat stunned and angry. He felt like telling him how he really felt and that he didn't want to own any slaves anymore. He felt like telling him that he would help his terrified negroes North, since he had heard from Will that they didn't always treat them nicely. He remained quiet, collecting himself for what he really ought to say. He was curious as to what it was Dawson thought so important to ride all the way to his plantation so late in the evening.

Dawson didn't appear bothered by his silence; he took a large sip of his drink and continued,

"There has been a runaway. The Sheriff came to me yesterday afternoon. A nigger from a smaller plantation south of here has run off, a buck. Gone for three days already and worth a lot of money, at least 1200 dollars. He is extremely strong and hardy and brought in crop at a rate twice as high as other negroes. He was also used for breeding and brought his owner a high yearly income just for that," Dawson said.

"Breeding?" James couldn't keep the distaste from his tone.

Dawson lifted his eyebrow and gave him a curious glance.

"According to the Sherriff there have been some stirrings on that plantation that points to a rebellion; rebellions can spread like wildfire if they ain't curtailed immediately. Especially if the women find out and start acting nervously around their negroes, who in turn notice and take advantage of the situation." He sighed deeply and relit his first cigar.

"James, I have to say…when I saw you with your niggers yesterday I couldn't believe my eyes. You have no idea how dangerous it is. You are putting us all at risk with such behavior. If they rebel they could rape our women, or worse." His voice became shrill and he got up yet again. "There was an incident in North Carolina just a couple of years ago where a woman was raped by a nigger and got pregnant! Can you imagine the horror? The pickaninny was gotten rid of course, but no woman should have to be shamed like that. It is disgusting, sickening."

Yeah it is. I've seen what happens to raped women, some men protect those babies at the risk of their own lives. James thought of Johnnie and Martha and finally he reacted to all the insults.

"You know, Dawson, I am offended by this. How dare you insult my parents' memory like this, tellin' me that they didn't raise me right and that I'm putting you all at risk? I tell you that they did raise me a lot better than you will ever know, taught me to treat everyone with compassion. We have never had a runaway on our plantation. I'm sure you are well aware of that. We have servants who are happy to work for us. My parents taught me that if I treated them with respect there would be no rebellions. *You* on the other hand have no idea whatsoever what it was that we spoke about on the porch last night, and my wife has every right to do what she sees fit to up the morale after their beloved mistress and master died just a few months ago. We are leavin' right now, Dawson. I thank you for invitin' us for breakfast, but I'll decline today, maybe another time.

James put the cigar butt in the ashtray and gave Dawson an icy look as he got up and left, not bothering to look back. Instead he caught the almost unnoticeable nod of approval from the house negro who just happened to be dusting the books right outside the office at that very moment.

He quickly located Katherine whom he found quietly talking to Mrs. Dawson as they were drinking coffee.

He hastily made an excuse and took Katherine lightly by the elbow, and then they left.

Katherine followed a little surprised, but rather relieved to be leaving. She looked at him to say something but James shook his head and to his relief Pap was already ready with the carriage.

"Pap, go!" James urged and then they were off.

He was so angry that he couldn't speak. It wasn't until they were all the way past the tobacco fields and almost at their own property line that he was able to turn to Katherine.

"I will have nothin' more to do with him, Katherine. You know, we are tellin' everyone tonight. If anything I'm more convinced than ever." When he finished telling her everything she started laughing. "Up the morale, huh? If he only knew what we were really talking about."

James nodded but he didn't laugh. "Yes, if he only knew. Thank God he didn't hear it, Katherine. I have to tell you that hadn't you gone to fetch the wine at that very moment he might as well have. We have to be very careful."

Katherine looked scared and moved closer to him on the seat. "What do you think he would he do if he found out?"

"I don't know, but if he was so angry at me for lettin' you serve them wine I can only imagine."

Katherine shivered and sat silent for a while and then she turned to him again. "What about the man who is running away? We ought to help him."

"I thought the same thing, especially if there is talk of a rebellion, cause then they want to catch him to make an example out of him to curb it. We ought to find out where there are safe houses around here and see if we couldn't help out. I'm not sure how we would do that though."

"Don't you remember what they said at Plymouth? How people put out lanterns and quilts? We ought to ride around at night to see if we see any of those signs and then we just go back in the morning and talk to them."

"We can't just ask them, Katherine."

"No, of course not, but we can ascertain a lot by just casually asking certain things, to see where their sympathies lie."

James didn't respond, instead he motioned silently to Pap who sat stock still on the driver seat. He was obviously listening to their conversation.

"Pap, stop the carriage for a moment, will you?"

He did and slowly he turned around towards them. He looked nervous.

"Were you paying attention to what we have been talkin' about?"

Pap cleared his throat. He looked scared and mumbled, "Yes sir. No, Mas…Mr. Waynewright, I can't help but be overhearin' some of what you said."

James smiled a little. "Pap, don't worry yourself. Please be honest with me. Do you know if there are any places around here where your people hide? You know we are on your side. We want to help. Don't be afraid, we are accustomed to helping, we have helped several people in our church in New York that came from down here."

Katherine reached out and touched Pap's arm. "Pap, James has changed; he really has. I made it very clear to him that I would not marry him unless he did. You should know that my sister and I have been involved in helping your people for years, long before I met James, though I'm more familiar with safe houses in New York. We don't know the area here and if we are going to help it's important that we have the right information. Surely you understand that, Pap?"

Pap looked astonished and for a moment it looked as if he would speak to them, but then he shook his head.

"I mean no disrespect, I sure don't, but I prefer not to answer that question."

James was about to demand that he did when Katherine answered.

"I understand, Pap. It's fine. Let's just go home."

"Yes, Mrs. Waynewright," he said and shook the reins getting the horses to a trot.

Chapter 08

Everyone was in the tobacco storehouse except for Will who was keeping watch outside. All of them had gathered in there when Pap told them that their master had something important to tell them.

James had been so very sure that he wanted to do this when he had spoken to Martha and she told him how Loch had raped her. He had been sure yesterday when Dawson insulted him, but as he stood here in the barn, he was wondering how angry his father would be if he knew what he was doing. Not only would he be angry that he was letting valuable property go, but he would have said that it would be cruel to set them free because they would not be able to fend for themselves.

Then he thought of how Pastor Beecher had quoted Jesus and reminded him of how Jesus had stood up against corruption because God had called him to do so and he cleared his throat. Katherine smiled at him from where she was standing on the side.

Pap, Auntie Ellen and her children were leaning against the wall in front near the door and he could see the excitement on their faces. As he looked at everyone else, closely packed together, looking expectantly at him, he could sense fear and anxiety in their faces.

Two women in the back of the crowd were clutching at each other trying to hold back tears, and a woman was hugging her baby to her chest. *They think I'm going to sell them all.* James thought and then he was finally able to go through with it. With new resolve, he began to speak.

"I have called you all here today to tell you something that I feel very strongly about...
I want you all to know that you are free. As of today you are no longer owned by me or by anyone else. I thank you all for all the work you have done for us, but I cannot in good conscience be an owner of my fellow human beings anymore."

There was a sound from someone in the crowd, but James didn't see whom it had come from. They were all staring at him. He tried to read their faces to see what they were thinking but their faces were blank as if they hadn't understood what he had said.

Some were shuffling their feet nervously and another coughed a couple of times, but then it was quiet again. James glanced at Auntie Ellen who nodded and walked up to him. *"Mr. Waynewright,"* she said with emphasis on his name and loud enough so that everyone could hear it. Another gasp was heard and Auntie Ellen nodded toward the crowd with a twinkle in her eye, then she looked at James again and repeated, "*Mr. Waynewright,* would you like me to explain it to them?"

"I would greatly appreciate that, Auntie Ellen," James said.

"I was shocked too when Massa told me 'n Will a couple o'weeks ago. But it true it is. Mr. Waynewright an' Mrs. Waynewright is good people and don't agree with slavery. Mrs. Waynewright never has; she even met Sojourner Truth." At that Auntie Ellen paused and looked around for a moment before she continued, "Mr. and Mrs. Waynewright want none of us to call them Massa and Missus no more, unless neighbors be around, then he ask us to pretend we still his slaves."

She paused and looked at everyone, but they were still too stunned to say anything. James noticed how excited she looked to be the one to tell them. "Auntie Ellen is right; please call me Mr. Waynewright unless one of our neighbors are here, at least for now. We'll see what happens after a while. As I have already told Auntie Ellen, Pap and Will, Hettie and Mary, if you want to stay here you still have a home here, but I will pay you for your work."

Finally Morris, Matilda's father spoke up. "Massa Jr. is this true? We could leave right now and you would not stop us, not send them dogs after us?" Morris looked uncomfortable when he realized that the last part about the dogs wasn't the nicest thing to say under the circumstances.

James shrugged and said, "I surely would not. In fact, we will help you to get away if you want. Just to be on the safe side. It is probably a good idea to organize things a little so that you can leave safely. Even if you carry freedmen papers, I'm not sure what would happen if you leave all at once, to be quite honest. If you choose to stay, you are more than welcome."

Auntie Ellen glanced at James and began speaking again, "We are stayin', Pap and me. We're too old to move on. Pap and I have been talkin' much, and we think it probably be best that we tell none at no other plantations especially for Mr. and Mrs. Waynewright's sakes. Some Massa's gonna get real angry if they hear what they done for us," she said with a serious undertone to her words. She let her eyes glide from face to face nodding for emphasis.

Morris took a deep breath and pulled Jenny towards him and then he looked at James and said, "God bless you, Mr. Waynewright."

It broke the ice and there was a roar in the barn, "God bless you, child, God bless!" Then there was yet another pregnant pause and then suddenly everyone started talking all at once. James took a deep breath, and went over to embrace Katherine. Out of the corner of his eye he saw Nathan shake his head and quickly leave the barn. He thought he saw him spit, but it happened so fast that he couldn't be sure. He felt so relieved and exuberant, that he brushed it aside thinking that he hadn't seen it right. He mumbled into Katherine's ear. "I did it, I did it. It was the right thing to do."

He hugged her again, but she didn't answer. He felt her shaking. When he loosened himself from the embrace he saw that she was sobbing.

"Oh Katherine, are you all right?" he asked and gently touched her face.

"Yes...I'm so happy, James, so very happy that you did this. Thank you." She tried to smile but she just cried more.

James almost felt like crying himself, but instead he laughed and touched her cheek. They remained there, standing together just looking at everyone. Some of them were hugging too; others still looked as if they didn't really believe what had happened and stood around and talked among themselves in muffled voices.

Then two men came up to him and Katherine. James recognized them as field hands but he didn't know their names.

One of them was probably in his mid-thirties, a handsome man with a chiseled face and very short hair, and the other an older man with an equally chiseled face but his skin was much darker and sat taught over his cheekbones and forehead. His hair was longer and grey and James realized that they must be father and son. Again, he felt ashamed and embarrassed that he barely knew his field hands and made a mental note that he had to get better at knowing everyone and their names.

The older man grabbed James by the arm. He could feel the calloused skin on his underarm then he looked him in the eye with such a force of emotion that James felt his eyes get moist.

"God bless you, god bless you, thank you, thank you, Mr. Waynewright. I'm honored to call you thus. Now I can go back to my family in New York, I have prayed every day for the day when I'd be able to behold my dear wife and daughters again."

Just then, the large storehouse door opened and Morris glanced at James.

"Will ain't seen nobody out there. You mind if we get some air in?" James nodded as a sliver of moonlight appeared on the shed floor and he felt a cool breeze hit his face.

"You have family in New York?" he said turning to the older man again.

"Yes, sir, I do. I would like to leave immediately with my son if you wouldn't mind signing the papers right away, sir."

James looked at him curiously as he realized that the man spoke as if he was an educated white man.

"Of course, come with me to my office and I will take care of it." He patted his shoulder and started to walk out, gently touching Katherine's fingers mumbling that he'd be back as soon as he could.

Once outside the three of them remained quiet as they walked across the soft grass toward the house. The crickets were loud and the fireflies were lighting up all over the lawn.

It's so beautiful here, what if they all want to leave. Then I have to sell, I can't bear it. Please God, let some stay. Dear God, let many stay. I will pay them more than I planned, just please let them stay. I don't want to leave.

James prayed silently and glanced at the two men walking by his side. They too seemed overwhelmed and he saw tears glistening as the lights from the windows reflected in the older man's dark brown eyes.

James' pulse rose as they came inside his office and he pointed to the two arm chairs in front of his desk and then he sat down and pulled out a piece of paper and started writing. He paused for a second and looked up.

"I'm very sorry; I don't know your names. I'm quite embarrassed, I...my father knew you all, but I guess I didn't pay as much attention as I should have when I was younger."

"I understand. My name is Timmy and this is my son Tobias."

"All right," James wrote what he thought would be appropriate, and added their names, pushed the paper towards them with a pen on top. "Just write an X next to your names there." Timmy took the paper and looked at it for a minute and then without a glance in James' direction, he signed his name and handed the paper to his son who did the same thing.

James looked on in amazement as Timmy nervously, but proudly, looked back at him.

"You can both write?"

"Yes sir, Mr. Waynewright." Tobias spoke for the first time, and just as Pap had that first morning he grinned as he called him Mr. Waynewright.

James nodded and then looked to Timmy.

"I'm curious, you seem well educated, and you mention that you have family in New York. How has this come about?"

Timmy glanced at Tobias and looked unsure for a moment, but he took a deep breath and looked James straight in the eye again.

"I used to belong to Master Dawson. I was a house negro and my wife worked in the tobacco fields. When our twin girls were weaned my friend overheard him tell a buyer that he was plannin' to sell them at the outcry, two girls for the price of one. We all ran that night, sir." He paused to see how James would react. James listened calmly and he continued. "We made it all the way North. Spent time with a very nice negro family for about a year and we were taught to read and count sums and such." He paused again, looking a little unsure and nervous again.

"Please go on, I'm truly on your side as surprising as that may seem to you."

Timmy didn't reply for several seconds but then continued with his story.

"My wife got a job as a nursemaid where she could bring our girls, a nice white family who had twins of their own, twin boys. Tobias and I—Tobias is my son from a woman who died when he was only two—well, Tobias and I worked at a carpentry. I learned book keepin'. We were there for five years and then one day Master Dawson got wind of it, it was the same year as the Fugitive Slave Act came about and he sent someone to fetch us. He almost killed me with the lash to have me tell him where my wife and daughters were but neither I nor Tobias gave in, even though Tobias lost two fingers on his right hand because of it."

James looked at Tobias who held up his hand, and for the first time he noticed that the middle fingers were gone. James clenched his teeth and was about to say something really nasty about Dawson, and at the same time wondering to himself how Tobias could still work with the tobacco with two missing fingers, when Tobias spoke for the second time.

"Massa Waynewright bought us at auction when Massa Dawson tried to sell us after he couldn't get us to speak. We have been nicely taken care of here, but we would *really* like to leave to join our family."

James stared at them and remembered how angry his father had been at Dawson over this. He had never understood until now, only that his father had bought negroes from Dawson and that there were things that his father didn't like. Now he understood.

"That misbegotten mongrel, he is truly evil; I want nothin' to do with that animal. One thing after the other confirms it for me."

James abruptly got up from his chair. "I don't have much respect for people like that. I'm surprised that my father was a friend of his. My father would never ever approve of something like that."

"That is true, Mr. Waynewright, I can attest to that," Timmy said.

James cleared his throat. "I ought to get back to my wife and the others. First, let me just say that I understand that you want to leave, I truly do; especially after what you have told me, but I urge you to wait until...,as a matter of fact, Katherine's uncle is coming down shortly to visit and look at Will's woodwork. Why don't you go back up with him? It'd be a couple of weeks but it'd be a safer trip back. We don't know yet if we can tell anyone that you are all free. I got the sense from Dawson just the other day that it would be foolish, and you certainly confirmed it. I realize that I haven't fully understood the implications of what we are about to do here."

Tobias grabbed his father's hand with his three-fingered hand, "It may be wise, Papa."

Timmy looked heartsick and all of a sudden close to tears, but he nodded.

"It probably is." He stood up and hesitated for a moment and then he leaned over the desk and held his hand out to James, "Thank you, from the bottom of my heart I thank you, may God bless you and your family. I owe you a debt that I can never repay you. I pray that God will repay you in multitude."

James stood up, walked around the desk, and touched the older man's shoulders.

"Seeing your happiness is all the payment I need."

James felt his eyes moisten and had to blink to stop them.

Timmy looked him in the eye for a moment and then with a nod he and Tobias left the room.

Chapter 09

On the surface not much had changed. Everyone worked as they always had except for six who decided to leave right away, Timmy and Tobias not included as they were waiting on Katherine's uncle.

The six that left were all field hands, three brothers, two women and a fourth man. They wanted to try to start a new life in a free black community not too far from the plantation they said. James was surprised to hear of it and not sure if he entirely believed them and told them that should it not work out they'd be welcome back at any time and could work for wages.

Ever since he had told them, there had been a current of happiness bubbling under the surface; someone could burst out laughing for no reason at all, for example. It took him of guard about two weeks later when he was stopped in his tracks by angry voices behind the stable.

He immediately recognized Nathan's voice. James pressed himself up against the stable wall to make sure he wasn't seen.

"Who he think he is? Comin' here telling us we're free! Now we should all be grateful to him, not callin' him Massa no more, I say not me. I ain't trusting him one bit. He always been a spoiled brat, don't even know our names. Now he think he gonna come here and be the hero and we all gonna love him? Then he has the gall to say he is gonna help us flee. Who is he foolin?"

Then James heard Will's familiar voice.

"Nathan, I see what you are sayin' but I know Mr. Waynewright. He has always been a kind man. He was always kind to everyone he met even when we was children. He and I played together all the time and he was always nice to everyone, animals and plants even. I ain't too surprised to be honest."

James felt himself go hot at Will's words. He knew exactly what he was talking about. He and Will used to have an insect and plant hospital behind the raspberry bushes. They fed injured bees and flies lumps of wet sugar. He hadn't thought of that in years.

"Ain't no matter!" Nathan exclaimed, sounding even angrier. "I'll never trust no whites, that's for sure. They might seem nice, but when it comes down to it, they are just turncoats; they're all evil.

"Really, Nathan, they ain't all evil. Massa 'n Missus Waynewright was both nice people, as far as massa's go," Will said sounding a little unsure of himself now.

"That's just a load of horse poop," Nathan said. "They just seem nice, always talkin' so nice on how it's their responsibility 'n all that." James heard him clear his throat and could actually hear how the spit landed on the ground. "They own us, that ain't, nice and they sell us too. 'Massa Waynewright sold my Mama, you remember? Then they have the brass to say that it was *only* as far as the Wilson plantation. It still a day's walk at least to go visitin' I was only ten! Only see Mama a couple of times a year. It ain't like we could go borrow a horse every Sunday we have off. No, I say they was evil too. Just like every white person. Massa Waynewright didn't lash, but he got mad just the same, yellin' at us for the smallest mistake. Treatin' us like we were dumb. I know I'm as smart as he was, or smarter... I was the one who always had to help him understand the equipment, he never remembered no matter how many times I show him."

James swallowed; he felt ashamed. As angry as Nathan was he was not telling untruths. His father did get mad and easily frustrated by things that confused him, but he also got over it fast. Nathan didn't mention that, but he did say out loud that what James could barely voice to himself, that they would see him as ridiculous who thought he could singlehandedly come here and save them all.

The truth in Nathan's comment, that he was spoiled and didn't know their names was true. James felt his pulse rise, he was scared to move lest they hear him so he remained standing, praying that they would leave soon and take the hill leading to the stream and not come back up in his direction.

He heard Will sigh, and he could imagine him shaking his head like he always did.

"Nathan, it true that Massa Waynewright had his weakness as everyone does, but Mr. Waynewright *is* a nice man and he does want to help. The world is changin' he ain't alone. There are many whites who don't like slavery."

"The Bible is for it," Nathan replied, sounding deflated suddenly.

"It also says that it's wrong, God punished the Pharaoh with famine when he wouldn't give up his slaves... I've re..." Will said, but the last of his words were drowned out by their feet on the pebbles that they must have stepped on to walk down to the stream as James had hoped.

James remained standing not sure what to do. His head was spinning. What Nathan had said made him feel nervous, but he couldn't let on that he had heard it and decided that he just had to let it go.

Chapter 10

Two weeks later Katherine's uncle arrived.

Katherine and James had decided not to write to anyone other than Pastor Beecher about their decision to grant freedom to their slaves. Maybe it was paranoia, but they were nervous that the letter would somehow end up in the wrong hands and they couldn't take the risk.

Therefore, when Uncle Peter stepped off the carriage he looked around with an air of mixed emotions. Auntie Ellen saw him through the kitchen window where she was busy baking pies and she immediately wiped her hands and ran out to greet the handsome New Yorker who would take her son and daughter with him to the Promised Land.

She was outside before James and Katherine had even noticed he had arrived.

"Dear Mr. You must be Uncle Peter. I myself is Auntie Ellen," she said with a conspiratorial wink. "Do come in, do come and have yourself a seat on the porch and will fetch you somethin' to drink."

Uncle Peter was too stunned to say anything and blindly followed her, leaving his luggage right where the driver had put it on the ground.

Seated on the porch, Auntie Ellen sent Matilda to get Will and Katherine and James as well. Soon all three of them walked up together. Will took the luggage and carried it inside while Katherine hurried up the porch steps and kissed her uncle.

James shook his hand.

"So nice to see you again; it's been so long."

"Indeed it has. Thank you for inviting me," he said coolly, his feelings about stepping foot on a plantation apparent in his expression.

"You must be tired after your journey," James said and sat down opposite of him.

"I'll manage."

Katherine broke the awkward silence that followed. "Uncle Peter, we are so happy that you have come. We have a lot to tell you. I can imagine what you are thinking right now. I remember when I first came and saw all the workers greeting James as if he was their own family. Well he is, we are all family, but it may please you to know that we have freed them all." Katherine beamed and James could see that she was almost bubbling over with pride at what she was telling him. She certainly had come right to the point, less than five minutes after he arrived.

Part of James was proud of himself, part of him wondered again if he was disrespecting his parents' memory.

Uncle Peter's reaction was unmistakably one of relief. "That is splendid. What courage; I'm very glad to hear this. So you are saying that the distinguished lady who served me lemonade is not a slave?"

James looked at Katherine and let her answer. "No, Uncle Peter; not anymore. She has chosen to stay with us, but Will her son, whom I've been writing you about... Where is Will?"

She turned to James who shook his head. "He probably stayed with Auntie Ellen after he brought your luggage in," he said turning to Uncle Peter.

"Oh I see," Katherine said, "Will wants to go with you, I'm sure you'll have him when you see his work, and there are two men, Timmy and his son Tobias, who would like to go as well. It is safer for them to travel with a white man, even if they have free papers. If they travel with you most likely there won't be any questions asked."

"If there are questions, you can confirm that they are indeed free to travel, if you wouldn't mind?" James asked. "Though no one will ask as they surely will think you are their owner."

Uncle Peter looked overwhelmed and a little scared, but before he could say anything Will appeared on the porch.

"This here is Will. He can show you his work now if you would like, Peter," James said.

Uncle Peter nodded and immediately stood up to shake Will's hand and then they disappeared into the house.

Only a minute or so later they heard a shout from inside.

"Astonishing, absolutely astonishing..."

The voice quieted down and James and Katherine could hear only mumblings from the open window in the living room.

"It looks like he likes it, eh?" James said with a crooked smile.

Uncle Peter and Will were inside for such a long time that Katherine went to speak to Auntie Ellen about the evening meal.

She found her stirring a pot that smelled delicious as she was staring intently at something on the wooden bench next to the stove.

Katherine smiled as Auntie Ellen startled and pushed a basket of apples on top of the newspaper she had been reading. She turned around with an embarrassed look in her eye.

"Afternoon, Mrs. Waynewright," she said quickly.

Katherine laughed. "Don't worry, Auntie Ellen. I figured you could read, I told James but he didn't believe me. Hettie and Mary are able to also, are they not?"

Auntie Ellen looked uncomfortable and didn't say anything at first, but then she finally nodded. "Yes, I...we can, don't have much time to practice readin', but Mr. Waynewright had just thrown this here paper in the garbage this mornin'."

"Do you read fluently, Auntie Ellen?"

"What do you mean?"

"Are you able to understand everything in the paper that you are reading?"

Auntie Ellen shook her head and replied, "Not all the words but I understand most anyway."

"Who taught you?

"Timmy. He had learnt when he was up in New York before Dawson caught him again."

Katherine shook her head at the thought of Dawson.

"I'll be happy to help if you'd like. Does Will know? He'll need it in New York."

"He does, he…I…" Auntie Ellen burst into tears and turned her back from Katherine as she sobbed into her red and white checkered pinafore.

"What's happened? Why is she cryin'?" James appeared behind Katherine and touched her shoulder.

"She is sad that Will and Hettie are leaving."

James went over to her and brought her close. "Auntie Ellen, you know you can leave with them if you want to. We'll miss you terribly but you don't have to stay."

She shook her head and said, "I want to stay…I'm just so sad that they are leavin', but I'm happy, too. Did Katherine's uncle like the cupboard?"

James nodded, "Seems so, they are still talking in there and we heard Mr. Greenfield shout so I would think yes."

In fact Uncle Peter could barely contain his excitement, just as Katherine had predicted. "I don't know how such a talent can have stayed hidden down here for so long," Uncle Peter said, pausing as he enjoyed a large piece of Auntie Ellen's sweet potato pie, "I cannot tell you how happy I am. I was thinking, Timmy and his son? Are they going to be situated in New York? I'll be happy to help them get settled. I know from just looking at Will's work, that I will have at least three clients who will pay me in advance." Uncle Peter was feeling so excited that he forgot his previous hesitation, though the third glass of wine that he had just finished probably had a lot to do with it. He had been rather nervous about bringing everyone north with him earlier in the afternoon.

"The Henry VIII client, Uncle Peter? Who is he anyway, why does he want to have an old murderous king's bed?" James asked.

"The very one, he is going to be beside himself when he sees his work. Well...what can I say; he is an interesting fellow that is for sure. He is wealthy as a king himself. No one knows where his money comes from, but they say he hasn't worked a day in his life. He is a collector and acquired a drawing of the bed that Old King Henry supposedly slept in. Or one of them; Henry had many castles, I assume several beds in each." Uncle Peter chuckled. "He is a nice enough fella' he comes to my shop every so often. As I said he will be beside himself when he sees Will's skill with wood. I think we should leave as soon as possible."

"Oh, no you are not," Katherine said, "You have to stay a little while at least."

"To answer your question about Timmy and his son, I think you ought to talk to them, but I believe they have family who are already doing alright in New York. We should ask. It is really nice of you to offer to help." James said and turned to Katherine. "I know you want Peter to stay, but Timmy is itching to get back to his family."

"I know. But, I hope he will give me a couple of days with my Uncle since he is giving him a safe journey back."

Later James would wonder if he simply had been so overwhelmed by his grief, his new marriage and his newfound passion for abolition that he hadn't been thinking clearly.

The morning after Uncle Peter arrived James was in the office rummaging around in the drawer for a pen when his eyes fell on a piece of paper.

September 1, 1845 Emancipation Bond for Henry, signed with his X, signed by Mr. Wilbur Waynewright. Secured by Ezekiel Hobbs.

He remembered it as if it had been yesterday, and cursed at his own stupidity for not thinking of it sooner.

He had been eight years old and was very excited to go into town with his father and Henry.

His father had explained that Henry had met a slave on a plantation four days ride from theirs and had begged his father to free him so that he could go and live closer to her and marry her. His father had been reluctant. James remembered discussions with his mother that he had been able to hear from his bedroom when they thought he was asleep. Finally his father had agreed. It surprised James now, and he wondered why his father hadn't sold him to the people whose plantation the woman lived on. His father did have a kind heart—maybe he would not dislike what James was doing after all? On the way into town so long ago, his father had explained to James that a freed slave had to register with the county clerk if he was to legally remain in Virginia. This was to prove that he was orderly, hardworking and not a drunkard.

James actually hit himself on top of his own head wondering why he had been so terribly stupid to not remember this before. Had he been thinking clearly, he would have realized that the township obviously would have laws about this and he couldn't suddenly just set them all free and have them live here as one large happy family.

In other words, it was illegal for all their friends to stay on their plantation unless they were slaves or unless they had permission from the country clerk, which would mean that all the neighbors would find out eventually. He could imagine Dawson panicking over it, probably thinking that his own negroes would pressure him to free them, or worse, cause rebellions.

Anxiously he yelled for Katherine. He yelled several times, but she didn't hear him and he had to go find her. She was resting on their bed with a book.

Her smile faded when she saw the look on his face. "What is it darling?" she asked and sat up with a concerned look on her face

"You married a fool, really you did. I'm so ashamed I did not realize this sooner."

"No, I surely have not," she laughed. "Don't be fatuous James."

When he told her about his discovery, she became pale.

"What does this mean, James?" she asked.

"Well, first I have to go to this free community and find the people who left and warn them, or rather I guess I need to go to town to speak to that country clerk, to see if I can get a hold of the law first, and then go find them. I cannot believe how I could be so terribly naive."

"Well, you remembered at least," Katherine said, petting his hand as she tried not to look too upset.

Chapter 10.5

The bent old woman held her hand out to her so she could crawl out of the trap door. Once up, she handed her a parcel and whispered, "There is a stream jus' past the main house, follow it. You will feel with your hands on the trees along the bank. When you feel the bark scraped off get out of the stream and follow the path. There is a little farm on the right hand side; they'll take care of you. If they have lit the candle in the window it is safe to knock.

"Run along north now, where no whip shall ever touch you."

Chapter 11

James and Katherine went into town the next day and knocked on the door to the Sheriff's office at the courthouse. When they didn't get a reply, James resolutely opened the door, and once inside they found themselves in a long hallway that led to a room on the left.

James shrugged and pulled Katherine with him and found the Sheriff at a large desk scratching his elbows furiously.

"Good mornin'. What can I do for you?" he said but made no motion to get up when he saw Katherine. He began to scratch again. "These blasted mosquitoes, makes me crazy. I can't stop, I know I should leave them alone but..." He sighed audibly, "Here 'ave a seat. What can I do for you, Mr. Waynewright, and is this the Mrs.?"

"Yes, sir."

"Pleased to make your acquaintance. I must express my sincere condolences, I had meant to come up to your plantation to do so, but things have been busy here and I..." He got quiet and looked genuinely grief stricken and finally stood up to greet them properly. James realized that the Sheriff had probably known his father pretty well, and must have been called to the scene when the accident happened. He clenched his jaws as he sat down in front of him.

"I assume you are here to find out what really happened. I have a note on it here somewhere," he said and shuffled some papers around on his desk

"To be honest, it hasn't crossed my mind that you may have some information that I ought to look at," James mumbled, looking at Katherine as he was trying to get his bearings. He cleared his throat. "I'm here to find out what kind of negro laws we have in our state. I need to know everything since I'm responsible for...um, so I was hopin' to speak to the county clerk or someone."

"Oh of course, the negro husbandry. Indeed, you need to know all the laws now that you are the new owner. Of course, well, I assume you probably know most of it, but I'll tell ya..."

He became silent and thought a while and then he said, "I should have it written down somewhere, but first off you cannot let one of your negroes out for errands or anything like that without written permission from you. It's illegal for them to carry firearms of any kind, so if you hunt, you cannot let them shoot....hmm, what else. You cannot let them hire themselves out to make money. Dawson mentioned that you have a negro who is skilled with woodwork, eh?"

James nodded, surprised that Dawson had spoken of it.

"'Became law back in 1793. Apparently lot a people allowed their negroes to make their own money, but I imagine it's not safe. They'll get all uppity and think themselves more important if they have their own money."

"Hmmm," James glanced at Katherine who looked back with the faintest roll of her eyes.

"What if I free some? I remember my father doin' that a while back and there was a registration process."

The Sheriff looked up, startled. He stared at them both for a brief second.

"I would sell them instead, Mr. Waynewright, instead of freein' them. From what I remember you have a healthy stock. Most of them are young, strong and healthy, only ole Pap and Ellen are a little older. You could get hefty sums for them if you feel that the responsibility is a lot to deal with. I know you have no overseer anymore since the new man left when you came back," the Sheriff said. He had a slight tone of disapproval in his voice. "You may consider keepin' all your negroes and hire a new one who can deal with them properly. Y'all have a lot of tobacco up there."

He knows everything, we really have to be careful. At least he doesn't seem to know that some have left already. James glanced at Katherine again, pleading with her silently, *Should we tell him? If they have to register, we have to.*

The Sheriff didn't notice his glance but went on.

"You know, Mr. and Mrs. Waynewright, I do understand your sentiment of setting some of them free, especially the older ones who ain't able to work anymore. If they are free they are no longer your responsibility. Since you can't sell the older ones anymore they cost you, but freeing younger healthy ones is very foolish, Mr. Waynewright. First of all, if they stay around here, if they pass registration and are orderly, sober and such, they may fraternize with other negroes and put ideas in their heads. Ideas of freedom and such that ain't good for business. Imagine negroes runnin' off both left and right. Nah, Mr. Waynewright, the young ones you have to sell, or as I said get a good overseer."

James jaw clenched again and he could sense the agitation from Katherine, he didn't dare to look at her.

"I understand your sentiment, Sheriff," James said stiffly. "My father had promised some of them their freedom when he passed on and I want to honor his word." It was a flat out lie, but he had to say something to get the correct information out of him.

"Oh, I see. I didn't realize that there was something like that. Well, I should'a known, your father was very soft on 'em. I remember how upset he got when his fieldhand got killed."

"Excuse me," Katherine said. James heard a bang and when he looked up Katherine was already out of the room.

"Oh, is she in the family way?"

James lifted his eyebrow, but didn't respond. *What, you think she just happened to feel pregnant at this very moment? It has nothin' whatsoever with the fact that you think my father was too soft for reacting to someone being tortured to death in front of his child and wife!*

"Sheriff, I do appreciate your time, but I must carry out my father's wishes. Now, if you would kindly tell me what I have to do.

The Sheriff shook his head, "Well, if you insist. I understand that you want to honor your father, but where are they going to go? They are feebleminded, stupid creatures, how are they going to survive?" He shook his head again and reluctantly got up from his desk and went to a small chest of drawers behind him. He opened the third drawer from the top and pulled out a paper that he began to read as he slowly walked back to the desk, humming a little as he read silently.

"All right, well it says here that they have to register with the Court every three years if they are to stay within our state. You'll have to vouch that they are orderly, able and ain't the thieving drinking sort. If they stay here and don't register then they'll be enslaved again."

"By whom?" James asked.

"Oh, by anyone. If they are found wandering round and their owner don't want 'em back, anyone could take 'em," he grinned. "Umm… and since '34 you have to describe how they look, if there are any scars etc. so that we can tell who is really who. You know they are conniving and borrow each other's papers to run. I usually serve as the Court Clerk and handle this myself. That's why I had the papers handy right here for you," he said proudly. James felt cold in the pit of his stomach. This was not what Katherine and he had been dreaming about those nights they had been up talking before they finally told them.

James stood up and said, "Thank you, sir. I should go find my wife, good day." James sounded insolent, but he couldn't hide it. He left the room not bothering to see the Sheriff's reaction.

He saw Katherine and Pap talking quietly in the shade behind the post office as he walked across the wide dirt road and the large open space leading to the post office, the saloon and the store. He had a feeling that the Sheriff was looking at him through the window. He could almost feel his eyes burrowing into his back, but he didn't look back and just continued walking towards his carriage.

He could see that Katherine had been crying when he reached them.

“Sweets, I’m so sorry,” he said, and grabbed her hand.

“That man is vile, horrid and wicked, James. He spoke of the murder,” her voice became shrill at the word, “as if it was a horse losing his shoe, and calling your father unnatural. I’m sorry I ran out like that, but I would have started screaming at him if I’d stayed.”

James smiled in spite of himself. “Well, I almost did myself, or worse.” He looked at Pap. They had not said anything to him when he drove them down, not knowing what would come of it. “Pap, I’m afraid we have bad news. We need to talk to you, but let’s get out of town first.” James lowered his voice and continued. “We will have to speak to everyone again tonight.” James took a deep breath and shook his head. “Let’s just go home, shall we?”

That evening James called everyone to the storehouse again. This time he had decided not to tell everyone at once but in two groups of thirty, and then the third group of eighteen. Pap must have said something, because the way they looked when they walked in was heartbreaking. He could see it in the way their shoulders slumped and in their eyes.

James found a wooden box to sit on as they all sat down on the ground in front of him. “I…my heart is breakin’ telling you this, I really didn’t know the full extent of this. My wife and I spoke to the Sheriff today and it seems that it isn’t as easy as we had thought.” He sighed.

"The situation is this...Virginia has laws that say that a freed slave has to register with the county; our Sheriff takes care of this here." James cleared his throat, trying not to look at anyone as he delivered this horrible piece of news. "This is so that you can prove that you ain't drunk, or disorderly in some way. If he thinks you can prove it, you may stay in the state, but must register every three years. If you don't register at all, you could be enslaved by anyone after a year." James swallowed hard and this time he looked at Will who looked as if he felt sorry for him. "I...this would be doable if...but the Sheriff was extremely reluctant to let me register the people who left already, he made it very clear that he doesn't like it. He thinks it could cause rebellion and disobedience on other plantations. I am not goin' back on my word. I still want you all to be free, but the way the Sheriff was talking, I don't think he would...agree to register all of you. It seems that the only way we can do this is for you all to leave, or if you'd rather stay..." James voice almost broke but he took a deep breath and managed to say it.

"If you want to stay, you will remain slaves. It seems at least for now."

The air instantly felt heavier, similar to the feeling right before a thunderstorm. An older man whose name James couldn't remember shrugged, as if he had expected it. Others looked dumbstruck and some women cried openly. It was too much to bear and James clenched his teeth. He regretted that he hadn't told them all at once, now he would have to repeat this two more times.

He looked down on his hands and a single tear escaped and landed on his thumb. Quickly he rubbed his eyes and cleared his throat.

"Please, everyone. My friends please. I ask you to be patient. We will figure this out somehow. I'm telling you this, even if the Sheriff and the Court won't think of you as free, you *are*. We will simply not register. That's it. We will not register you. You are still free in my eyes," he said in desperation, but he knew how ridiculous it must sound. If they were not legally free what were they going to do if he changed his mind or if he or Katherine were to die? Pretending to be free meant nothing at all. They were trapped, trapped by the laws of their state, no matter what their Massa's son thought.

"With your permission," James offered, "I would like to find the six who left for the free community and inform them of this. The Sherriff wasn't happy, but he would register them at least, he thinks that my father promised them that they would be free when he died. Then we'll see. Will, Hettie, Timmy and Tobias are leavin'. Katherine's Uncle and I will make sure you will get to New York safely," James said and glanced at them where they sat right next to him.

Timmy nodded gratefully and then he said, "We know that this isn't your fault, Mr. Waynewright." He looked at the group, everyone looked devastated but many nodded their approval in the midst of their devastation.

Nathan stared at Will. The, *I told you so* was unmistakable.

"We appreciate your honesty and that you are doing what you can for us and are willing to help us even if the law isn't on our side," Timmy said looking at him again.

"That's easy for you to say, Timmy, you is leavin'!" Nathan spat out the words and got up to leave.

James felt his emotions talking hold of him again and he cleared his throat several times to suppress it.

Chapter 12

Things moved swiftly after that last meeting. Pap and Will found the six in the free negro community and James brought them into town to register. Sticking to the lie that these were the men and women who his father had promised to set free.

The Sheriff handled the matter for the court as he had said, but took James aside and questioned him, wondering if these were really the negroes his father had meant, so young and healthy looking. He stared into James' eyes with suspicion as he said, "I thought they'd be the older ones that worked for your father most of their lives, like Pap or Auntie Ellen, did your father leave this in writing, or did they just tell you that he said he'd free them?"

"Yes," James stared right back, knowing that if he so much as blinked he would be caught in a lie, "indeed, these are the very ones, my father's favorites as a matter of fact. I'm sure my father didn't plan to die so early. Thirty years from now they would not have been so young," he said icily ignoring the comment about having it in writing.

The Sheriff sighed, and at that he took down their names looked in their mouths and at their skin to see if there were any scars that would identify them. James was grateful that he made Katherine stay at home so that she didn't have to see this humiliating affair.

When they were done and they walked out the door together they heard him grumble behind them, "Thousands of dollars are walkin' straight out of my office."

James and Peter locked eyes but neither of them said anything. They took the carriage back to the plantation so that the freed people could leave from there. There was no need to leave a fresh trail from the station for the Sheriff to follow.

James wrote freedom papers for Will and Hettie then a letter stating that he had freed them as well as Tobias and Timmy and allowed his wife's uncle to escort them to New York.

The night before they were set to leave, Will and James took one last walk around the tobacco fields, a tradition they had begun again shortly after James and Katherine arrived on the plantation.

They walked in silence taking in the view of the neat tobacco rows in the evening sun, the vistas behind them framed by the wetlands and the wooded area to the west. The cicadas were loud already even though the sun hadn't gone down.

"Look, Will," James said touching his shoulder, as he pointed to the sky where an eagle was slowly gliding across the darkening sky, "he is looking for his last meal before night time."

Will looked up and nodded, then he sighed. "It probably sounds strange, but I will really miss this place. I can't believe I'm leavin'. I will miss you too, Mr. Waynewright." He stopped talking and swallowed before he got control of his emotions. "I used to dream of being free when I was a child, but Mama always told me not to get my hopes up. She told me to be grateful that we had a Massa and Missus' who was nice an' took good care of us. I don't know if you realize how scared we was when they die and you weren't here We didn't know if you were goin' to come back at all. Most were sure that Dawson would sell us. Then you show up with your pretty wife an'..." Will's voice almost broke and he swallowed again.

"Here, let's sit here." James took the opportunity to sit down mostly as he didn't know how to respond. There was an old fallen tree in the little glen overlooking the tobacco fields that was a perfect resting place. He and Will used to play there as children as well. Once they found a sparrow there that they had brought to their insect hospital, but the sparrow didn't make it.

Imagine if he hadn't met Katherine, or Mr. Gilbert for that matter, then he would never had visited Plymouth Church and might have come down here to sell them. James shuddered. "Will, I think that God showed me the way. I had never thought much about any of this until I went to a church service in Plymouth Church. At first I felt shocked," James paused and waved at a fly that kept buzzing around his face, "I couldn't believe that all these people were against my family's livelihood; to me they seemed uneducated and ignorant." He waved the fly away again and looked over the vista as he thought back on that very first day, it seemed so long ago now. "Then when they started singing... They have this way of singing where the whole congregation responds. I have never heard anything like it, I became strangely moved, and it was so beautiful. Right after everyone sang the Pastor brought a young negro couple up to the podium. I saw how the congregation reacted and I saw grown men cry openly." He shook his head and glanced at Will who sat silently looking straight at him.

"The first time I went to the Church a couple from Virginia brought me there. We had something to eat and we were talkin'. I remember feeling different, as if I couldn't connect with them, the way they were speakin' about everything, I thought of all of you here, and it didn't feel right anymore."

"Who were with you? Are they also abolitionists?"

James laughed harshly and shook his head, "Oh no, you will not believe it. They saw this church as entertainment. They went just so they could see what abolitionists think. I don't think they would believe their eyes or ears that it is partly thanks to them that *I* too am one now."

Will laughed but looked as if he did not believe him and didn't comment.

"How is New York? How is it really like up there?" he asked, changing the subject.

"I'll tell you, it's very different, but after you get used to the smell and the noise it grows on you. I miss it."

Their conversation continued until it was completely dark, then Will walked James to the main house.

The full moon came out from behind the clouds and they were able to see each other very clearly. James looked into Will's face. His eyes were large and dark brown, and angled a bit, it was an unusual look, making him look very handsome. A feeling came over James that Will would marry shortly after arriving in New York.

"Thank you, Mr. Waynewright. I will never forget you." Will looked him deeply in the eyes and then he turned around and ran down the path disappearing in the darkness under the trees where the moon light couldn't reach, and the only source of light was the twinkling of fireflies.

"My name is James," James whispered.

Chapter 13

Another month passed, and then another. Their friends were paid for the first time as they had sold the first crop of tobacco. The mood after that made up at least somewhat for the disappointment of them not being completely free yet. They had begun to talk about registering a couple of more people and see how the Sheriff would react, but they were moving cautiously as everyone was nervous about it.

Katherine's trunks finally came full of dresses, books and issues of The Liberator.

James shook his head when he saw them.

"I can guarantee you that the writers didn't imagine those coming to a plantation without being thrown in the fire. I'd be interested in reading them."

Katherine smiled and pulled out two hatboxes and handed them to James. "Look, my Mother hid Uncle Tom's Cabin in hand towels, and see, she has embroidered our initials on them: J and K."

James bent down and looked at one of the beautiful white hand towels. Their initials were made with tiny red stitches. "The letters looks so shiny?'

"It's the thread, James."

He fingered the book and turned it this way and that. It had a black and white drawing of a little cabin with a negro family in front. An overseer with a whip in his hand was walking behind a man who painstakingly moved forward.

It was a stark image and James shuddered. "UNCLE TOM'S CABIN or LIFE AMONG THE LOWLY," it wrote.

"Mother probably hid it just so that no one would see it that oughtn't to. Just in case one of our lovely neighboring wives would be present during my unpacking, but why didn't she hide The Liberator?"

"That is strange," James said and lit the lamp on the bedside table by his side of the bed. They had redone his old room to be the master bedroom. The room was smaller, but James couldn't bear to sleep in his parents' bedroom. For now it was just left as it was. They would have to think of what to do with it at another time.

"She may not have hid the book on purpose then, or she did and then forgot whatever reason she had when she put the newspapers in, or Mother might have started the packing and then let Mrs. McNeary finish. She may not have thought about it at all. She might have been in a hurry and just got it into the trunks as fast as she was able." Katherine shrugged and sat down on the Turkish rug and pulled out two pairs of gloves, a muff, several corsets and undergarments. She flushed and put them on the bed so that she could put them away later. James grinned and was just about to say something when they heard a voice from downstairs.

"Massa?" James and Katherine looked at each other. Everyone had gone home for the evening already, even Auntie Ellen who had made supper early saying that she felt a little poorly.

"Comin'" James hollered and they both hurried downstairs.

Mary stood by the foot of the stairs looking nervous.

"We are alone, Mary," James said.

She looked relieved. "Mr. and Mrs. Waynewright, please come with me."

"What is it?" James asked, noting with horror that Mary was wiping her hands on her skirt and that it was streaked with blood.

"Please just come, come quickly." Without waiting, she hurried out the door, almost forgetting to hold it open for them and then she hurried down towards the quarters. Katherine shivered in spite of the warm night air but didn't say anything. James took her by the shoulders and then they hurried after Mary, down the trampled path past the lane and the road and along the cow pasture. They heard an owl hoot loudly and then a door slammed somewhere in the quarters in front of them.

"Mary, please tell me what is goin' on. Why do you have blood on your skirts?" James asked short of breath now, his voice sounding strained.

She didn't answer, but just shook her head. James looked at Katherine still walking tightly beside him and she stared back with a look of fear in her eyes.

After what felt like an unusually long time to get down to the cabins, Mary knocked on the door; four loud knocks and then two softer.

Why is she knocking at her own door? James looked at her curiously.

The door opened right away and Auntie Ellen appeared. She hesitated just for a second but then she stepped aside so that they could come in.

At first nothing seemed amiss; a small fire was lit in the hearth and remnants of an evening meal sat out on the small wooden table in the middle of the room. There was a half-eaten apple and some of the same stew that they had for dinner in a bowl.

Then suddenly they heard a cry and as James turned, he saw a skinny mulatto man on a pallet on the floor. "No, please no," his eyes darted back and forth and he tried to draw himself backwards on the pallet. He grimaced as he did so and James could see that his right foot was bandaged.

Auntie Ellen rushed to him and hushed him. "No need for worryin' they are on our side, they ain't no regular Massa an' Missus." He didn't look as if he believed her, he started to rummage around for something around him, and made motions to get up.

Auntie Ellen resolutely pushed him back down. "You ain't goin' nowhere, you are stayin' right here or you gonna die. We got help now and you needn't worry no more."

Then she turned from him and looked at James and Katherine. She was silent for a long time and just stared at them before she finally took one long and deep breath and spoke;

"We dared not tell you at first, we should apologize but it ain't easy to always trust what white people say, but this man is traveling on the railroad. This here is a stop."

James stood dumbstruck and not a word came out of his mouth. He heard Katherine gasp beside him and saw clear fear and worry in Auntie Ellen's eyes.

Everyone stood stock still; even the stranger on the bed had stopped rummaging and was staring at them.

A railroad stop...? I...it's... Is Pastor Beecher? James couldn't think clearly. For a fleeting moment, he thought that Pastor Beecher had something to do with it and had traveled down here as a surprise. Then the reality sank in.

"Auntie Ellen, are you sayin' that your cabin is a station on the railroad?"

"Yes sir, Mr. Waynewright, it is, and has been for years." She looked nervous, her voice was shaking and she quickly glanced at Mary who stood by the window, keeping a lookout.

Katherine broke the spell and she turned to James with her eyes shining. "Had you only told me that dear, I would have married you even faster."

"Thank the lord," Auntie Ellen said as her tears seemed to actually spray straight out.

James shook his head in shock, almost feeling dizzy at the way everything was falling into place. His own change, his travels, Katherine's abolitionist passion, Plymouth Church, and now his own plantation; it was as if he had been led firmly along a path all along. He could almost feel God's hand on his back.

"Auntie Ellen, I remember the men running past the porch one evening. I remember you said that they should run so no whip could hurt them...was that...?"

She nodded, "I'll tell you more later, we need to help this man.

She pointed in the direction of the pallet where the stranger looked as bewildered as they all looked and felt.

She told them what had happened. He had come all the way from Georgia. Everything had gone well and he had rested for a day or two at each stop and sometimes under trees. He had been out for weeks and he felt a little more confident that he wouldn't be recognized, so one night he had ventured into a village to buy a belt. His trousers were beginning to get too loose from his weeks of wanderings and not eating as much as he was used to. Had he only asked for a rope or even an old belt from any of the station masters he would have been all right. Instead, the shoemaker who sold him the belt had become suspicious and told a slave catcher who sent his dog after him.

He escaped but the dog bit him, the teeth gnashing off a big piece of flesh in his calf.

Now he was feverish and from the look of it, the leg was in real bad shape.

James swallowed, "Let me take a look." He walked over and sat down next to the man as Mary began to unwrap the bandages. It looked horrible. The leg was swollen and pus was oozing out from what looked like a blackened mass on the calf, red streaks crawling upward toward his groin. James' year and a half of medical studies had no way near prepared him for anything like this. He felt nauseous and quickly turned away.

"He needs to see a doctor as soon as possible." *They will most likely have to cut the leg off, or he'll die. I can't cut it off myself,* James thought.

Auntie Ellen shook her head, "The doctor knows everyone around here. He will notice that he is new. There could be a warrant out for him."

"I have not seen any in the papers lately. Not in town either." James turned to the man on the bed. "What is your name?"

"Carl, Massa."

"Carl, did that slave catcher see you when the dog bit you?"

"Don't think so. I ran up a tree an' waited. The dog barked under it a long time, but the catcher never came and then it left. It a miracle..." His voice was labored but it was clear enough so that they could understand him.

James sighed. "It's a risk, but we have to take the chance. Just to be safe we ought to move him into an empty cabin."

James laughed suddenly, "Well, actually it's very simple. I have just bought him. Since I freed six of ours, obviously I bought a new one. Then he was bitten by a stray dog."

Mary nodded approvingly.

James smiled. "Let Pap leave as soon as it gets light with a note from me. I'll go write it right away." James nodded as if to himself without waiting for an answer and left.

The cabin became silent. Katherine and the other women looked at each other and Auntie Ellen lowered herself down on a chair. She looked exhausted.

"Please sit, Mrs. Waynewright," Auntie Ellen said as she pulled her hand through her graying hair. It occurred to Katherine that she was getting too old to spend so much time cooking and they ought to ask Mary to do more of it.

"Auntie Ellen..." Katherine grabbed her hand and glanced at Carl on his pallet, he seemed to be asleep, then she looked at Mary. "Mary, please come and sit with me."

Mary approached with hesitation but sat down opposite her mother.

Katherine kept her voice low, just in case Carl wasn't completely trustworthy and said, "I think you ought to call us Katherine and James now that we are all working at the same station."

Auntie Ellen shook her head and shrunk into her chair. "Oh no, Mrs. Waynewright, I ain't comfortable with that."

Katherine didn't reply at first. She was a little hurt by it, but she could understand how they must feel. "All right, Mrs. Waynewright is fine, too. Thank you for trusting us and telling us this. I assure you that you have nothing to worry about."

Katherine glanced at Carl. He looked as if he was cold; he was sleeping in a tight ball on his side with only his hurt leg pointing straight out in an awkward position.

Auntie Ellen nodded but didn't say anything. It was an awkward silence and they just sat there looking at each other smiling now and then. Katherine kept looking around in the room. It was so small. She could not believe that four adults had lived here when Will and Hettie was still there.

Then there was a knock on the door, four loud and two softer.

Mary laughed and went to open the door.

"Mr. Waynewright.,,he learns fast."

James hurried inside and handed Auntie Ellen two pieces of paper. "A traveling pass and a note to the doctor. I'm sorry that I still have to give him the pass," James said uncomfortably. He pulled something out of his pocket. "I found Laudanum, I'll give him this, and wrap the leg, but the doctor should have a look as soon as possible. "

A few minutes later he was done. There was not much he could do without proper tools; the cut needed to be sewn at least.

"We should leave, Katherine. Wake me tomorrow when the doctor arrives if we ain't awake yet," James said with a quick glance in Auntie Ellen's direction, took Katherine's arm in his and they left the little cabin.

Pap was standing in the darkness outside the cabin that he had shared with Timmy and Tobias, but they didn't see him.

I always knew there was somethin' special bout the Waynewright boy, he mumbled to himself.

Back at the house James collapsed in the armchair in front of the fire. He waved his arm toward Katherine. "Please get me a scotch, darlin'. I'm parched."

"Sure will." Katherine got two small glasses and filled them to the brim with the brown liquid. She handed him one and sat down on the couch next to him leaning on the armrest.

James felt so bewildered that he just shook his head and downed half the scotch in one gulp.

"I don't know what to say, Katherine. When I walked up to get the stationary, I was thinkin' that it's like this has been the plan for me all along. Of all the things that could happen, my own negroes are stationers on the railroad? I can barely believe it, of all the plantations around here, the very one where there happens to be an abolitionist, me," he said and pointed to his chest and took a small sip of the remaining scotch. "The one where the son turns abolitionist is the very one where there is a secret station. It's just too bizarre, isn't it?"

Katherine nodded sipping her own scotch as he continued.

"They are so different. It's like they are a completely different people when we ain't around; they read, they hide people, I don't know what to say."

"I don't understand, James, where do they keep them? Where have they kept all these people all this time? Didn't you and your parents come and go at all hours? Didn't you see anything?"

He shook his head. "Never, it's a mystery, a complete mystery."

***

When Auntie Ellen woke him to tell him that the doctor had arrived, the grass was wet from the morning dew and it smelled fresh and clean as if mother nature herself had washed the very ground to get rid of his illusions.

The doctor was leaning over the leg and poking it with his fingers when James came in. Carl he stared at him with fearful eyes behind the doctor's back.

The doctor looked up and took his pipe out of his mouth. "Mr. Waynewright, this doesn't look good at all. Why didn't you call me sooner?"

"Well, Doctor Johnson, to tell you the truth, I didn't know he was hurt."

"Ah, I see, not surprising. They always hide it from you, scared of gettin' lashed. Well I'll tell ye, you have two choices, either let him live out his days... I give you a vial, I don't believe in lettin' them suffer needlessly. You ain't going to have much use for 'im anymore cause that leg has to come off if you keep him."

James clenched his teeth and tried not to see how scared Carl was. *What a preposterous thought to just let him die cause he would be of no use.* James thought.

"Save him," James said and tried to sound calm.

"As you wish, sir. I'll go get my tools." He briskly walked past James to go out, but paused at the door. "Is this one new? I haven't seen him before."

"Just bought him a couple of weeks ago, then some blasted wild dog bit him."

The doctor looked troubled. "How did a wild dog get so close to him? You don't let a new negro wander loose do you?"

"Certainly not, I have no idea how it got so close. I guess it was starvin' and lookin' for food, may have belonged to someone at one time and not been so scared of people." James shrugged; surprised that he could lie so easily.

"Well, well, too bad on such a fine buck to be useless so young, but you may be able to use him for somethin'." The doctor paused, and then lowered his voice.

"Get your wife out of here, he'll scream."

"Can't you give him something for the pain?" James asked, cringing inwardly at the man's coldness, but he wasn't as cold as he sounded.

"I know, I will give him whiskey and laudanum, but unfortunately it will only help a little. I don't like to see the creatures suffer, but to save his life it's..."

"I understand."

"He may not survive."

James didn't respond. He walked back to the house so that he could take Katherine to visit the Burnham Plantation. Today was as good a day as any to visit the place of his parents' death.

Chapter 14

The Burnham Plantation was about half an hour away and they decided to ride over instead of having Pap drive them. Katherine had become a confident rider and she loved the exercise. They didn't speak much. James was trying to sort out his thoughts. Part of him kept thinking that he ought to be upset with Auntie Ellen and that he should be afraid of the consequences of having a station on his plantation. In fact he felt elated, as if it proved beyond a shadow of a doubt that he *had* chosen the right path and that Pastor Beecher had been right that it was his responsibility to do what was right. He was thinking that they ought to speak to Auntie Ellen and find out where the other stations were around here. She had mentioned that several stationmasters had helped Carl. Maybe they could befriend them and learn from them. He wondered if Auntie Ellen told her passengers where to go from his plantation. Maybe there were other people that he already knew that were abolitionists right here in his own county.

He was so deep into his philosophizing that he almost missed the turn to the small road leading up to the Burnham's plantation. Whereas most of their neighbors had large lanes that gave the impression of grandness before you reached the home, Burnham's was just a small country road barely wider than a trampled horse path. It circled around a natural mound that they called the Burnham Hill and around the bend, you came directly upon the stately home with three floors and an ornate wraparound porch. Below that, down a slope, lay the stables, tobacco fields and negro cabins.

"Oh, James, this is beautiful, how unusual. It looks as though we ought to have come upon a little farm but instead there is a grand estate, it's like a secret."

"It used to be a smaller farm at one point, Burnham's father rebuilt it. They too have lived here for generations. It's nice but very inconvenient when they have large gatherings," James mumbled feeling overwhelmed. He hadn't fully realized the impact of seeing the place where his parents had fallen to their deaths.

"Katherine give me a minute will you?" he said and slid of the horse, turning from Katherine and patting the neck in the warm place under the horse mane. He could hear Katherine's horse trample behind him and Katherine struggling to get off the lady saddle by herself, but he couldn't face her yet. Miss South, his horse, sensed his emotions and slowly turned her head toward him and looked at him with her enormous brown eyes. She nuzzled his shoulder and looked as though she was trying to say something. She must miss them too, and the poor girl probably had no idea why her favorite humans didn't visit or ride her anymore.

"Oh Miss South," he mumbled and kissed her muzzle. She moved her velvety lips and breathed at his face in response and he stood there letting her sniff him for several minutes before he sighed and said, "Miss South, I have to go help my wife."

Katherine looked teary when he approached and when he pulled her of her horse and into his arms she hugged him and nuzzled her face into his shoulder, just as Miss South did. "You smell like horse slobber," she said and looked into his face. "Are you all right?"

"I'll manage," he said swallowing his emotions and taking the reins from her. They silently walked around to the front of the house.

Mrs. Burnham sat on a rocking chair on the porch with a tall glass of iced tea. Right beside her a negro woman was having iced tea as well.

"Fraternizing with her servants now is she," James mumbled and winked at Katherine.

"She better watch it or Dawson will get upset," Katherine whispered.

Mrs. Burnham got up as soon as she saw them and rushed down the porch and said, "Oh James Waynewright, I'm SO very glad to see you." She threw herself into his arms and started sobbing, "I'm so sorry that we haven't visited, so terribly sorry. I didn't know how to face you. I..."

Her voice broke and she sobbingly broke herself loose trying to collect herself.

"Isn't your fault Mrs. Burnham," James said awkwardly.

"Oh, yes it is. There ain't a day that I don't think about it. If we had only had the veranda properly checked after the winter, we hadn't even noticed. There ain't a day that I don't regret it," she sniveled, barely able to form the words, but she turned to Katherine and managed to greet her. "I'm so sorry dear, you must be Mrs. Waynewright. I have heard so much about you."

"You have?" Katherine looked surprised and Mrs. Burnham laughed with her eyes still teary.

"You are the talk of the town, my dear, the pretty Yankee turned plantation owner, and from what I have heard you are handlin' it mighty well. Welcome Mrs., please, do come sit down and Esther will get you refreshments. Esther, come let me introduce you dear," she said and turned to the heavy set dark skinned woman who hurried down the porch.

She curtsied in front of them, "I'm so very sorry for your loss Massa and Missus Waynewright."

"Thank you, Esther," James said. "It's very kind of you."

She nodded to both of them and went back inside to get their iced teas.

"Oh isn't she a darlin', so well behaved and always happy," Mrs. Burnham said as they walked up to sit on the porch.

James tried not to notice the fresh looking wood and new paint on the veranda above them and didn't reply to her comment.

"Mrs. Waynewright, how are you faring with the responsibility for your house negroes? I know that Auntie Ellen and her daughters are the sweetest. James' mother always spoke so highly of them."

"They are wonderful, I'm very happy with them," she said and only James could hear the uncomfortable tone in her voice.

"Good," Mrs. Burnham replied as she turned to James. "My husband is down in the fields. I'll have Esther get him for you after she serves you your tea. I assume you want to speak with him. Again, I feel so awful. If there was anything I could do to have that night back so that I could have preve..." Her voice broke again and she began to cry, dabbing her eyes with a handkerchief that she pulled out of her pocket.

James and Katherine didn't know what to say.

After several minutes had passed, Katherine cleared her throat and spoke honestly.

"This is odd for us all, but I think that James' parents would be happy to see us together. I imagine them smiling down on us right now."

James took her hand and squeezed it before he let it go again. He wasn't able to think of anything to say. Mrs. Burnham nodded and looked gratefully in Katherine's direction and they just sat there silently watching the view in front of them.

A stable hand loosened the saddles on their horses where they had left them at the tying pole. He brought them water and gave them just enough to drink so that they could quench their thirst without getting colic. He nodded and smiled as he walked past the porch, lifting his finger as if he was pushing a cap upward.

It is certainly different here, not like it is at Dawson's, but still not right. I wonder what the Burnham's would think if they knew what Katherine and I are doing, and their negroes, so happy and well behaved like she said; maybe they are reading and helping runaways. We have been so blind to fool ourselves into thinking that we rule the world and that the negroes need us, that they can't do anything by themselves. We don't even notice who they are. We are trapped by our own hubris.

James looked at Mrs. Burnham, suddenly nervous that she would be able to know what he was thinking from his expression, but she sat as before, completely unaware.

Esther appeared with their iced tea on a silver tray. He could smell the mint leaves in it as she handed him his glass.

She smiled at him and for a moment James wondered if she knew something and if she helped with the railroad, but the feeling passed and he dismissed it.

"I see Massa Burnham now Missus, he already on his way here."

"Oh you have an observant eye, Esther. Thank you," Mrs. Burnham nodded and Esther curtsied and left, taking the tray with her.

Mr. Burnham walked briskly and was soon close enough to make eye contact with James. He nodded and kept his eyes locked on him the whole while until he reached the porch, then he embraced James without a word.

He held him so long that James felt the heat from his sweaty arms and chest radiating through his shirt, smelled the distinct smell of tobacco and earth, before Mr. Burnham let him go and stepped back. He looked emotional.

"So good of you to come, we have meant to call on you...I..."

"I just said the same thing, Thomas. I told him we had meant to but couldn't face him," Mrs. Burnham interrupted him as tears began to flow down her cheeks again. Katherine handed her one of her own handkerchiefs as Mrs. Burnham's was completely soiled by now.

Mr. Burnham sat down heavily and put his head in his hands taking a deep breath. Once he looked up his voice sounded thick, "James, I don't know what to say. There isn't a day that goes by that I don't wish that we had canceled our party, or that I had thought to stop them from walkin' upstairs, or wished that it had been cloudy that day. Most of all I wish that I had had the veranda looked over so that we had known..."

"Just what I told him," Mrs. Burnham interjected and blew her nose loudly in Katherine's handkerchief.

James swallowed. “Please tell me about them. Were they happy that evening? What did my mother wear? Was my mother laughing as she usually is…I mean did? I have been going over and over in my mind how their last hours were, if they were dancing’, if they were…”

James’ voice broke and he felt Katherine put her hand in his and he grabbed it gratefully, but kept his gaze on Mr. Burnham.

“I believe they did, I do. We had so many guests but I did see your mother laugh and your father and I were talking for a while.”

“About what?”

Mr. Burnham smiled, “As a matter of fact, we spoke of you. He said that he was very proud of you studying medicine all the way up in New York and how glad he was that you were able to meet some of the business associates and merchants up there. He mentioned that he had always meant to travel to New York more to meet his associates himself but never had the time.”

James could only nod.

“Oh, your mother wore a beautiful gown, dark yellow, almost orange or dark peach. She looked beautiful. She was wearing her pearls too, the ones your father gave her on their tenth wedding anniversary,” Mrs. Burnham added. “She too spoke of you and your letters, how you remembered to write and describe everything about the big city for them.” James sat silent for a moment taking it all in. He tried to breathe calmly and evenly.

“Mr. Burnham, can you please tell me exactly what happened when they died, please.”

"Of course, James, I was expecting this. It was a beautiful night and several people noticed the moon rising, it was one of those large moons on the horizon. Your parents, Mrs. and Mr. Pierpont and Mrs. Moore, she is a widow," he explained to Katherine, "were all standing by the window downstairs marveling at it. My wife and I were sitting down on our couch when they all decided to go upstairs. We were considering it, but we had just sat down and after being on our feet all day we felt too weary. Then it happened so fast, we heard a crashing sound and then we saw them both fall right in front of us. Since we were lookin' at the moon, we already had our eyes to the window and we saw everything. I....it's..." he cleared his throat, "I will never forget it, but I still cannot remember gettin' up. I just remember that I was out the door and yelled for someone to run for a doctor. But your dear mother..." he choked up and swallowed several times before he could continue. "She...it was clear from the beginning that..."

"How?" James asked and it sounded fiercer than he meant it, but Mr. Burnham continued calmly.

"It was clear from first glance that her neck was broken, she died instantly." He needed to clear his throat, but ignored it. "Your father landed on his back with his head hitting the stones right below the porch here." He gestured with his arm behind him. "I sat with him, holding his hand until...he was conscious off and on, but there was much blood. He asked for his wife, and I told him that she would be all right. I'm not sure if it was the right thing to do, James, but I didn't have the heart, I couldn't tell him. I...," Mr. Burnham cleared his throat, "by the time the doctor and the Sheriff arrived it was too late."

Mr. Burnham leaned forward with his arms on his elbows rocking back and forth until Mrs. Burnham took his arm and looked at them.

"We don't know how to ask you to forgive us. Please just know that we'd do anything for you, anything at all."

James stood up and pleaded with Katherine with his eyes to do the same. "I understand, and I appreciate your candor."

Mr. and Mrs. Burnham made motions to get up but James shook his head.

"No need to get up. We ought to get back; we have a sick negro at home to see to."

They left, not looking back, but could hear Mrs. Burnham's silent sniffles and Mr. Burnham soft voice as he tried to comfort her.

When they came back home they found the doctor waiting for them. He sat under the tree in one of the lawn chairs smoking his pipe. On the lawn table was a cup of tea and an untouched sandwich on a plate that Auntie Ellen must have served him.

He got up as they approached and shook his head.

"I'm so sorry, Mr. Waynewright. He didn't make it. I tried my best but he was too weak from the fever and couldn't take it. He looked skinny. He must not have been given enough to eat before. Who did you buy him from? I hope you didn't pay too much for him."

James shrugged. It was all too much and too overwhelming. He needed a scotch.

"Take care of Ellen, she seems distraught, must have gotten very attached to the boy already."

"I will speak to her," Katherine said as the doctor came up to help her off her horse.

Chapter 15

James and Katherine hadn't realized the full extent of Auntie Ellen's operation. For one thing, only four other friends knew about it, Pap, Hettie, Mary and Will.

Auntie Ellen said that if the traveler had not been bit by that dog and become so sick she would never have said anything to anyone else, but due to the circumstances, she felt that she had no choice. She didn't dare to think of what she would have had to do without James and Katherine.

When James and Katherine had gone calling on the Burnham's, Auntie Ellen had spoken to everyone else on the plantation saying that Mr. Waynewright had bought Carl at the outcry as no one else would since he was sick and had such a severe dog bite. She said that he had been afraid that someone would either shoot him or leave him by the road to die and that's why he bought him, even though he had vowed to never own anyone again.

It made James nervous since it was a slight bend on the lie that he told the doctor. He had to pray that the doctor or no one else would ever check up on it, or ask at the outcry if a sick slave had been auctioned off.

They had a small funeral for him that evening and though most didn't know him they all paid their respects.

James could barely look Jim in the eye when he spoke to him after the funeral and expressed how kind he had been to do what he did. That he had never ever heard of a white man buying a sick negro and that he shouldn't feel bad that he had to do it.

A couple of days later James asked Auntie Ellen and Mary to stay after their chores and have dinner with him and Katherine.

James locked eyes with Katherine. It was a big step, he knew that by becoming involved with the Railroad there was no turning back. Freeing his own slaves was different than helping others who were running. It was a crime and he knew very well where it could lead.

The silence was pregnant with unspoken emotion and James wished he could hear everyone's thoughts, instead he could hear the wind howling outside, the sound of the curtains fluttering slightly in the breeze. He could hear rustling from the trees outside and something squeaking out there that needed to be oiled.

He let several minutes go by and then put his fork and knife down.

"Auntie Ellen, Katherine and I have been talkin' a lot about this. We want to help you with the railroad and with your station.

We were wondering about a couple of things, Auntie Ellen. You mentioned that after your station you direct the passengers to another station. Do you know who these people are? How far is it?"

She hesitated for a moment, swallowed hard and said; "I will tell you Mr. Waynewright... The people who are responsible at the next stop is that little farm where the old couple livin'. The ones who everybody talk about a couple of years ago, cause they wouldn't let the Sheriff leave a man by their road when there was all that talk of another rebellion. Remember Mr. Waynewright?"

James whistled and lifted his eyebrows in surprise, "I'll be damned, Old Mrs. and Mr. Petersson, the Swedes?"

"That be the very ones."

"I do remember it was about six or seven years ago wasn't it? There was something goin' on south of here, Katherine. An incident where someone had challenged his master they tied him up, then took his horses, and rode off with about five of the slaves. I remember my father wouldn't let me talk with Will unless we did it here in the house. It lasted a couple of weeks, but then people stopped worrying about it and everything got back to normal. Did those people come by here, Auntie Ellen?"

"No, but I imagine they didn't want no man at guard in case another runner would need the station."

James shook his head. “Imagine so close to us, all this secrecy goin’ around. Have you been to their farm? It’s far, how do people get all the way there?

“No, I ain’t been there. Will went once or twice; they are real nice people he said. I tell my passengers to go round the back until they come to the stream right back behind the stable, then they follow it north and they need to feel with their hands on the large trees along the bank. Once they get to one that has the bark scraped off, they are there. Then if the candle is in the window, it be safe to go inside.”

“That must be at least an hour or two of walking in that river?”

“Take about four and a half. Would be much faster if they could walk on land. There are lots a plants and shrubbery growin’ over the stream in places, they have to take care to not disrupt it, or the dogs might smell it.”

James glanced at Katherine who knew exactly what he was thinking.

“We should drive them from now on. Can’t have them do that anymore, there are snakes in that water. I saw one just the other day when James and I were riding along it. A large one, too, I screamed so loud that James thought I’d hurt myself,” Katherine said a little embarrassed.

Mary looked scared. “Poisonous ones?”

“I couldn’t see what kind it was. Might have been a cottonmouth, they are poisonous, but I wasn’t sure. She screamed so much that I couldn’t concentrate on what kind the poor fellow was.”

Katherine shivered. “It was enormous and I still have nightmares about it. I’m scared of stretching my legs out in the bed, in case there is one under the blanket or under the bed. James has to look sometimes. I wake him up.”

“I feel like stranglin’ her every time, lookin’ for imaginary snakes.” He laughed and jokingly shook his finger at Katherine before he got back to the subject. “Auntie Ellen, do you know Mrs. and Mr. Petersson? Do you speak to them?”

"No, Mr. Waynewright...I haven't been there as I said. The station master before us contacted me cause it's too far for everybody to travel all the way to Peterssons' from the earlier station. They needed a stop in the middle to rest first."

James felt more and more amazed at the unbelievable truth that unfolded by the minute.

"Do you know *them*...that station?"

"No, Mr. Waynewright, I don't. It's a free negro who came by here who help them from somewhere else...is better if we don't know too much...just in case. The Massa's has a way to get us to talk..." Auntie Ellen looked flustered, she was sweating but she kept telling them more and more.

"How long has this been goin' on? My parents never knew anything of this?"

"No, Mr. Waynewright, they didn't know nothin'. They had no reason to suspect anything They been very good to us. It's the other negroes 'round here that was not so lucky who needed to run. One time a whole family came cause they were goin' to get sold apart."

"Where did they hide exactly, Auntie Ellen?" Katherine asked, patting her arm.

Auntie Ellen glanced at Mary.

"They all hid in a hole we dug out under our cupboard, Mrs. Waynewright." She looked scared as if after everything she told them, this particular fact would be too much.

James didn't know what to say at first, there was so much that was revealed that he had never known.

"Auntie Ellen, Mary, I feel quite overwhelmed by all this, but I'm grateful to you. It may surprise you, but this makes my task here on my plantation a lot easier to bear. I have changed too much since I left. I wouldn't be able to bear handling the plantation the way my father did."

After much discussion, they agreed that Mary would make the sound of an owl calling four times to signal when they had a new visitor. Mary showed him and Katherine how to fold their hands just so and blow into them to make the hooting sound of an owl, but no matter how they tried they were not able to. Katherine managed a small sound once, but James couldn't do it at all. Therefore, instead of calling back he would go out on the porch and slam the door leading into the small dining room. He would slam it four times to signal that he heard and that there was no one calling on them that night. If it was clear, Pap, Mary or Auntie Ellen would come up to the house. They would send food, clean clothes or whatever was needed. If they did have company at that time they wouldn't slam the porch door.

James and Katherine would drive the passenger the next evening, or after a couple of days of rest, but none of the travelers would know that they were the owners of the very plantation in which the slave cabin they were hiding in resided.

They hadn't met the Peterssons yet; there had been much debate of how to go about it. Since Auntie Ellen hadn't actually met them and Will was away in New York, they didn't know how to approach them or if the Peterssons would trust them.

PART III

Chapter 01

In the early spring after the year of mourning came to its end, James and Katherine decided to hold a small gathering. Officially, it was to introduce Katherine to the neighbors. The real reason was so that they had occasion to be acquainted with Mr. and Mrs. Petersson and so that all the neighbors would see that there was a relationship between the families and would not wonder if they went calling on the Peterssons late at night.
It was only about an hour until the guests would arrive. The house had been prepared by not only Auntie Ellen and Mary but three of the women who usually worked in the tobacco fields had been inside, setting tables and putting out vases with freshly picked flowers that had already began to grow around the plantation and in their flower beds.

Candelabras were ready to be lit, the fire ready to kindle and all James had to do now was to pour Katherine and himself a scotch and join her upstairs and change.

"Do we really have to do this, Katherine?" he said and handed her the scotch as Mary pulled her corset tightly before she laced her up in the back.

"Thank you dear, I need this, she said as Mary quickly left the bedroom.

"You look gorgeous, like a real southern woman. Blue is such a beautiful color for you." James said and kissed her. The scotch burned their kiss and distracted them for several minutes until Katherine pulled away laughing. "I hope so," she said and looked at herself in the mirror, pushing the round wooden frame backward to get a better look. Her stomach looked flat but the dress bellowed out in a very large bell shape.

"Mary used one of your mother's underskirts with a bustle; it has a wired frame to make the skirt so big. See?" Katherine lightly ran her hands around her hips, slowly spinning so that the skirt swung and rustled. "I have never worn such a large bustle. Actually, I have never worn a bustle at all, just underskirts. I feel strange. Do I really look pretty?"

"Stunning," James said as he began to wash himself with the soapy water in the bowl on their dresser, sponging his face and hands, underarms and armpits. He looked at her through the small mirror on the wall in front of him.

"Katherine, I'm very uncomfortable. I haven't seen Dawson since we visited him that day. He's never liked me, I know it, and I certainly do not like him. I feel like hitting something each time I think of what he told me that day. Still, I feel that I may have been rude to leave before breakfast. He did invite us to eat with them," he said and took another warming sip of the scotch and proceeded to put on his shirt.

"Don't worry yourself about that now; they accepted *our* invitation, so I'm sure it's fine. How do I sit with this?" Katherine tried to sit on the bed but the bustle kept getting in the way.

"I think you have to lift it up in the back with your hands. I think I've seen women do that, but I'm not certain."

Katherine nodded absently and went back to the subject of their neighbor.

"I'm scared that our friends have been talking and that they already know something. Remember how Mrs. Dawson somehow knew that little Matilda is always hanging around the kitchen? How did she know that? Who told her?"

"I don't know, people always seem to know everything about everyone here but we have to hope that our friends will have been quiet about this. For their own safety, they must know that. I made it pretty clear when I spoke to them."

Katherine tried to take a deep breath, "Oh, I'm laced too tight. I think I should ask Mary to redo it. You are right, Auntie Ellen was very eloquent when she told them why it was so important that everyone stay silent, and she should know what to say. She has been used to keeping secrets for years and years with the railroad. Maybe they won't say anything."

"Probably not, but I still can't believe that we invited Dawson here. We shouldn't have, I'm regretting it again now. What he said to me that day about raped women and fraternizing, I…."

Katherine looked pained and handed him her glass with most of the scotch remaining. "Yes, but we decided it was for the best or people would wonder why. Have this and then we'll go downstairs. The guests ought to arrive at any minute."

Soon the front was full of carriages with drivers in fancy chauffeur attire dropping of their mistresses and masters.

The women wore elaborate dresses in incredible colors with glittering jewelry and their parasols held high.

James felt elated in spite of himself as he stood on the steps next to Katherine and remembered all the balls he had been to as a young man. Today he and his wife were hosting and he felt proud, albeit with mixed emotions and a different worldview.

He smiled at Katherine and winked, "Welcome to my world, darlin'."

She laughed and then they moved inside enjoying the scene of their guests receiving drinks served on silver trays, their friends making it look completely natural and they both began to relax a little.

Mr. and Mrs. Dawson arrived making a merry entrance.

"Oh, this is dandy. Thank you for invitin' us! What a splendid idea to introduce Katherine. Is your family here as well, Katherine?" Mr. Dawson asked. He looked relaxed as though he had forgotten about their argument months before.

"We considered it, especially since we married rather quickly due to Mr. and Mrs. Waynewright's passing, but we…" she hesitated and James continued, touching her arm.

"We decided that instead of makin' everyone travel we would have an occasion to go back to New York and have a similar invite there at Katherine's parent's home. I have business up there that needs attending to anyway. Now when I see everyone here I almost regret it, it would be so nice to introduce everyone." *It sure would, wouldn't it? Your family and mine would have so much in common.*

"Oh I would love to meet your family, Mrs. Waynewright," said Mrs. Dawson

"And they you." Katherine began but before she heard her response, James nudged her in the direction of the open door.

An older couple arrived that James barely recognized, but guessed they were Mrs. and Mr. Petersson. They drove themselves and James saw Mr. Petersson hand his horse and small carriage to Pap. *I wonder if they both know that the other one knows,* James thought and said loudly, "Oh how lovely, Mr. and Mrs. Petersson are here."

The look of surprise on the Dawson's faces was unmistakable.

Mr. and Mrs. Burnham, who had just approached, heard James and turned around. "Oh, did you invite them? That is very nice; they are always so polite and kind when we happen upon each other in town. We have thought of doing the same, but it has just been talk." Mrs. Burnham left her husband standing with Dawson and walked over to stand closer to Katherine and James.

Mrs. Petersson wore a nice but plain gown in dark green, no bustle. She looked small and unnaturally skinny compared to all the other women. She carried no parasol and squinted in the setting sun as they walked up the stairs.

James shook their hands, "Welcome, it's so nice of you to come. Please make yourself at home and go inside and have some refreshments." *Please don't say anything about abolition when you are served, you wouldn't do that, would you?* James thought suddenly, wondering how political and outspoken they were, but he didn't think that anyone would be so careless at a ball full of slave owners if they wanted to keep the skins on their backs.

"We will be delighted, thank you Mr. Waynewright, and this must be Mrs. Waynewright?"

Mrs. Petersson kissed Katherine on the cheek and then they made their way to the back receiving a drink from Mary. James and Katherine barely dared to look at each other.

After about half an hour of pre-dinner drinks, Katherine told them that the dinner was about to be served in the dining room. James took her arm and motioned for the guests to go first. It was beautiful; the chandelier was lit, its crystals glittering in the light as did the crystal glasses in front of each gold trimmed plate placed with napkins folded into the shape of swans.

Mary and Jenny served dish after dish and the conversation around the table flowed naturally.

James and Katherine sat at the head of the table with Mr. and Mrs. Wilson on one side, Mr., and Mrs. Petersson at the other, then the Dawson's and the Burnham's next to each other at the opposite end. On both sides the Davenports, Mr. Frost and the Templetons. James had known Mr. and Mrs. Templeton as well as Mr. Frost since childhood. They lived on the other side of town and he had not seen them for many years. Mr. Frost had been a widower for as long as he could remember. The Davenports he barely knew at all, but his father and Mr. Davenport had been writing to each other regularly.

"Katherine," James said and smiled at the Wilsons. "I didn't have much time to introduce you earlier. Mr. and Mrs. Wilson live very close to town. You may remember that I pointed out their beautiful plantation to you. They have three sons, William, Eric and Reginald; all grown now if I'm not mistaken?" James said raising his eyebrow in question.

"Indeed, Reginald and William are both living at home and planning to take over when the time comes. We have enough space for two families when they marry. Eric is in England handling the business from there." Mrs. Wilson's round face shone with happiness as she spoke of her sons. Her graying hair was styled high on top of her head with sapphires and pearls glittering in an elaborate braid. She was wearing a yellow gown probably meant for someone younger but it suited her somehow, highlighting her personality perfectly.

Mrs. Wilson changed the subject and spoke plainly, "Dear Mr. Waynewright, I'm very glad to see that the Burnham's are here. It is *very* gracious of you to invite them."

Mr. Petersson nodded. "We haven't offered our condolences; we heard of course, and we are truly sorry."

"Thank you," James replied simply and glanced over at the other table where the Burnhams sat at the far end. He never knew quite what to say when condolences were offered. "We felt that they should be here, it was just an accident after all."

"Tragic, very tragic..." Mr. Wilson said and shook his head, but changed the subject. "What about your medical studies? Are you planning to move back to New York again to continue?"

James shook his head. "Most likely not, not with the responsibility for the plantation. I...my life have taken another turn."

"Indeed, it is wise that you remain. You have a beautiful place here."

James smiled gratefully and turned towards Mrs. Wilson who leaned forward towards Mrs. Petersson. "We are very glad to meet you. Why haven't we seen you at any other soirées? Where do you live? Where is your plantation?"

"We have no plantation, just a smaller farm," Mr. Petersson interjected.

"Oh, you say? How sweet, you sell no tobacco?" Mrs. Wilson went on sounding slightly inebriated by the drinks already and she got a dismaying look from her husband who interrupted her.

"Small farms are nice. I grew up on a smaller farm myself about two hours from here. My father had only five negroes helpin' us, but it was sufficient. I remember being very happy there."

"We are fine, have enough for ourselves and enough land that Ebba can sell some vegetables and eggs to the town store, pies as well. If you have ever had sweet potato pie or apple pie at the salon it's my Ebba who has made 'em," he said proudly.

"I *have* had the pie there in fact and it's delicious. Every time I check on my mail, I have a bite to eat as I read my paper," Mr. Wilson said, smacking his lips as if he was actually eating it.

Mrs. Petersson laughed, a pearly laugh, sounding almost like a young girl.

"How many negroes do you get by with?" Mr. Wilson asked and Mrs. Petersson's smile faded as quickly as it had come. James saw her glance at her husband and the barely noticeable shake of his head before he answered.

"We get by just fine without."

"Oh how quaint, completely self-sufficient, unless you of course hire a couple from Mr. Waynewright during the harvests?" Mrs. Wilson added, nodding as if she assumed that the answer would be yes.

"We don't hire people's negroes," Mr. Petersson answered curtly.

Katherine glanced at him and threw him a quick nervous smile. James tried to think of something that he could say to change the subject. *Oh god, this was not a good idea at all, how could we have been so foolish, we are going to ruin everything. I have to say something fast.*

He abruptly got up from his chair and banged his dessertspoon in his glass. "Everyone, I would like to take this opportunity to introduce you all to my dear wife, Katherine. I'm the most fortunate man in the world to know such a kind, compassionate and wonderful woman. We met in the great city of New York, or rather I should say that I met her father and sister first. I managed to impress them simply by talking about our raspberries; for a city dweller, they are quite exotic. Had it not been for those succulent Virginian berries, I would not have met my wife. Please, let's have a toast in her honor." James smiled at Katherine, trying to look like the loving husband and not someone who was terrified that a debate about slavery might take place. He then made eye contact with everyone at the table with his glass raised, and waited for the gesture to be returned. He came to Dawson last. "Here here!" Dawson said and raised his glass with a polite nod.

After the toast, James sat down and locked eyes with Katherine. She clinked her glass with his. Touched by his sweet words she touched his arm. "Oh James, you make me blush. Really all, I thank each and every one of you for coming this evening, I am most honored."

The conversation naturally changed to another subject and the rest of the evening went smoothly and without incident.

People enjoyed themselves, clustering in smaller group and talking amongst themselves, drinking and eating pastries served on little plates that Mary had placed all around the parlor. The men, with the exception of Mr. Petersson, slipped out to James' study for more small talk over brandy and cigars; he stood by himself looking at the décor, which was a bit too ostentatious for his taste.

As the guests prepared to leave James allowed himself a deep breath. So far the evening had been a success. Then his thoughts turned to preparing for what was to come next.

Pap had discretely arranged it so that the Peterssons' small carriage was been parked in such a way that they had to leave last.

If they were dismayed by it they didn't show it, but stood patiently in front of the house small talking with the rest of the guests as they waited for their drivers to turn around and pick them up.

James glanced at Pap who grinned at him as Dawson left last then made a show of going to get the Peterssons' carriage.

"Thank God, that went well," James whispered.

Mr. Petersson gave him an odd look and opened his mouth to say something, but James interjected.

"Katherine and I would very much like it if you wouldn't mind joining *us*, Pap and Auntie Ellen for a night cap by the fire before you leave?"

Mr. Petersson looked at his wife with an expression of surprise and alarm.

"No thank you, we really need to go home, Mr. Waynewright, if you please."

"Yes, we need to get home," Mrs. Petersson repeated and moved closer to her husband.

They both looked extremely uncomfortable and when Pap came back without their carriage Mrs. Petersson's knees buckled and she would have fallen to the ground had her husband not held her up. James realized that they thought that they would confront them, Auntie Ellen, and Pap together; it was probably not the best idea to suggest a night cap. James had assumed that it would make them comfortable, but it had had the opposite effect.

Pap smiled, pointing to Auntie Ellen who came up the road from the quarters having rested after preparing all day. She waved at him and slowly walked over to the Peterssons.

"Sorry I couldn't send word earlier, I'm Auntie Ellen. I know that you know who I am. Is all right, don't be scared now."

Katherine walked over to Mrs. Petersson and whispered something in her ear. James saw her eyes widen in surprise and after a quick glance in her husband's direction she nodded.

James motioned for them to go inside first. He felt his pulse racing. He took Katherine's hand in his for a moment and felt that it was clammy and cold.

Once they sat down James began to talk.

"I know that you know Will, our *friend* Auntie Ellen's son," he said and nodded in Auntie Ellen's direction before he continued. "He is *employed* by my wife's uncle in New York now, working professionally as a woodworker and carpenter. I signed his freedom papers."

They looked a little less terrified but still full of disbelief but Mr. Petersson nodded slowly.

James took a deep breath.

"I apologize. I'm so sorry to alarm you. I...we...Katherine and I, we are on your side, we want to free all our servants... About ten have left already, including Will whom you know. The reason we invited you here was so that we could talk to you about helpin' you with the runaways. We are thinkin' that Katherine and I could drive them to your place so that they don't have to walk in that cold, snake infested stream."

The look of shock on their face was almost bigger than when they first told Auntie Ellen and Pap.

"You are abolitionists?" Mr. Petersson asked incredulously.

"Very much so," Katherine replied.

Chapter 02

Mr. Petersson spoke first, hat in hand.

"I don't know what to say, we certainly had not expected this. I mean no disrespect but..."

James laughed, "With us having a plantation full of slaves, yes I can see how that might be confusing."

"If you don't mind me asking, Mr. Waynewright, how did you come to understand...I...what made..." Mrs. Petersson stammered giving up on finishing her sentence.

"I spent over a year in New York and being away caused me to see things differently. I had never left our county before, never questioned anything at all." James shot Auntie Ellen and Pap a glance and continued. "I was raised to believe that we were supposed to take care of our servants, that it was our duty as Christians, it never really crossed my mind that it isn't right. I had occasion to go to a service at Plymouth Church while I was in New York, and Pastor Beecher made a very strong impression on me." James turned to Katherine and patted her arm. "Then I met my wife and she wouldn't have me unless..."

"You have met Pastor Beecher?" Mrs. Petersson exclaimed looking flustered. She waved her hands in the air and dropped her handkerchief on the floor; she almost fell of the couch when she reached for it.

Katherine leaned forward to lend her a hand, but seeing that Mrs. Petersson was all right she relaxed and said, "Yes we sure have, he married us as a matter of fact."

"I'll be darned!" Mr. Petersson slapped his knee with his hat, grinning happily.

Auntie Ellen and Pap laughed.

"My sincere apologies, Ellen, I should have said something sooner. I'm just in such awe that I forgot." Mrs. Petersson easily got up from the couch and went over to where Auntie Ellen sat; then she took her hands in her own.

"You are my sister in this fight. Many a guest has come our way because of you throughout the years and every one of them arrived safely," she said and tenderly touched Auntie Ellen's cheek.

Auntie Ellen's eyes brimmed with tears and she said, "And I have sent them all knowing they be finding a safe place to lay their heads, Mrs. Petersson."

James and Mr. Petersson looked at each other and smiled, not noticing Katherine wiping away tears.

"How did you get involved in this endeavor, Mr. Petersson?"

"Now you call me Oskar, Mr. Waynewright, and my wife Ebba."

James felt himself relax.

"Thank you, Oskar, you as well. I'm James and my wife is Katherine."

Oskar nodded happily. "I came here as a young boy, havin' journeyed on the big ship from Sweden with my parents. They built the farm but were never interested in buying negroes. My Pa said he felt that he was fully capable himself and didn't want the trouble. There were a lot of goings on when I was a small boy, rumors of cruel treatment and even burnings in the area."

Pap cleared his throat in discomfort.

"My father always spoke of how he had moved from Sweden to America because it was said that here all men were treated equal, without rich landowners that could force you to work or who took your crop. He had not come here to see men abused. In fact he almost made us move back. Well, I guess I share his sentiments. We support the American Anti-Slavery Society, though we dare not get their almanacs; you never know who get wind of it and begins to investigate what it is that the postman brings."

"We have to be careful. I have *Uncle Tom's Cabin* and a couple of issues of *The Liberator* should you be interested. Mother sent them in my trunks," Katherine informed them.

"Oh, dear Katherine, yes please," Ebba clasped her hands together in delight.

Oskar turned to Pap but looked thoughtful for a moment before he spoke.

"You said that you have freed your slaves, but that only ten of them left?"

Pap began to explain about the sharecropping and the legal complications if they wanted to stay in the state.

"We have decided to wait for a while to apply with the county clerk and take it on a person to person basis. If someone wants to leave then we'll do it, but he made his views pretty clear that it wouldn't be so easy," James added. He remained quiet for a moment before he continued. "Frankly, we ain't sure of what to do. Pap and Auntie Ellen want to stay, but as of now it does not seem possible for them to do it as free people."

Auntie Ellen reached across the table and gently patted James' arm. "We know what's in your heart, Mr. Waynewright, that's what important." *Yes but you are old Auntie Ellen, for you it is easier to take,* James thought to himself but didn't say anything.

Ebba looked disturbed. "I never imagined that it would be so complicated to do the right thing!"

"Neither did we," Katherine said and sighed with agreement.

Chapter 03

No new travelers had arrived, and by the time November approached, it was getting colder so they didn't expect anybody.

James and Katherine snuggled in bed, having retired early for the evening. They had hoped for a baby by now but there was still no sign of one. James wasn't too concerned, his mother had only had him and Katherine had only one sister. "Maybe it's a family trait. We have only been married about a year and a half and we have our whole life ahead of us," he said and kissed her gently on her nose like she loved before she had time to respond.

That's when they heard it; four loud hoots in quick succession.

Katherine's eyes rounded, "James you have to slam the door, hurry!"

Quickly he got out of the warm bed, pulled on his trousers and shirt and hurried down the stairs in bare feet. He ran across the cold floor to the porch door.

He slammed it hard once, twice and then the last two times, wondering if it was loud enough for them to hear. He buttoned his shirt as he looked out the small window in the door to see if Mary was coming.

He heard Katherine patter down the stairs in her slippers. She was still in her nightgown having just thrown a robe over her shoulders, her dark hair askew and loose over her shoulders. As usual when he saw her like this he was struck with her beauty; it didn't matter what was happening, he couldn't help noticing her flushed skin and thick mane of dark hair, but he didn't say anything and looked back out the window.

"Don't see anyone yet. How long should we wait do you think? Do you think they heard me?"

"I think so, James, it was rather loud. Wait a little longer then you can go down. Maybe they are feeding the poor soul and he or she hasn't hid yet. It's dark, and they don't have to hide them right away since we know."

He nodded silently.

"James, let's get some lemonade, I'm thirsty. I'll light the lamp so that they see it," she said and leaned forward over the little side table, her face lit up as by a halo in the darkness as she struck the match.

They walked silently through the house in the darkness. "I should have brought a candle from upstairs," Katherine whispered. "I don't think we should light all the lamps. What if someone rides by and wonders why we are up in the middle of the night?"

James shrugged, but couldn't help but feeling a little paranoid about what she said.

"We have the right to be up as late as we very well please!" he said sounding more irritated than he meant.

"I only meant..." She sounded hurt.

"I'm sorry, you are right we should be careful, Sweet. But it isn't late, just about nine." He touched her shoulder and leaned against the door in the kitchen as Katherine poured them each a glass from the pitcher in the icebox. Auntie Ellen had traded lemons for pies with the cook at Dawson's plantation some weeks ago and they still had some left.

Just then they heard a scraping sound and suddenly the door in the kitchen opened from outside and Mary appeared in front of them.

Katherine let out a sound and almost dropped the pitcher. The lemonade spilled out of it and James heard it land on the floor with loud splat.

"I thought you would come through the porch door in the front." Katherine said.

"Sorry to startle you, Mrs. Waynewright. I didn't think of that. I didn't think it'd be appropriate, we always walk through this door. I'm sorry, Mrs. Waynewright," Mary repeated.

"No, no it's all right, Mary, you are right. We weren't thinkin'. When I slammed the porch door I just assumed you would come in that way too." James added in a lowered voice, "Do we have a visitor?"

"Yes, sir, a man…." she hesitated, "he is no worse for wear, just tired cause he has walked a many a night in the cold. His shoes were all worn out and he took 'em off."

"We'll have to see what size he wears and find him a pair. When did he arrive?"

"Just now."

Katherine got a basket from under the table and started filling it with food; eggs, a loaf of bread, dried apples and a bottle of milk that she handed to Mary. "Take this. Do you need anything else?"

Mary glanced into the basket but shook her head, "Should be enough for now, Mama wants him to rest himself for two days before he move on."

James cleared his throat, "We should plan to drive to the Peterssons' the day after tomorrow then. We'll leave around seven p.m., as if we are going to visit them for dinner," James said, sounding more confident than he was.

Mary looked content and with a quick nod she disappeared out into the dark night, the basket securely in her arms.

James and Katherine stared at each other without saying anything; they listened to Mary's quick footsteps as she hurried down the path and the sound of a light rain pattering on the windows. James reached for Katherine's hand.

"Come, Sweet, let us go back to bed. There isn't anything else we can do now. We have to wait it out and pretend that everything is normal." He grabbed her around her waist and pulled her close, and she sighed leaning into him. "You are right, James, but I don't think I'll sleep. I want to go visit that poor man and see who he is and where he is from."

James didn't reply until they were back upstairs and back under the warm covers. He grabbed the newspaper from his bedside table and pointed to an Ad on one of the pages.

"**Fredericksburg, October 29th 1858**
100 dollar reward.

Negro named Alfred ran away from the subscriber October 20th. Is strong, tall and muscular, almost 6 feet, has no scars, but has a slight limp on left foot. Dark skinned, around 30, all his teeth and no gray hair. Wore grey clothing last seen.
Return to C Williams

"It's probably him, Katherine, don't you think? The timing seems plausible if he's had help and hasn't walked all the way here."

Katherine shivered and crawled in next to him. "If it's him, then he has been on the run for almost ten days. Did you get the buggy ready, James? Is the extra compartment big enough for such a tall man to hide?"

"If he lies bent or curled up I should think so yes. Pap pulled off the panel under the seat and the space under it is big enough I think, and then you can just put the panel back after he crawls in. It's crude, not as nice as if Will had made it, but it'll do."

"You are a genius. Will there be enough air?" she asked, her eyes shining with excitement.

"I hope so; there are some natural holes in the wood. I should have shown it to you. I'll show you tomorrow." He yawned and pulled the covers over himself and Katherine, hugging her close. He felt her hair tickle his nose; it smelled of soap.

Chapter 04

James and Katherine waited in their buggy by the edge of the woods just behind their property line. They would have been able to see the graveyard in the distance if it had not been so dark. It was chilly, the wind howled and the trees rustled in such a way that it was impossible to distinguish the sound of footsteps on the mossy ground. *What would you say, Mother and Father, if you knew what I'm doing, literarily on top of your graves? Are you turning over?*

James shook the morbid thought from his head and took Katherine's hand; her glove felt cool against his skin.

"They ought to be here any minute now," she whispered. "What time is it?"

James pulled his watch out of his breast pocket, but it only appeared as a flat smooth stone in his hand, "It is too dark to see."

"Oh, I didn't think," she whispered. Their voices were almost inaudible with the wind. Still, they felt nervous that someone would hear them. The darkness seemed oppressing and frightening. *How did runaways muster up the courage to be out here for weeks?* James wondered to himself and thinking that Harriet Tubman herself might be in the forest right now, bringing people back north.

They heard the sound of an owl hooting three times, startling them even though they had expected it. Katherine pressed her hand to her mouth to muffle an involuntary yelp.

As agreed, James responded with his signal, clearing his throat three times.

Then they heard a man's low careful voice. "Evenin,' sir."

James jumped down so that he faced the man. His eyes had become used to the darkness and he could perceive that the man was very tall and dark skinned, the whites of his eyes appeared clearly in his face. James didn't say much, just helped Katherine down. He touched the man's shoulder and gestured for him crawl in underneath their seat.

"Crawl in there." James whispered as low as he could, but the man heard it and wiggled into the tight space without hesitation. James felt him search for his hand in the dark, when he found it he squeezed it in thanks. James felt a tightening in his chest at the gesture and squeezed it back. He tried to push the panel back to close it, but just as Katherine had worried, the man was too big. His knees protruded out just over the edge where James and Katherine's feet would rest; the panel closed on one side but it couldn't close on the other, it would have had to bend in the middle for that to happen. They stared at each other in frustration. Her face looked almost translucent in the darkness as her pale skin contrasted with the hollows of her dark blue eyes. "Katherine, hand me your shawl." James whispered.

He threw it over their seat so that it was hanging down over the uneven side. It was far from perfect but it would have to do. Barely daring to breathe, James helped Katherine up so that she sat on the side where the panel actually closed, and he jumped up next to her and they were off.

Once out on the road they stopped again and James got off and lit the lamps in the front. They had to appear as if they were out for a reason and were not sneaking off somewhere. Katherine held a pie in her lap as a gift for the Peterssons on whom they were calling. Are you cold, Katherine?" James asked in a normal tone of voice now. "I'm sorry that you forgot your shawl. You can borrow my coat if you need it."

"I'm all right, James. My own coat will do just fine. The shawl is just an extra layer for the wind."

He squeezed her hand in response and then they remained silent, not knowing how to keep a normal conversation going with their cargo right beneath their feet. James was physically holding the panel in place with his legs.

After about twenty minutes they heard hooves coming at them in high speed. Katherine gasped and grabbed his arm. "We are goin' to dinner, we have every right to do so," James mumbled trying to sound confident, even though he felt as if he could soil himself out of sheer terror.

Soon they saw a man on a white horse in front of them. James pulled the reins bringing the buggy to a stop, and then he heard a familiar voice.

"James! Howdy, how do you do? Fancy meetin' you here, where are you goin' on such a cold night?"

Peter Dawson, James' childhood friend whom he hadn't seen since before he left for New York, had the horse cantering across the road towards them. As Peter came into the light of the lamps they could see him grinning as he gingerly slid off his horse.

"Peter, you are back, what a pleasant surprise," James said, trying to sound as happy as Peter did and not daring to jump off, afraid that the panel would come loose if he did. He leaned down and shook his hand heartily, praying that Alfred, if that was his name, would lie still as a mouse.

"When did you get back to Virginia? Your father told me you were in Europe."

"I was, then I spent time on Safari in Africa as well."

"You don't say?"

"Yes indeed, a mighty adventure it was. The fever almost killed me but my trunks are full of prizes that I have not unpacked. You should come see!"

"I'll be delighted, another time. Peter, I want you to meet my wife. Katherine this is one of my oldest friends, Peter Dawson," James said and turned to Katherine who looked perfectly white. "We are on our way to dinner, running a bit late to be perfectly honest, but..." *Why did I say that? It's obvious that we are on our way somewhere. Why else would we be out here with a pie? I'm an idiot.*

Peter Dawson didn't seem to notice anything out of the ordinary and smiled as he walked around the carriage to Katherine's side and reached for her hand so that he could kiss it. "Mrs. Waynewright, I'm delighted to finally meet you. I hope you find us to your liking and have been made welcome."

“I sure have, Mr. Dawson.” Katherine smiled pleasantly, but James could see that she looked terrified underneath her perfectly composed face. “I’ve had the pleasure to meet your father several times, I see the resemblance.”

“James, I was so terribly sorry to hear about your parents, please accept my condolences. I remember your father so fondly.

“Thank you, Peter. I appreciate it.” James changed the subject, “We would both be delighted to have your company at our home, please do call on us.”

I will in a day or so. Enjoy your visit,” Peter said with an exaggerated bow and a wide grin.

“We will, thank you,” James replied and shook the reins, swallowing his fear as they left him standing there.

His hands felt weird on the reins as if they were holding on to something else entirely. He kept staring ahead until he suddenly became aware of Katherine crying softly beside him.

“I know, Katherine, I know, but we are alright. Peter didn’t suspect anything at all.” He shifted the reins to one hand and took her hand in his. “Don’t cry, he was friendly. We must prepare ourselves; we might meet others nosier than Peter. We will be there soon in about fifteen minutes or so. Are you cold? You are shaking.”

“I’m just nervous, but I’ll be fine. I can’t find my handkerchief.” She sniffled and tried to smile. “You’re right James. We have to steel ourselves for all kinds of meetings on the road and just play along. The best we could hope for is to encounter a friend. I must bear in mind the courage of the people we are trying to help, and get strength from them.”

James grabbed her hand. “Indeed you are right, and we have to keep in mind that people would never ever suspect us of this, so even if they heard something they would assume it was something in the woods, or something falling off the carriage wheel or something. They’d never think of it unless the person sat up and showed himself.

Finally they came to the fork in the road that led to the Peterssons' farm. There was a candle in one of the windows and lamps were lit in a room on the side.

It felt like an eternity before they heard somebody move inside after they knocked, but finally they saw a curtain shift in a window and then the door opened wide.

"Oh, there you are, welcome, welcome, dinner is almost ready." Oskar said as if he had been expecting them. "Katherine, why don't you go inside? James and I will put the horse in the stable for a rest, eh?"

James nodded as Oskar put on his boots and came out.

"So nice of you to call on us, Ebba has been cooking all day, you know womenfolk," Oskar said with a wink. James began to relax a little.

The stable was in a small barn behind the house and when the horse was safely in the stable and the buggy hidden in the darkness next to the barn, James took a deep breath and with a cautious look around him he removed Katherine's shawl and pulled out the panel.

The man didn't move at first and for a dreadful moment James thought that he had suffocated, but then they saw his legs stretch out, his hand grabbed the edge of the seat and he painstakingly sat up. He gave James a bewildered look as if he had just woken up. He tried to climb out but he was so stiff from lying curled up that both James and Oskar had to help him. His knees almost buckled as his feet found the ground but he steadied himself and stretched.

"Come inside dear fellow, we will go in though the back here," Oskar said and walked ahead of them to the back of the house.

James turned to him and touched his shoulder. "I'm James," he said giving only his first name.

"Alfred," he said hoarsely. *It is him, just as we thought,* James said to himself.

Inside Ebba and Katherine waited for them.

"Welcome, you must be weary. Please have a seat in the kitchen and we will get you something to eat. Then you can sleep in the attic. You are safe here, don't worry about anything."

Alfred nodded and sat down. He looked scared but relieved at the same time. He massaged his back and then gratefully accepted a tall glass of milk from Ebba.

"Were you all right when we met our acquaintance on the road?" Katherine asked, not mentioning Peter Dawson by name, even though Alfred must have heard it.

"I was, tried not to breathe, and didn't move a muscle."

"You met someone on the road?" Ebba asked.

"Yes, we did," Katherine said and Ebba understood not to ask who it was and just nodded.

"Close call, eh?" Oskar added and sat down next to her. "It's your first time; you get used to it. Should have seen Ebba's and my first time. We hid a young girl in the attic but we were so nervous that we didn't dare to have her down here in the house, even for her meals. We ran up and down those stairs every two minutes to check on 'er, then suddenly the Sherriff knocks on our door." He paused for effect and looked them each in the eye with a raised eyebrow before he continued.

"Turns out that there was a runaway horse loose; a stallion that was panicked and was running around raising havoc. I about had myself a heart attack. All I heard was runaway and the Sheriff had to repeat himself twice before I understood that he wasn't taking about the young woman in my attic."

"Oh, I remember that," James said, "It ran past our house and scared my mother. I wasn't too old then, maybe six."

"That is probably right; it was years ago, we've been doin' this for a long time. You get used to it, and after a while you will be less scared about it." Ebba answered and then turned to their runaway and asked; "What is your name?"

He smiled, almost laughed. "Alfred, Ma'am."

“Would you like some eggs and bread before you go to sleep up there? Even if it’s early in the night yet, it’s safer that you are up there us much as possible, then late tomorrow night we’ll have you on your way to the next meetin’ place.

James let loose a sigh locking eyes with Katherine, relieved that everything went well.

Chapter 05

As it often does, several things seemed to happen all at once at the worst possible moment.

Just a couple of days after the "visit" with Ebba and Oskar, James was doing some work in his office. He had pulled out his notes on sharecropping and was trying to make sense of it, figuring out how much money would go to each person or family that were now *working* on the plantation. To his surprise, at least the way it looked at first glance, they had done so well that even though he would share the profit with his workers they would still be fine. Maybe his father wouldn't turn over in his grave after all. Just then there was a knock on the door.

Auntie Ellen appeared. Uncharacteristically, she walked all the way over to his desk instead of remaining by the door.

"Massa," she said, "you have a visitor." Then in a lower voice, "Seems I do too, only not in the cabin." She had an odd look on her face.

"Who is it?"

"It's Mr. Peter Dawson."

"Oh," James gave her a quizzical look, "and?"

Auntie Ellen shook her head and quickly glanced behind her then she took yet a step closer and whispered, "His driver is in the kitchen, he isn't alone."

James didn't know how to respond or what it meant. He just looked her in the eye as he slowly nodded, then he said in a louder tone, "That will be all, Auntie Ellen. Prepare us refreshments."

"Yes Massa."

James hesitated for a moment wondering what was afoot; then he left his office and walked out to find Peter standing by the fire.

He turned around as he heard him, "There you are my long lost friend, I've missed you old married fellow. Where are the babies? See none toddling around here yet."

"Not yet, not yet. You didn't find a wife on your travels?"

"Nah, I'm in no rush for it. I want to travel more, kind of got the itch for it. I thought you were crazy leaving here and going to New York, now I can see why, I'm..."

Both Katherine and Auntie Ellen interrupted them.

Auntie Ellen came in with a tray with steaming cups of tea and a plate with biscuits, Katherine with several pieces of mail in her hands. Her cheeks were rosy from the cold and her eyes sparkled as she put all of the mail except for one of the packages down.

"James, Mary and I had a nice time in town, and we have a lot of letters..." She stopped midsentence, "Oh I'm so sorry, Mr. Dawson. I didn't see you."

"Pleased to meet you again, Mrs. Waynewright," he said and bowed with a flourish. "I'm the one who should apologize. I came over on a whim without an invitation. I don't mean to intrude."

"Not at all, and we did invite you, just the other night, didn't we?" Katherine said glancing at James who cleared his throat.

"In fact, Peter, why don't you stay for dinner? Call for Auntie Ellen again Katherine and have her make something special."

Katherine nodded and causally threw the package on the couch next to James and then she rang the bell on the wall.

When Auntie Ellen came back, she curtsied and listened carefully to what Katherine was telling her. "Yes, Missus, that be a pleasure. Could you please come with me for a moment and look at somethin' in the kitchen, so you can pick the meat that is the most suitable."

Auntie Ellen who had been gazing demurely somewhere midair lifted her eyes and looked Katherine straight in the eye.

"Certainly," Katherine said throwing a quick glance at James.

What is going on? James thought.

"How does she take the husbandry? I take it she ain't much used to it, not having any servants up there in New York?"

"Well, that's not entirely true. Her family has a housekeeper from Ireland, Mrs. McNeary, but no it's not like it is here where we have so much help. She is doing fine. She feels that running a plantation is a lot less overwhelming than she had expected with having them. It's a change, of course. Living quite isolated down here compared to city life was a bit of a challenge at first."

"Ah, yes but you are making the most of it visiting with the neighbors. That's good. Did you have a nice time? Can't say I know the Peterssons well, but Papa told me that they were here when you had your banquet."

James swallowed trying to hide the uncomfortable feeling that was coming over him.

"Well," he laughed. "I would not exactly call it a banquet, more like a small gathering, but it was nice. I felt very proud to introduce Katherine. I remember standin' on the steps feeling proud and very much at home... though it is a very sad reason I was hosting instead of my parents." *What is happening in the kitchen? Where is Katherine?*

Peter's expression changed and he cleared his throat and took a sip of the cooling tea. "I was still in Africa when it happened, heading back to Europe to get on the ship back here. Devastating, I didn't know what to do when Papa told me when I came back. I felt horrible for you and wanted to call on you right away, but—" He touched James' shoulder, "James, how are you feeling, really? I'm sorry that I didn't ask you earlier; I can be a buffoon sometimes."

"It's all right, Peter."

"No, really it's not; I should have been here for you earlier, James."

Before James could answer Katherine came back. She looked at Peter and sat down on the couch opposite them and absently opened her mail parcel and started to pull out its contents, only to stop again with a sudden panicked glance in James' direction.

James saw the corner of a newspaper sticking out from the torn packaging: "The Li..."

Jesus, it's the Liberator! Chrissy must have sent it. Why in God's name did she open it now?

Peter did not notice anything, probably assuming that the tense moment had to do with them speaking of the tragic death of James' parents.

Katherine discretely put the package to the side; pretending that nothing had happened, she turned to Peter. "Please do tell us all about your travels in Africa. It must have been a marvelous experience."

"Sure was. I saw some things that I could never had imagined before. Elephants and lions, zebras...I had not really believed that they had horses painted in stripes. Well, they ain't horses but they are really astonishing. I saw savages livin' in huts naked and runnin' around shouting in a language that no civilized person could understand. Those who don't think that we are doing the right thing with our negroes here in the south should just go visit Africa and see how they live there. It'd change their tune right quick."

"Indeed," James nodded, not daring to look at Katherine who rose from the chair tucking the package with The Liberator under her arm.

"Let us move to the dining room shall we?"

Peter followed and James stepped aside so that Peter could walk ahead. He and Katherine looked at each other. "If you will excuse us for a moment, Katherine will change for dinner. I'll take that to my office," he said and took the mail from her.

James hurried into his office and put the mail in a drawer, then headed into the kitchen finding it empty of anyone other than Auntie Ellen who sat resting by the table with a teacup, their dinner puttering both on the stove and over the hearth.

"What's afoot, Auntie Ellen?"

She motioned for him to shut the door and to come close. As he sat down she pushed the tea cup forward so that she had space to lean her arms on the table to get closer to him.

"Without knowin' of my hideout, Jonah had overheard you and Dawson talkin' one day, and got the feelin' that you is a nice Massa and that maybe you wouldn't notice if he hid here a while before he goes north. He came right into the kitchen after the driver...they went to my cabin now, not sure yet if we should show him the hidey hole. He had this plan a long time; he hid himself under the carriage with a rope!" she clicked her tongue and grabbed James' arm. "Can you believe it, the rope tied round himself so he could lie underneath and not get scraped up, still his arms were so weak he could barely move them from holding on so long."

James got a sickening feeling in his stomach, wondering how much he had given away of himself that day in Dawson's office. He remembered the negro who was dusting outside who nodded at him as he left the office. It must be the same one that was in Auntie Ellen's cabin now.

He had been very clear and outspoken about his views on being kind and compassionate. He remembered that he had wanted to tell Dawson what he really felt, but that he had not.

There was probably not more to it than that. The man had noticed that he wasn't cruel and seized the opportunity to find a place to collect his thoughts before he ran on. But to risk it by going straight into the kitchen seemed a bit much. James touched Auntie Ellen's hand. "We'll have to talk about it later. Are you sure that Peter didn't see anything, nor know anything regarding what we are about?"

"Mr. Dawson, Jr? He ain't seen nothin.' He knows nothin'," she shrugged.

"Good, I'll go out to my guest and we'll talk later." Auntie Ellen squeezed his hand and nodded silently, and James went to join his childhood friend whom he didn't seem to have anything at all in common with any longer.

They remained in the dining room for the rest of the evening. Peter told them story after story of his adventures in places that he had visited, some of them they had not even heard of.

"Oh, it was incredible, Egypt especially. I think it might have been the most interesting place I have ever seen. The Pyramids, no matter how many drawings or photographs you have seen you cannot quite understand how large they are and so...well, it feels ancient to stand there, as if you are part of something," he shook his head. "I can't explain it, but when you visit I'll show you the stereoscopic cards that I bought. Have you ever seen those?"

"I have once or twice," James said. "They are quite remarkable."

"It's like you can walk into the place. I don't understand how they do it. I have heard that Prince Albert and Queen Victoria are supposed to love them and have several," Katherine said with a slightly dreamy look.

Peter laughed. "Mrs. Waynewright, had I known how much you like them, I should have brought you some. I should have thought to buy several to give as gifts," he said, not even looking at Mary who refilled their wineglasses and brought out a plate of sweetmeats, moving silently as she served.

"Please, James. I've been talking too much. Tell me instead of you and your travels in Yankee country. Is it as they say, full of radicals?"

James glanced at Katherine. She looked perfectly composed, but he could see her hand shake slightly as she reached for her glass.

"Well," he began but was interrupted by Peter.

"Can you imagine that I was approached by several people in Europe about that horrid book about that Tom, Uncle Tom's Cabin? It's already translated and spreading propaganda all over the world!"

"Are you serious?" James thought of the copy that Ebba had borrowed from them.

"They should read *Aunt Phillips Cabin* instead or even better *Uncle Robin in His Cabin in Virginia, and Tom Without One in Boston,* well at least it gets our beautiful women in the south to use their penmanship, though my father does not think that women should dabble in politics."

Peter paused and took a sip of his wine, smiling wide. He looked none worse for wear even though he must have had at least three large glasses.

"Have you read those, Mrs. Waynewright? I'll be happy to lend them to you if you haven't, my sisters love them."

"I would be delighted, thank you," Katherine said evenly.

James sat silently and tried to focus on the conversation. He didn't like the direction it was taking, especially not as they had one of Dawson's negroes hiding in their quarters. What if Jonah panicked and caused a commotion when Peter was here? Or what if Dawson noticed he was gone, or someone had seen it and told him? Then it would only be a matter of time until Dawson himself came over here to have a look.

"Are you all right, my friend?" Peter asked. "You look as if you have seen a ghost! You are so quiet."

James laughed, hoping it sounded natural. "Not at all, but I may have had too much to drink," he said feigning a yawn.

Peter looked at him oddly, used as he was to his and James' evenings with loads of drinking.

"Plantation responsibility gettin' to you I suppose," Peter said and stood, but hadn't quite lost the questioning look. "I should be goin'. I thank you for your hospitality; it was a delight," he said and smiled genuinely now. "I better fetch Adam so he can drive me home. I assume he isn't sitting in the kitchen still? Do you think he went to the quarters?"

For God's sake, don't go down there on your own!

"Possibly," James said trying to sound calm, and walked over to the bell on the wall and rang for Mary. "I'll have Mary find him for you. It's getting late, maybe he is waitin' in your carriage already."

Peter rolled his eyes. "I get the sense you want to get rid of me." He grinned and boxed James playfully in his shoulder.

James laughed feeling a bit more relaxed. He needed to calm down; Peter was obviously his regular old self and didn't know the drama he had unwittingly caused by calling on them.

A few minutes later Katherine and he waved at Peter as he sat himself in his carriage. Adam closed the door behind Peter and stiffly climbed up behind the driver's seat without a look in their direction.

It must have been extremely uncomfortable for Jonah under there and how incredibly impossible it was that no one had noticed.

Chapter 06

James fell down in the armchair with an exasperated look at Katherine.

She stared back equally bothered and sat down opposite him on the sofa. She sighed and shook her head.

"I'm so sorry about the package, I know it was stupid."

"Yes, Katherine, it was, for god's sake, we could have been exposed right then and there as we are havin' one of their servants hiding in our damn kitchen. What the hell were you thinkin'?" he said, his voice sounding angrier than he had intended. "Didn't you know your sister would send them; I assume it's her. It's illegal, you know that don't you?"

Katherine looked startled and as though she would cry, "Well, had he seen it? I'd just tell him that I was curious to see what it is people say about us, especially now when I see the truth and how nice everyone is to their servants."

"Well, you say? Don't you think it would have been *just a bit* too risky? He could easily have seen through your charade."

"Maybe, but maybe not," she said and waved her hand in the air. "Plus, it actually might have been interesting to see what he would say about it if we read it with him."

James shook his head and didn't respond, "What are the odds that you get this mail just as he visits? How much do you think they know at Dawson's? What if they have spoken of our *loose* husbandry and their servants have begun to suspect what we think?" James said.

"Or do you think that the word is getting around that Auntie Ellen has her hidey hole and is helping people along?" Katherine asked instead of replying to James question. "I didn't get much time to ask when I pretended to look at the steaks."

"Was the man still in the kitchen?"

"No, he had gone."

James nodded. "Auntie Ellen has done this for years without anyone knowing. It's probably unlikely that people should know now. We better get them up here at once. I'll bang the porch door, and if they don't hear it I'll go down there."

Katherine nodded. She looked scared but didn't say anything. The air felt icy as James opened the door, and he wondered whether something had happened at their plantation for a Dawson slave to run away now when it was so cold. He really thought that Alfred would be the only one. It'd be real cold up north now, could even be snowing already.

Only a few moments later they both heard the hooting of an owl three times.

Katherine laughed. "It works both ways apparently!"

About ten minutes or so later, both Auntie Ellen and Mary appeared.

Mary looked shaken and nervous and Auntie Ellen a little bewildered.

"Mind if we sit?" she asked but sat down right next to Katherine without waiting for their reply.

"How much does this man know? Does he know about *your* operation? Does he know about us?" James asked.

"Seem to be a complete coincidence. Like I said he overheard you talkin' to Massa Dawson and figure that he could hide here, safer than runnin' from there. Thinkin' they catch up with him faster. He don't know I got a place for him to stay. I ain't feel comfortable with them being so close to you and all, should he get caught and made to talk."

James took a deep breath of relief. "That was my thought exactly. I don't think that we should drive him to Ebba and Oskar either. Let him stay tonight, but no longer. It'll only be a matter of time before someone from the Dawson place is back here asking if we have seen anything. God forbid the driver is made to talk, and then we are all in trouble. Even if it's for nothin' more than that the servants feel that we are nice." *Which is exactly the thing that Dawson warned me about that day, that fraternizing with them would make them uppity and they would take advantage of us. If he puts two and two together?* James thought feeling his jaw clench and his chest contract. "We are on dangerous, dangerous ground here. To be quite honest, the right and safest thing would be to tell Dawson about him."

"For God's sake, James!" Katherine exclaimed.

James didn't say anything, instead he got up to pour a drink but changed his mind thinking that he needed his head clear and sat down again, this time right next to Katherine on the couch. He took her hands in his, looked her in the eye for a moment, and then shifted his gaze to Auntie Ellen and Mary sitting next to her.

"Really, I don't like it one bit either, but it just hit me right now that it may be the safest way. We just bend the truth a little bit. You go down and tell the man, what is his name anyway?"

"Jonah."

"Oh right, Jonah, you said...you tell him to run tonight, give him some of your food and tell him to run as fast as he possibly can. We wait until tomorrow mornin', then I ride over there and tell them that I noticed something amiss and got the truth out of you Auntie Ellen, the truth that he had sat in the kitchen with you saying he was planning to run."

"James, again for goodness sakes what do you think this will do?" Katherine pulled her hands out of his.

"Well, Katherine, for one it will remove all suspicion from us, should there be any, to make it a safe station for other people who may come our way. Second, it would keep you and me safe. What do you think they do to traitors in these parts?"

"I don't feel it's right," Katherine got up and began to pace around the floor. "You may be right that we should say something, but at least we have to help him to the Peterssons' first."

"It'd be too dangerous, Katherine."

"No, it won't, if he just runs they'll find him and question him just the same. He has a bigger chance of getting away if he can hide in their attic for a couple of days or however long it'll take."

"He will recognize me if we take him, and he has seen me since I was a kid I'm sure, even if I didn't recognize him," James said. "He saw me leave Dawson's office that day, and he may have seen you too, Katherine."

"We will have to wear something so that he won't recognize us," Katherine said quietly, but with desperation in her voice.

"Mr. Waynewright, I think she is right. If we get him right now before they start missin' him over there, we can do it. Just make sure he ain't seeing you. Put the carriage somewhere and I'll help him in myself before you drive him, and don't talk to each other none."

James sighed, and then remained silent for several minutes. Finally, he nodded reluctantly. "You have a point, you two. But, Katherine you are staying here. There is no way you would be outside at this hour. I want you here sleeping like nothin's amiss. Should I get stopped I'll think of some excuse. We have to pray to God that he isn't caught and is made to tell that you helped him into some carriage."

Auntie Ellen was silent for a moment. "I'll ask Pap. Jonah doesn't know him very well, ask him not to show his face none, and to be silent."

Only half an hour later James got into the driver's seat after Pap had given the signal that the "cargo" was loaded and ready.

Like they had done the other night, James drove to the edge of the clearing by the road and got off to light the lamps. He was scared and wasn't sure if he was doing the right thing. He worried that Dawson had seen right through him in the office that day. Who knew if he hadn't checked up on his activities in New York? It wouldn't surprise him after his experience with Loch.

He felt that he was playing a dangerous game and that he had gotten himself into something he should have played very differently.

The fact was that he *had* shown what Dawson called Northern Bullshit, even if he had done more than showing a side of compassion; he should not have shown that side of himself, at least not to Dawson anyway.

James realized that it was very likely a given that the Sheriff had spoken to him about the unusually young negroes that James had freed. James had told the Sheriff that his father had promised them their freedom, but what if Dawson knew it not to be true? James felt almost nauseous from fear as he was sitting there analyzing on the empty road.

It was dead quiet in the woods except for the sound of a light rain rustling the leaves; the raindrops felt icy and sharp on the skin of his face. He was praying that nobody would pass him on the road and stop him. It was 12:15 when he left and must be close to 1 AM now. He prayed that no one was leaving a late party and wondering why he was going in the opposite direction of his home this late.

He went back and forth in his mind but couldn't think of any reason why he would be out like this, especially not with this carriage. Had he been on a horse he could have had some excuse of not being able to sleep because he thought he'd lost something on the road earlier and went to look for it. Surely they would wonder why he would look for it in the dark.

The longer he was out the more paranoid he felt. He thought he heard the sound of hoof beats in the forest following him. When he passed the open fields belonging to Wilson's plantation he almost turned back,but he forced himself to continue.

There was still a candle lit in a little lantern in the window and James quickly jumped off his seat. By sheer chance last week he had happened to take note of which of the rooms was the bedroom, and instead of knocking on the door he went to the bedroom window and threw a couple of small rocks at it. They landed with a loud tap - tap and James waited.

In spite of the sound, they did not wake up and he had to do it again and then again before he saw the curtain shift to the side and Oskar peering out at him. James eyes had become so accustomed to the darkness that he could see Oskar's sleepy and worried eyes. They popped open right away as he recognized him and then the curtain was pulled aside. Oskar opened the window and motioned for him to come closer.

"Oskar," James whispered. "I'm sorry to come so late, we have had an incident, or rather we had guest that didn't take the regular route. Can I speak to you inside?"

"Go 'round the back like last time. Is the passenger safe in the carriage?"

"He was instructed to stay until he heard three knocks on the side, but we should hurry just the same," James whispered not sure if he'd been heard or not. Oskar had already pulled his head inside so that James could go meet him by the back door. Before he reached it, it opened and both Oskar and Ebba stood in the doorway and motioned for him to hurry over.

Inside, James quickly told them everything and impressed upon them the importance that Jonah could not know that it was James who had driven him over here.

They both nodded and Ebba grabbed his arm and pulled him closer to her. "Dear, seat yourself down in the livin' room, have a cup of tea to warm yourself. Wait a minute 'til he is safely in the attic. Then you go home and relax. We'll take care of him." She stopped and swallowed, looking as if she was considering something,"Nothin' I wouldn't do to get at Massa Dawson. I have not heard good things about that plantation over the years." She put her finger to her lips as they heard the door open and Oskar leading Jonah straight up to the attic so that he wouldn't see James.

Chapter 07

Not only did James drive over to Dawson's the next morning, he brought Auntie Ellen with him. Pap drove them in the fancy carriage.

"Are you nervous, Auntie Ellen?" James asked her as they got closer. She shrugged, "I know what I know, Mr. Waynewright. They can't hurt me. Doin' it this way is the best way to get them off our back. I lay awake all night thinkin' on it, and this way we broaden the way for everyone else. As long as I can do as we say and put in a good word for the driver, and make sure they understand it's not his fault."

"Of course, I will too. I will pretend I saw Adam and how surprised and scared he looked."

"He did, it ain't a lie."

"Good," James said and Pap spurred on the horse as they turned into the majestic lane. The birds were chirping and the morning sun was warming the air, even though it was so late in the year. A slave was raking the leaves in the front and smoothing the ground after the rain. As soon as they approached, Mr. Dawson came outside and was waiting for them. He was all smiles, "James, what a pleasant surprise, come in, come in. What leads you to call so early in the mornin'? Is everything as it should be, James?" he didn't acknowledge Auntie Ellen with even a glance.

James decided to do the same and didn't say a word about her, instead he instructed Pap to wait and walked up to Dawson. He swallowed his fear and spoke clearly, "Not sure how to say this, Mr. Dawson, but something came to my attention early this morning. Can we go somewhere more private?"

Dawson raised his eyebrows. Clearly he had not noticed anything amiss as of yet.

"Certainly, can I offer you breakfast?"

James hesitated, "Well, you may not have much time after I tell you what I've become aware of." James glanced around him. The slave who had been raking had gone on to something else and the only persons who were still within earshot were Auntie Ellen and Pap.

"I may as well say it now. This morning I found out that last night when Peter called on us, unbeknownst to Adam, your Jonah had hid himself underneath the carriage with some kind of contraption. He appeared in our kitchen just a few minutes after Adam dropped Peter off and was getting refreshments and visiting with Auntie Ellen."

Dawson's brow furrowed. "Those bloody niggers. Taking every chance they get to sneak off to socialize," he shook his head, "I'll deal with'm."

James cleared his throat. "Well, that's just it. According to Auntie Ellen, she thinks he ran off." James paused again as Dawson's jaw dropped and he stood seemingly speechless as James gestured for Auntie Ellen to come over. She slowly made her way toward them. *You ain't that old and decrepit, Auntie Ellen.* James thought as he watched her walk.

"She can tell you herself, as she did me this morning," James continued, "Jonah pretended need of the outhouse and hasn't been seen since. It may be that he is back here just doin' what he did for an outing and to skedaddle from his work yesterday as you said, but I have an inkling he ran away, sir."

"God have mercy!" Dawson said losing all color in his face, but keeping his composure.

"You have something to tell me, girl?"

"Yes, sir." Auntie Ellen replied. She looked nervous and hesitated before she answered. James wasn't sure if she really was nervous or if she pretended so that she didn't appear obstinate.

"Go on." Dawson crossed his arms over his chest.

"Yesterday, I invited Adam in the kitchen for a bite to eat when Mr. Dawson Jr. came to visit. Massa Dawson, he came in and sat himself down on the chair having just got a sip of coffee when Jonah appear. Adam looked so surprised he near drop that coffee in his lap."

She stopped for effect and quickly glanced at James who ignored her, keeping his gaze on Dawson.

"Then sir, he told us that he hidden himself underneath the carriage with a rope to hoist himself up with a'..." she hesitated, looking real insecure now and looked to James for support.

"It's alright, Auntie Ellen, it's better for everyone if you tell Mr. Dawson exactly what took place. You go on now."

She took a deep breath and looked to the sky as if she was pleading with God.

"He didn't say much, just that he wanted some water and a piece to eat. I gave it to him, then he say he needed to use the outhouse and he was gone, mumblin' somethin' 'bout running but I ain't sure I heard it right."

Dawson kept shaking his head, moving his weight from one foot to the other. "You sure Adam knew nothin' of this?"

"It didn't look as if he did Massa Dawson, he was as surprised as I."

Dawson looked at her quizzically for a full minute. "You are sure that he didn't plan this *with* Adam? Adam didn't see anything or notice that something as large as a nigger was stuck under his carriage?" Dawson said his voice full of disdain.

James cleared his throat and touched Dawson's shoulder. "I can attest to that. I went in the kitchen for a moment putting a package away and I saw Adam lookin' completely bewildered. I thought it a bit odd at the time, but didn't pay too much attention to it. Peter was there, he was telling us about his wonderful and interesting travels and I hurried back to hear the rest of his adventures."

Dawson nodded. He looked very serious. "Did you see the carriage?"

"No, I didn't. I was in my study when they arrived."

"That son of a bitch!" Dawson exclaimed angrily. Then he whistled loudly. The door opened immediately and a house negro came out looking expectantly at Dawson who told him to get Adam up there immediately.

"Thank you for bringing this to my attention. How did you find out? How did you get this bit of information out of her?" he asked James as if Auntie Ellen wasn't there.

"She looked odd and nervous this morning when she brought us our breakfast. She tripped on our rug and dropped things, wouldn't look at us and such," James lied looking Dawson straight in the eye. "It was clear that she was hiding something and I got the truth out of her real quick."

Dawson looked both impressed and a bit surprised.

About ten minutes later Adam came walking toward the house. It was plain to see even from afar that he was dragging his steps and was probably completely panicked.

"Let's go into my study," Dawson said and motioned for the house negro who did his bidding earlier to show them inside. Dawson remained outside and waited for Adam.

James and Auntie Ellen eye's locked for fleeting moment as they were led into the study, but they had no time to say anything to each other before Dawson and Adam joined them.

Dawson looked gravely at Adam and sat down behind his desk. Then he pointed to a small wicker chair for Adam to sit on and motioned for James to sit in a chair next to himself. Auntie Ellen remained standing.

Dawson sat silent but the undercurrent of anger was palpable.

Adam was looking down at his hands. Even though he was clasping them together to keep them steady, they were still shaking.

Finally Dawson spoke, "Adam, I presume that even though you are just a nigger, you have figured out why you are here?"

"Yes, Massa," Adam replied, his pulse racing so fast that James could see it at the nape of his neck.

"Why didn't you tell me as soon as you got back last night?"

"Massa...I...it was late Massa, I didn't want disturb—"

Dawson stood up and picked up a paperweight holding it in the air, then slammed it down on the wooden surface with such force that his newspaper went flying. James startled at the sound and he heard Auntie Ellen gasp.

"Were you even going to tell me at all?" he thundered.

"Course, Massa. I was on my way up this mornin' already, you can ask Hob. I was not in the fields when he got me."

Dawson calmed down somewhat at that and sat down, shaking his head.

"If this is a lie, boy, I'll have you whipped, you understand."

James swallowed hard, resisting the urge to tell Dawson that he would rather buy Adam from him than leave him there with him, wondering if coming here had been such a good idea after all.

"Yes, Massa."

Dawson didn't acknowledge his answer, instead he stared him down silently to intimidate him. Sweat was beading on Adam's forehead as he sat there silently waiting.

"So, boy, you tell me everything that happened, you hear."

"Yes, Massa," the words were barely audible.

"Speak up, boy!"

"Yes, Massa," Adam replied, struggling to speak louder, "I didn't notice nothin' before I drove young Massa Dawson to the Waynewright plantation and went in to speak with Ellen, then suddenly Jonah walk in and he could barely open the door cause his arms so hurt from holdin' on."

"Holdin' on? So you knew, you knew already."

"I don't understand, Massa?"

Dawson shook his head and pulled out a cigar and slowly, painstakingly he proceeded to cut the end with the cigar cutter. He turned the cutter over in his hand a couple of times, looked sternly at Adam and put it down in front of him before finally lighting his cigar. He offered one to James, but he declined, clenching his jaw hard to hide his disgust.

There was something so threatening in his mannerisms that James realized that he could very well decide to cut one of Adam's fingers off with it. He had to steady himself by holding on to the armrest as the memory of Tobias showing him his hand and Timmy telling him that they had been tortured to get them to tell Dawson where Timmy's wife and daughters were. *I'm glad I drove him to the Peterssons' last night. Should have taken Adam, too.*

"Adam, you said that he couldn't open the door because his arms hurt from holdin' on. How did you know that?"

"Massa Dawson, if I may interrupt." James glanced at Auntie Ellen as she looked Dawson right in the eye and said, "He didn't know sir. Jonah told us both when I had to open the door for him to get inside."

Dawson looked at Auntie Ellen with a frown. "Is that correct, Adam?"

"Yes, Massa, he told us everything after Ellen help him in the chair and gave him something to drink, said he hung under the wagon the whole time."

"You are sure you didn't see him crawl under there?"

"No, Massa."

Dawson stood up again, walked over to Adam, grabbed him by his collar, and pulled him out of the chair.

James couldn't resist any longer and got up himself and touched Dawson's arm.

"Mr. Dawson, please."

He didn't even appear to notice. He pushed Adam against the bookshelf.

"Why didn't you tell Peter this as soon as it happened? Why didn't you tell Mr. Waynewright? How could you let all this time go by? By now he could be as far as Tappahannock. What the hell were you thinkin'? And you, Ellen, isn't it your responsibility to tell *your* Massa if something is amiss?"

"Yes, sir, it is, and I did this here mornin' when he ask me." Auntie Ellen's voice shook a little and she didn't dare to look at him.

Dawson grumbled something and then he let go of Adam who sank down on his haunches. He remained there looking defeated.

"Mr. Dawson, if I may interject here. From speaking to Ellen this morning, I understood that it wasn't entirely clear that he had run away. They are just negroes. They don't always understand everything as you rightly know. It's clear to me now that neither Ellen nor Adam were sure if he just wanted some fun for an afternoon. Even though he had mumbled about running, they were not sure if he really had meant it. As I found out this morning they looked for him when it became dark and our dinner was drawing near its end. When they didn't find him they thought that maybe he had decided to walk back home. My Ellen here didn't want to cause unnecessary trouble if she wasn't sure. I of course understood this to be a serious matter right away."

James paused for effect, thinking that he had become uncannily good at this lying game. "I'm so sorry to have to be the one to tell you this."

James didn't dare to look in Auntie Ellen's direction, but he sensed awe in her gaze.

Dawson took a deep breath and nodded, "No need for apologies, thank you for bringin' it to my attention. Adam, get up, I believe you. Go look in Jonah's cabin and round the area in case he *is* still here. In the future, always tell me or my son everything, no matter how late it is."

"Yes, Massa, I'm truly sorry that I didn't and I cause this here trouble. It won't happen again."

"Good. Take Ellen to the kitchen for a visit with Erla. James and I will have a talk."

"He has run away, I can feel it. God damn it!" Dawson said after they left.

"Probably," James agreed, hoping that he looked convincingly upset about it. "There is of course a slight chance that he had a reason to go to our plantation. Could he have a love interest among ours? I suppose it's possible that he is still there. I'll look when I get home again, or is there a reason why he might have run?"

Dawson shrugged, "Don't know. He was ungrateful for all we do for them, I suppose, like they all are. Don't realize what we give them here, thinkin' they are better off on their own. Don't think he has a love interest. The only one who leaves here is Adam when he drives me or Peter. We don't allow fraternizin' on other plantations. I buy wives for them."

Dawson grunted with annoyance. "I better get on with it. Thank you for bringing it to my attention. I'm sorry that it had to involve you and cause inconvenience."

"It's all right. I hope you find him. Just let me know if I can be of service," James said, barely allowing himself to think of him hiding in the Peterssons' attic, but to play the game out he asked one more question. "I'm surprised that Adam didn't say anything to Peter yesterday when he drove him home."

Dawson shrugged, "No matter, he was probably too scared to tell him. Wouldn't have told me either had you not come here. You have saved us hours in the search. We'll find him. Don't believe he can have gone that far in a night, but we are wasting time so I best get on with it."

James nodded, "I understand. I should get on home. I'll of course ask to see if anyone has seen anything," James said and thought of Jonah crawling up the stairs to the attic.

Chapter 08

They didn't hear anything from either Dawson or the Peterssons, and there was nothing to do but to go on with their daily tasks. It was hard, though. Both Katherine and James were nervous and wanted nothing more than to call on the Peterssons to see if Jonah was still hiding there, but they decided to wait at least a week. They assumed that someone from Dawson's plantation would let them know if he was caught and hoped that no news was good news.

Then almost two weeks later James came back from town and found Katherine sitting with Ebba in the small dining room.

"Ebba, that's *your* horse out there? You were riding on your own?" James bent down to kiss her cheek, surprised.

Ebba laughed, "I'm not as frail as the young women round these parts that wouldn't dream of riding without an escort. I'm sixty-two, I can handle it just fine," she said with a peevish wink.

Just then Mary came in with a tray full of freshly baked scones and coffee.

"Oh, Mr. Waynewright, I didn't know you were back. I'll get you a cup. Sit down and I get your wash cloth," she said and left before he had time to answer.

When she came back James wiped his hands on the moistened and soaped cloth and handed it back.

"James has been in town today," Katherine explained.

Ebba nodded without commenting, she turned to James and pulled something out of her skirts. She handed it to him and he saw that it was the same invitation that had arrived for them just a couple of days ago for a winter ball at the Dawson plantation.

"You too, eh? First please tell me how your guest fared?"

"Oh, I'm sorry James. I told Katherine already and didn't think to tell you." She lowered her voice and continued, "It went well as far as I know. He stayed for a week and then he left. I gave him enough food to last for a while and we attached horseradish, turnip and pepper bags on his shoes to distract the dogs. We can only hope he got safely to the next safe house." She sighed and glanced at Katherine with a look of fear.

"She is nervous that they were invited because Dawson caught him and he told them where he was hiding," Katherine added and reached for Ebba's hand over the table and squeezed it.

"Hmm...well, I have a feelin' that's not the case. First of all, they would have come here to tell me right away since I told them about it, and since we invited you I think that they just thought it was a nice neighborly touch that they do, too."

"That's what I said as well, James. But what if Jonah noticed that it was you who drove him after all and what if he told him? Then this ball could just be a ruse to get us all over there at the same time."

"They always have a winter ball."

"They didn't last year, James." Katherine sounded afraid and got up and started to pace around the table, snatching Ebba's invite from James' hands.

"Katherine, calm down. I'm sure they did have it last year, but we were not invited because of being in full mourning still."

"Oh," she fell down in her chair with a sigh of relief.

It didn't last long. "But, James, are you sure? Isn't it a little odd that we get the invites so soon after the rescue? Ebba were you invited last year?"

"No, child, but I think that your husband might be right, thank God. I didn't think of the mourning. Last year we didn't know them. They had no reason to invite us."

James looked at Katherine and said, "If they say anything we'll deny it. We have an advantage of being white, Katherine. That's just the way it is. They will never take a negro's word over ours, no matter what he says. They'll think he made it up. Besides I really think he made it. I don't think that Dawson even looked for that long to be honest, too much of a bother for him. He probably just bought someone else, or someone else is workin' double over there now, probably Adam."

"Adam?" Ebba asked.

"He was the man who unknowingly drove Jonah over here under the carriage. James said that Dawson was horribly mad at him and vaguely threatened to cut his fingers off with a cigar cutter," Katherine said and shivered.

Ebba looked horrified and put her cup down on her plate with such force that the spoon jumped off the saucer. "We were never invited to things like this before. I don't know if I like bein' so involved suddenly, we used to live our own life in peace."

James caught Katherine's eye.

"Well, Ebba, I understand it's hard but Katherine and I talked at length about this. If we are goin' to help and make it safer for everyone we have to establish a non-secret relationship between us, or people would talk if we were seen with you."

Ebba didn't say anything; she stared out the window looking as though she would cry.

Finally she spoke, her voice catching in her throat as she did, "I understand, James, I do, but to have to socialize with such people who do such things. If you only knew what Jonah told us during the week with us. I...it's unspeakable. I...to treat people like this it is..." Tears began to trickle down her cheeks and she rummaged around in her pockets looking for a handkerchief but didn't find one.

"Here, take mine," Katherine said and glanced at James again. He could very well imagine what Jonah might have told them. Nothing would surprise him after what he had seen of Dawson lately and what Timmy told him that night when he signed their papers and Tobias showed him his hand. He shuddered.

"You are right, Ebba, but what you are sayin' makes our work even more important, and we have to play the game if we are going to continue unnoticed. At least Katherine and I have. You and Oskar could understandably say no."

Ebba dried her tears and blew her nose. "I'm sorry, Katherine. I'll wash it for you." She looked embarrassed and turned to James. "I shouldn't have lost my composure like that. It must be so much harder for you. I should help you and encourage you and not sit here and complain. I...I'm an old woman and I've seen a lot. I don't know why I'm so upset because of a winter ball."

"It's all right, Ebba. I understand. Think about it. We would love to have your company at the ball, but if not I'm sure you can come up with a valid excuse."

James did understand, but she sounded as if she blamed them. As if she'd rather have the runaways walk through the swampy, snake-ridden river for four hours as they had in the past so that she didn't have to deal with them or Dawson. He felt defensive as if she counted him and Katherine in the same crowd as Dawson. The way she said that she should encourage him; it was as if she thought herself better than him.

Finally he excused himself and left the table telling them that he had paperwork to do in his office. He did, but he poured himself a scotch instead.

He had just about finished it when there was a knock on the door. It opened slowly and Isum peered inside, clearing his throat.

"Mrs. Wayneright said that you be here and I could just go in."

James feeling relaxed, in a better mood after his drink smiled and motioned for him to sit on the chair in front of his desk. "Come in. What can I do for you?"

Isum cleared his throat again and sat down; he looked uncomfortable as if he didn't know how to begin but finally he spoke.

"I... Martha and I are wonderin' if you would let us jump the broom?"

"I'm very happy to hear that Isum. Of course you can, but you don't need to ask my permission for this."

Isum tried to smile, but he still looked nervous.

"There is another matter too, we...Martha and her little girl...and I, we would like to leave. We are thinkin' on stayin' another year but then we'd want to move north. We feel we should' let you know our plans, we owe you that."

"Thank you. Just let me know when and I'll give you the papers, I appreciate that you are letting me know now." James smiled and swallowed, unsure of what to say next. He was very happy for them, especially since Martha who had been through such trauma at Loch's hands was doing well and moving on with her life. Still it was bittersweet, reminding him that no matter what he had told everyone, no matter how welcome they were on his plantation, or whether they were paid, it was not enough. To be truly free they had to leave.

Chapter 09

Pap drove them in the fancy buggy. Pap in a brand new suit and a hat that made him look as if he could have attended the ball himself. He sat high up on the driver's seat proud of his "Master and Mistress" who had promised him and Ellen to remember every single detail and share with them over dinner the next day.

James took Katherine's glove-clad hand and looked at her. She was wearing a beautiful black felt coat attached at the neck with a large brooch. The dress underneath it was incredible, dark green and silky, it had almost taken his breath away when she had come into his office wearing it. It accentuated her dark blue eyes and pale skin so that she seemed to be glowing. James had wanted to take her right upstairs and pull it off of her, but he had taken her by the arm like a proper husband and led her to the waiting carriage.

The end of Dawson's driveway was lined with torches that flickered in the cool evening breeze and several lanterns were lit around the house, not only by the main entrance but also on top of poles around the large rotunda in front. It looked festive and inviting.

They were escorted inside by a negro wearing the finest livery. Inside things were organized just as effectively. It seemed as though every negro from Dawson's plantation was inside, unless he had hired house negroes from somewhere else for the occasion. They were taking coats, serving drinks and helping people find a place to sit. James and Katherine were handed tall glasses of bubbling champagne as they were escorted through a smaller room that led out to a very large ballroom.

"Enjoy yourself, make yourself comfortable. Massa and Mistress Dawson will call the dinner themselves," one of the servants said as he pointed at a small couch in the corner.

"Thank you," James said and smiled at Katherine. She looked rather stunned. "It's just one servant after the other, almost as if it's a royal wedding. They must have practiced for days," she said.

"You are probably right," James laughed as he let his eyes circle around the room. He hadn't been in here for a long time. The last time had been the year before he went to New York. He and Peter had become so drunk that they barely remembered anything the next morning when they both woke up on the couches in the drawing room.

Today everything was cleared out except for a couple of smaller tables where the guests were expected to put their drinks before the dancing begun. Slowly the room began to fill up with guests. He recognized most of them though he didn't know them by name. He knew that some people traveled for days to attend and spent several days staying as guests with the Dawson's.

"This is so grand, James," Katherine whispered. "Do you think Ebba and Oskar will show up?"

James didn't have time to reply as a couple beamed at them and began to hurry across the polished floor. James froze as he realized who it was.

"Mr. and Mrs. Gilbert, what in the world are you doing here? I don't believe my eyes!"

James hadn't seen them since that day when they went to Plymouth Church that first time. He didn't even remember if he had told Katherine about it or not. *If John or Brianna says anything she might misunderstand their meaning completely*, he thought as they came closer.

"Mr. and Mrs, what do you mean old pal? My name is John, thought we were over the formalities a while ago," he laughed, slapping James on the back.

"Who is this lovely woman next to you?" John looked full of admiration as he looked at Katherine. "Fancy meeting here. You're friends of the Dawsons?"

"She is my wife," James said and put his arm around her shoulders. "Katherine, this is Brianna and John Gilbert, we are actually old acquaintances from New York," James said and turned to John again. "I remember you tellin' me you were from Virginia but I had no idea we had friends in common. Indeed, the Dawson's were close friends of my parents," James said as Brianna and Katherine shook hands.

"Neither did I, I can't tell you how pleased I am. I went looking for you at your hotel a little over a year ago hopin' they had a forwarding address. They sent me to West 4th Street but the landlady said that you had left suddenly. Little did I know that you had married? I assume now that you moved to a larger home?"

Brianna touched James' arm with a merry look in her eye.

"Oh, I'm so happy for you, James. I wrote John that he ought to make sure that he invited you places. I felt so sorry for you being all alone up there in the north. Everyone is talking about slavery now wherever you go up there, John is telling me. There are a lot more of those abolitionists nowadays. We southerners need to stick together, and you are *married;* that explains why he didn't see you. You are here to visit family and celebrate Christmas I assume?" Brianna looked at both of them as she jumped from subject to subject.

James didn't dare to even glance at Katherine, but he could feel her shoulders tense under his arm.

He swallowed and pulled his arm from her shoulders and took a sip of champagne to give himself a second to collect his thoughts.

"Well actually, we live down here permanently now. My parents, they...they passed away over a year ago."

Briana's hand went to her mouth. John looked just as stunned as her.

"My dear fellow, we had no idea. I'm so very sorry. I should have enquired as to how you were faring before I went on assuming things. Please forgive us and let me convey our deepest sympathies and condolences for your loss," John said as Brianna slowly removed her hand from her mouth. She nodded and touched James arm.

"I am so sorry to hear that, may I ask...You said they both died, I...?"

Katherine cleared her throat, "It was a tragic accident. They both died very unexpectedly."

John and Brianna's eyes were full of sympathy. "I'm so very sorry James," John said and touched James' shoulder. "Why don't we wander 'round and see if we can sit down somewhere before dinner. We'll have a drink or two and you can tell me how you have been faring and our wives can get to know each other a little better."

James glanced at Katherine and nodded, "Why not, it sounds nice. It'll be a while before dinner anyway and it looks like the orchestra is getting organized," James said as several servants hurried past them carrying violins, a trumpet and another string instrument that James didn't know the name of. The musicians followed them with a worried look on their face as if they didn't trust them with their instruments. "Here come the musicians, Katherine," James said and then whispered as he leaned over her shoulder; "If the Gilberts mention Plymouth Church they ain't on our side, just play along." He paused, "Nice instruments these I wonder where the musicians are from, James asked aloud.

"Me too," Katherine said and then in a lower voice, "I understand, not a word." They followed the Gilberts across the floor and into a rather large sitting room where John pointed to a sofa with a beautiful quilt thrown over it.

Those are the quilts the woman at Plymouth Church—whatever was her name again, oh yes, Miss Emma—said that they sew messages in that tell them which way to go. Mr. Gilbert, if you only knew what you did to me by inviting me there. James thought as Katherine and Brianna sat down together on that quilt.

"I'll call for another round of champagne," John said and waved to a server passing by outside the sitting room.

Brianna touched Katherine's hand, "Mrs. Waynewright, I was able to discern from hearing you speak earlier that you are a northerner. I'm so sorry if I offended you with my comment about the north. It's just that the first time I met James we took him to Plymouth Church where those awful abolitionists preach, so that's why I brought it up. I understand that you obviously ain't one of them."

Heeding James' warning Katherine hid it well and feigned a gracious smile.

"No not at all. I completely understand. I love your dress by the way. We don't see such beautiful dresses in New York. It took me a while to get used to the large hoops underneath the fabric," Katherine said, blatantly changing the subject and touching a deep red rose attached to the front of Brianna's white dress. Layers of lace and red ruffles matched it beautifully.

John looked at James and laughed. "Leave it to women to leave politics behind and talk about more essential things."

"You could say that," James laughed too as Adam appeared with a tray with both champagne and scotch. Adam gave him a look that James couldn't quite read as he handed him a glass. It was hard to know if Adam thought that James was a malevolent ally of Dawson or if he had been grateful that James had at least tried somewhat to defend him.

Katherine didn't notice Adam but grabbed another glass of champagne with a mischievous look at James. They both knew that she'd rather have the scotch.

"So, James, how are you doin'? I take it that you are responsible for your plantation now?" John asked.

"Yes, goin' on two years now. The plantation is doing very well. I have been completing several improvements and if I may say so myself, it's more efficient, the negroes are happier and have more energy with a more organized workload." *Efficient, that's a good one, and why not? Even though several of them have left and I have fewer people, no overseer and they share the profit, yeah it's efficient, I may not have become richer but I have a better conscience.*

"There's nothin' like the younger generation with new thoughts. I'm glad to hear that it's going so well. May I ask how you have accomplished it?"

"Certainly," James, decided to stay as close to the truth as he could. "I have made some improvements in the way I work them, and to be perfectly honest I have given them more free time. We are working on larger gardens, more supplies for them so they can plant more of their own food, another half day off on Saturday afternoons and believe it or not, they work a lot harder now and as I said much more efficiently. A couple of small changes here and there made a remarkable difference. They needed encouragement I suppose. They were very heartsick when my parents died. It gave me a hunch, and it's worked amazingly well."

John looked at him thoughtfully and nodded slowly. "You don't say, you don't say, I have to say in lieu of our previous discussion, when I had too much of this," he grinned, reminding James of the embarrassing scene he had caused.

"As we so eloquently spoke of then, they need to be well taken care of to work properly. All these abolitionists, they simply do not know how it really is down here. You make a perfect example of how a plantation *should* be run. Could those Plymouth parishioners only see that, then we wouldn't have all these debates that have been so loud lately."

"Precisely," James said and glanced at Katherine. She and Brianna had left their clothing conversation and were listening intently.

James decided to change the subject.

"John, how about you and Brianna, are you still staying in New York, or are you back? Do you live near here?"

"Yes, actually we do live rather close. Fancy we never met here before. It's only the second time that we have been at their winter ball, but I've had business dealin's with Mr. Dawson several times. Bought a couple of his excellent negroes, as well. What's your plantation called, James?"

"Just Waynewright plantation. My parents could never agree on a name and now Waynewright has stuck."

"Well, that'll do won't it? Don't think I met your father."

Just then they heard a bell ring and then Dawson's baritone voice telling everyone to come and enjoy their banquet.

The Gilberts left the room ahead of them, leaving James and Katherine a short moment to themselves.

Bringing her close he whispered, "I cannot believe that they are here. I told you of them, right? They are the ones who brought me to Plymouth. I...it hits close to home. I like them, if he only knew what impression it had on me. I'm a *traitor* you know." Katherine touched his cheek, whispering, "You are doing fine. We'll be ok. Did the Peterssons arrive?"

"Didn't see them yet, so we'll see," James replied in a normal voice. "Let's join the others."

Someone that James recognized from childhood helped them to their seats at the table, Peter Dawson's nanny. He remembered her being very funny and sweet when he visited. James smiled in recognition. "Remember me, eh? No pranks now, no unsuitable things under the table, you hear," she said with the same wit that he remembered so well and he burst out laughing, making several of the guests turn around and look at them.

"I better tell you another time or you'll lose your appetite!" James explained to Katherine who looked at him merrily.

They found Oskar and Ebba already seated.

"We are delighted to see you," James said and touched Ebba's wrinkly hand.

"We are, too. Mrs. and Mr. Dawson received us personally when we arrived, makin' sure we were comfortable. They made a point of telling us that they were embarrassed that they had not invited us previous years. They *are* nice. It's...," she said looking James deep in the eye.

He sighed. "I know," James said simply, understanding her mixed feelings.

A server came around to their side and put a whole roasted quail on each plate garnished with parsley and other greens that the Dawson's must have been growing in their greenhouse to have fresh year round. A second server came right after and poured white wine in their glasses. James made a mental note not to drink more than a sip from each glass—assuming that they would be served red wine with the meat, then port with the dessert—so that he wouldn't accidentally talk too much and give himself away. He had not anticipated the toll his new and secret political views and their secret nightly adventures would take on him. It would be so very easy to ruin it all with just a slip of the tongue and everyone's life could be in danger, not only his and Katherine's, but the Peterssons and their workers. They all depended on him.

A little while later after the banquet, the mood was merry. There was dancing, excellent music and as most people became more or less intoxicated, no one seemed to take too much notice on what people were really saying. James began to relax a little bit as he slowly sipped another scotch. Katherine was talking to Mrs. Burnham and he was leaning against the wall by one of the tall paned windows with a view over the lake when Dawson came up to him.

James smiled and lifted his glass. "This is lovely. We are truly enjoying ourselves. Nice of you to invite the Peterssons, they were touched," James said and gazed searchingly into Dawson's face. Dawson nodded towards the dance floor where they were dancing just a few feet away from them. "It was your idea entirely. You invited them first and it got us thinkin' that we should have done so as well. We have seen them in town for years, but never thought to do it just because they have a smaller farm. Was it Katherine who thought of it?"

James cleared his throat and tried to smile convincingly. "Well, I'm afraid it was me. I was so besotted with Katherine, still am, but I felt that since we got married so fast without a proper party I felt I owed her something grand. Still wasn't as grand as this of course, but, well I tried to invite everyone I could think of."

Dawson laughed. "I should have known and there I was thinkin' Katherine had some northern sensibilities to teach us."

James tried to laugh, but wasn't entirely successful. He decided to plunge right into an even more dangerous area. "I haven't seen you since your boy ran. Did you find him? Katherine and I asked every one of ours, but no one saw anything…" *Damn, why did I say that? We didn't ask them…what if he checks? I've got to keep things together!*

Dawson shook his head. "Can you believe it, no we didn't. Sent out several search parties but have not seen even a trace of him. It's as if he vanished into thin air. I assume that he either made it north or froze to death." Dawson sat down on the chaise and patted on its velvety surface. "Have a seat, James. Sorry, my feet hurt. I've been runnin' around all day checking on everyone for this blasted ball.

"Well, anyway, what I find the oddest is that my dogs didn't pick up a scent at all, none. I've had runaways before and there is usually some kind of trail to follow, if nothin' else, to the swamp or the little brook behind your land where they lose the scent." He paused as in deep thought. "You know, James, I swear that he had help. I just have a hunch. It's odd, real odd the whole thing. I questioned Adam again after you left and he truly doesn't seem to know anything, but something doesn't sit right, especially that he went to your plantation first. It really makes me angry that he put *your* property at risk. You know how niggers are, if they hear that it's easier to run from your plantation than mine, then your niggers could get ideas in their heads and spread all kinds of rumors." James looked at him and felt as if something cold was pressing against his chest and he had to concentrate real hard to keep his face and body relaxed.

"James, if they have done anything at all to cause disruption on your plantation, you tell me, you hear? I am dreadfully sorry that you were involved like this. It's troubling that he went to you first, even if it was only to get away from me. Like I said, I had my dogs sniff 'round your property but nothin'. It's odd just, odd," Dawson repeated taking a big gulp from his wineglass. "Who the hell could have helped them? Do we have another of those helpers travelin' down here stealing our property? That man Tubman have been active again I heard somewhere, heard that he was up in Maryland stealin' twenty niggers at once about a month or two ago." Dawson shook his head for effect not noticing how panicked James felt. He looked for Katherine but she was still deeply engaged in her conversation. Mr. Burnham and Brianna had joined them and no one was noticing James and Dawson where they sat.

"You have heard of Tubman haven't you, James? I bet he is some wealthy radical nigger lover who has some false sense of altruism."

James began to sip his scotch but thought better of it and only wet his lips. His heart thumped loudly in his chest. *Dawson you have no idea that Tubman is a former slave. I used to think she was a man, too. Auntie Ellen calls her Moses.*

"I think I did hear that name yes, but Mr. Dawson, you said that your dogs were sniffing at my..."

"James, why do you alwaysh call me Mishter Dawhsson. You are like my nephew. I—" Dawson sounded wet as a whistle all of a sudden.

"Well, you are my dad's friend. You have always been Mr. Dawson to me," James said stiffly. "However, I am interested in what you said about having your dogs sniff around my property? Tell me the next time, will you?" James felt stone cold sober as he watched Dawson wave at one of his servants for another glass as he sloshed the last drip of his wine down his throat. Did Dawson suspect him? Why had he had dogs at his property without telling him? When was that? What if they noticed something? Jonah had hid in Ellen's cabin after all. The dogs must have picked up his scent and known that he had been there.

Dawson was so drunk by now that James couldn't get a straight answer out of him. An uncomfortable server who looked like she wished that she could deny it to him gave him a new glass of wine. He took a large sip as he grinned helplessly at James. It was the second time that someone had drunkenly told him that they were spying on his plantation.

"Here lad, help me up scho I can go assshk your wife for a dansch."

"Sure," James said and grabbed his arm. The panic began to flush over him once again. His heart beat so hard that he was sure that Dawson must be able to hear it and he felt sweat beading on his upper lip and under his armpits. He wanted to grab Katherine and the Peterssons and run. But Pap was probably nowhere near ready with the carriage, most likely getting a bit drunk himself and eating with the other drivers.

Dawson found Katherine and pulled her to the dance floor, something he did surprisingly well given how drunk he had become,

James took a deep breath to steady himself. He drowned the scotch and began to analyze their conversation.

It *was* possible that he had only had the dogs near the river behind their property for the mere fact that Jonah had gone with Adam, but it worried James that Dawson hadn't told him about it. The way he had offered James an apology might mean just that, that he was truly concerned that his servants would influence James' in a negative way by coming to his plantation before they ran. It *was* a legitimate concern. He might not suspect anything at all, might be genuinely puzzled and was just venting to James since he'd had too much to drink.

James decided to assume that everything was in order. If Dawson truly had suspected him he probably would have gone about it in a much different way. Maybe it was God who was showing him that they had to be a lot more careful, warning them that Dawson had his dogs out there. He sighed and said yes thank you as he was offered another scotch, forgetting that he had decided to drink lightly. His hand was shaking as he replaced his glass on her tray with a new one.

Chapter 10

The winter was quiet. James didn't see Dawson or hear anything that indicated that he was suspicious of him. Life went on as it usually did in the winter, a little less busy with more time to stay inside and read. Katherine's uncle had sent issues of *The Liberator,* information from The American Anti Slavery Society and issues of *The North Star* in hatboxes. They had an extra bottom added where he had hid them. When a hat was put on top nobody would notice anything amiss. Katherine and James spent hours reading them on their bed upstairs. James felt validated seeing that he was not alone in his anti-slavery philosophy. It encouraged him. He knew that he was doing the right thing, but he felt scared all the time. He hadn't told Katherine, but he hadn't been able to sleep through a single night since Dawson's party. He felt paranoid and jittery. It was as if he had eyes on him wherever he went. Once, in town, he thought the store clerk had acted oddly. He had barely looked at him when James paid for his supplies, just a quick crooked smile and a nod when he was usually so talkative. Did he know? If he did, why hadn't he told the Sheriff? Was the clerk against slavery, too? James even pulled on his earlobe as a sign that he was for abolition, but he didn't get any reaction from it at all, and that made him even more paranoid wondering if he had given himself away.

They hadn't had a traveler for several months now, which was expected given the colder weather, but instead of calming him because of the lessened risk, he had a gnawing fear that travelers *were* trying to come but were being stopped by Dawson on the way over. He knew it was irrational, but when he laid awake at night listening to Katherine's calm breathing the thoughts were spinning around in his head. He pictured them trampling through the frozen ground, walking right into the arms of Dawson's men and being tortured with his cigar cutter until they told him that James was a traitor.

But time went by without any incident or trauma. Spring began to sprout its new green life: trees budded, flowers sprang up and the birds began to chirp earlier and livelier.

It wasn't just nature that was growing. Katherine was finally expecting and James was so happy that he forgot about his fears.

He immediately insisted that Katherine should do nothing at all but relax, read and take gentle exercise in the fresh air, absolutely no horseback riding or any heavy lifting. Auntie Ellen promised to take care of her and make extra nourishing meals for her. They both fussed over her so much that Katherine threatened to go back to New York and stay there until the baby was born.

***

It was chilly, but a sunny and beautiful fall morning. James and Katherine had their coffee on the porch. Mary fussed with Katherine's blanket as Auntie Ellen served them their coffee and breakfast.

"Are you sure you are comfortable, Mrs. Waynewright? Can I get you a pallet for your feet? You ain't too cold now?"

Katherine laughed as she patted her round stomach. "We'll be fine my babies and me," she said. They suspected twins. Just a couple of days earlier, Katherine had experienced severe cramping. Thinking that the baby was early Auntie Ellen had prodded her stomach to feel if the baby had turned yet. As it turned out it was just indigestion, but Auntie Ellen was sure that she felt more than one baby. "I have a month or so to go yet. No babies are coming earlier just from me being a little cold on such a gorgeous day."

"You *are* cold then?" Auntie Ellen interrupted and looked sternly at Mary, "You go get her another blanket."

Katherine laughed. "No, it's not necessary, really. I'm not that cold. I will be fine."

James shook his head at the women and took a nice warming sip of the freshly brewed coffee. *There truly is nothin' better than a fresh cup of coffee in the morning,* he thought as something caught his eye. He squinted and noticed what he first thought was a lone rider turning on to their road. Their house was at an angle from it and the trees in the lane blocked James from getting a good view of the rider. According to family lore, they had built the house to the side instead of right in front of the road. It was for some sort of superstitious reason. James' mother used to say that it was so that joy would stay inside the house instead of flowing straight out again. James was sure that his Great Grandfather had some other natural reason for it. Maybe there was a natural road there already, and maybe there had been a reason that they couldn't build right below it? His mother's idea was sweet, kind of like a horseshoe hanging with the points up to keep the luck in.

"Someone is coming," James said and pointed towards the lane and then he could see that there were in fact two riders.

Everyone turned and looked as they approached. They were riding fast and as soon as they came out from under the canopy of leaves they could see that it was Mr. Wilson and Peter Dawson. They looked flustered and jumped off their horses at the same time. Mr. Wilson whistled and looked around for Pap as if he owned the plantation himself.

"Mr. Wilson, Peter. What gives me the honor so early in the mornin'?" James asked and stood up to greet them.

The pair left their horses where they stood, letting them walk where they may. They were apparently expecting Pap to show up at any moment, not knowing that Pap was visiting the free community and wouldn't be back for a day or two.

"You will not believe what we found out in town this mornin'."

"No you, won't," Peter interrupted as he hurried up the side steps to the porch and quickly kissed Katherine's hand. "We were both at the barber when we heard and I was just about to leave, *such* an outrage!" Peter's eyes shone with excitement and he waved his hands in the air, trying to continue but he was so upset that he stammered and Mr. Wilson took over a little more calmly. "As I said, you will never believe what a truly atrocious event took place just a couple of days ago at Harper's Ferry."

"Harper's Ferry? That is quite far from here, unless I'm mistaken. I have not read the paper in a couple of days, what's happened?" James asked moving back to his seat to get away from Peter's waving hands.

"It's in today's paper," Mr. Wilson said and pulled out a copy from his chest pocket. "Read this. Some bloody *abolitionist* tried to take over the armory to arm the negroes!" He almost spit out the word abolitionist and shook his head with a look of disdain. He waved at Mary to get her to bring him a chair though he could easily have reached for it himself as it was only a step away from where he stood.

James stared at him, and then at the paper, trying to focus on what it said as his heart pumped louder and louder in his ears. Before he had time to read it Mr. Wilson snatched it out of his hands. "Those blasted evil people. They'll hang him you know. He had eighteen men with him, mostly *white.* Can you imagine such traitors? He is white too. They had Bibles shipped to them, though they were apparently not bibles at all."

James looked at Katherine. She held her stomach protectively and he could see tears in her eyes. Beecher Bibles, Chrissy had hid a letter about those in one of the hatboxes. It was just as Peter said; the crates were labeled as containing Bibles, but were in reality full of rifles. They gazed into each other's eyes for a short moment as Mary brought both Mr. Wilson and Peter chairs. Katherine's eyes were full of fear, and James reached for her hand and squeezed it, trying to convey calmness he didn't feel.

Mary curtsied and quickly left the room, no doubt to run down to the quarters to tell the news.

"Would you leave us alone as well, Auntie Ellen?" James said quietly knowing full well that she would go and listen behind the curtain in the living room so she could report to everyone else.

"Of course, Massa Jr."

"Oh, for god's sake, I'm so sorry, I apologize," Mr. Wilson exclaimed, "I should've asked you to dismiss your servants first. They shouldn't be hearin' this. I'm so used to ignorin' them since they ain't an intelligent breed, but obviously it's not good for them to hear about a rebellion. I apologize."

"It's all right, they are gone now. Peter, please sit down and tell me exactly what has happened. James said and motioned at the chair that Peter was leaning on. He could see Katherine lifting her eyebrows in displeasure at Mr. Wilson's comment from the corner of his eye.

Peter sat down, his face full of disbelief and disgust. He pulled out a pipe and started to fiddle with his tobacco as he spoke. "Well, we found out from the man who came into the barber's that John Brown had been in the area for a while, rentin' a farm where he had his headquarters. A couple of days ago, on the 16th he said, didn't he?" Peter looked at Mr. Wilson who nodded.

"Well, as I said on the 16th he and some of his men—some he left at the headquarters—marched on the armory and tried to overtake it. He planned to go round Virginia and hand out rifles to our niggers so that they could shoot us all and then escape north, or overtake the whole south and enslave us. Who knows what that blasted traitor was thinkin', it's disgustin'!" Peter Dawson shook his head and discretely looked at Katherine's protruding belly. "I apologize, Mrs. Waynewright. This isn't fit for a woman's ears."

Don't get her started, Peter. She isn't nearly as feeble as you think, James thought shooting Katherine a warning glance.

"I will be all right, Peter, but thank you for your concern." Not even a hint of a smile came across her lips.

Peter turned to James but he just shrugged. "Thank God they caught them," Mr. Wilson interjected, "but to think that they wanted to come here and give the negroes arms, they were plannin' to travel all over the states and hand out rifles. They began by cutting the telegraph lines, can you imagine such gall? Do you know that they took several people hostage? Hostages, they bloody took Colonel Lewis Washington."

"You don't mean?"

"Sure do, Mr. Waynewright...*the* Colonel, President Washington's nephew."

"It's his great grandnephew, I believe actually," James said. He couldn't believe what he was hearing. It all seemed so surreal. He felt scared but elated at the same time.

"Well, they were caught, thank God. A train came into the station and its baggage master tried to warn the passengers but they shot and killed him in cold blood! A negro he was, too. Those stupid abolitionists don't realize that they hurt negroes."

Peter stood up and puffed loudly on his pipe, "Those bastards opened fire. Well, with all the arms they stole I guess it aint surprisin' some other men were shot too but somehow they got him and the men. It doesn't say much more in the paper and some of what we told you the man at the barber knew somehow. I take it there will be a trial and everythin'. My dad will panic when he hears this. He is terrified of rebellions and uprisings, especially since he had that runaway just last year."

"A runaway?" Mr. Wilson asked.

Peter nodded, "Ask James, he was involved."

James felt as though Peter had physically hit him in the stomach and all the air escaped from his lungs and he more sensed than heard how Katherine became rigid in her chair before he understood what he'd meant. He started coughing violently before he regained his breath.

"Oh, are you all right, James? Swallowed something?" Peter asked, completely oblivious and handed James his coffee that had cooled some time ago.

"I'm sorry, thank you," James said, and cleared his throat. "I must have swallowed air or a crumb. They did have a runaway that for some reason got it into his head to begin his journey by stoppin' by my plantation first. He tied himself underneath Peter's carriage one day and asked Auntie Ellen for something to eat or whatever. I forget now. Peter's father never caught him."

Peter shook his head, "No, he didn't, though I haven't stopped hearin' about it. He gets so worked up when they misbehave and then everyone is irritated. I wish he could just leave them alone and let them do their work. We would all be happier and I suspect more productive that way."

James raised an eyebrow but didn't say anything.

"He sure has reason now, though, as do I. I will have to have a talk with mine today and make sure that I make them obey. I'm going to have to restrict them again and forbid them from leavin' for visitin' or any other reason they may have to leave my property. I'll just tell them I'll sell them if they try. That usually gets them to do what I say. I advise you to do the same, Mr. Waynewright. You have not been here as Master for that long. I implore you to make sure that they know who is Master so that *you* don't have a rebellion on your hands. It could get real ugly, especially now when you have a little one on its way," Mr. Wilson said and smiled at Katherine.

James' jaw clenched, but he nodded and looked Mr. Wilson straight in the eye. "I will make sure of it."

Mr. Wilson nodded and looked to Peter, "Well, I better get home to my wife. You never know what the negroes have heard already. I don't want to leave 'er alone." He got up and looked around, surprised that the horses had slowly trotted over to the field by the stable. "Why hasn't anyone taken my horse?"

"Pap is sick, the rest of them are down in the fields," Katherine said. "I have kept an eye on them. They have walked around happily the whole time. No need to worry."

Mr. Wilson didn't answer, he just stared at Katherine for a moment and then he touched Peter's shoulder. "You ought to go home, too. You should tell your father."

"Yeah, I better," Peter said, looking rather uncomfortable at the thought.

Katherine and James watched them as they caught up to their wandering horses. "It's insane, such a young man runnin' the plantation. Why hasn't he gotten someone else to take the horses if Pap is sick? Freein' all those young ones he did, too." They heard Wilson as clearly as if he was still on the porch in the still morning.

Katherine took his hand and put her finger to her lips, reminding him to wait until they were out of sight. James swallowed, feeling both angered and uncomfortable.

Soon the men were at the end of the lane and they saw Peter make a left turn and Mr. Wilson a right. Auntie Ellen came outside and sat down on the chair in front of them. Tears were streaming down her face and she held a handkerchief in her hand that looked completely soiled.

James ignored her tears and angrily turned to Katherine. "Did you hear what he said, Katherine? They are all spying on us, cause I'm SO young and inexperienced. Why hasn't he...Why hasn't he found someone else if Pap..." he said, mocking Mr. Wilson's haughty voice. He paused for a moment trying to regain his composure. He felt paranoid and out of control, but grinned suddenly,"You know, that man is brave. What an idea bringing arms. We should do the same you know...imagine all of Dawson's negroes with guns turned towards him, he would surely piss himself."

Katherine hushed him loudly. "James, be careful, you don't know who might overhear. You just said yourself that they are spying."

Auntie Ellen looked uncomfortable.

"I'm scared, Mr. Waynewright. Those men, just like Peter said, Dawson, he gonna be angry and he gonna run around to every plantation scaring all the Massa's so that we can't go nowhere and Pap is out alone. He'll be travelin' soon." Auntie Ellen sniffled and blew her nose loudly.

James threw Katherine a glance. "Auntie Ellen, you are absolutely right. Can you please go down to the quarters and tell everyone to come up here. Then we have to get someone to hurry to the free community to warn them and Pap."

Auntie Ellen turned around without a word and hurried down the porch steps.

"We are not alone, James. It's bubbling just under the surface now. More and more people are fighting for what is really right," Katherine said as she painstakingly got out of her chair supporting her belly with one hand and pushing herself up with the other. She shook her head at James' attempt to help.

James nodded, smiling at her comment and looking thoughtful simultaneously. "Yes, but our neighbors are going to become extremely vigilant." He lowered his voice and said, "If we get a visitor, it's not going to be safe to get them to the Peterssons'. Besides, they will probably want me to be part of a watch team that keeps a look out at night." James began to have a panicked look again.

"Yes, but James, your wife is with child. You cannot be leaving her alone at night." Katherine said.

James stopped what he was doing and stared at her for a moment.

"You are absolutely right, my sweet." He pulled her close and kissed her, sighing a little as he drew in her scent.

Katherine's chin began to quiver and she let herself collapse into his chest.

"Sweetie, don't worry. I apologize for making it worse by thinkin' out loud, and worrying too much. You know how I am. Don't worry now, love. I will take care of you and everyone. I'm not as weak and wet behind the ears as everyone thinks." He stroked her hair and held his hand on her stomach feeling the babies kicking gently in there.

"Do you feel it? See, they agree with me. We will handle this. We should be encouraged, not scared."

"Yes, I feel it. How could I not? They are inside me are they not?"

James laughed and kissed her and then he saw all their friends hurrying up to the house. James waved and pointed to the barn as he opened the porch gate and walked across the lawn, motioning for everyone to follow along.

"I take it that Mary and Auntie Ellen have told you some of what's goin' on?" James said as loud as he dared so that everyone could hear but so that no one outside barn would if they were in the vicinity. They had left two men outside as lookouts. One by the road and one in sight of the tobacco fields where there was a path that Dawson and Peter sometimes took as a shortcut. Still, he couldn't be too safe.

"Yes, sir," several people said, but some looked full of questions and James began to tell them what they had just learned.

"We have to be very careful. Mr. Dawson and Mr. Wilson are going to tell everyone to stay close to the plantation and will most likely threaten them with being sold and with the lash if they don't do as told. They are goin' to be terrified of rebellions and I want you to stay clear of anyone you see," he said and looked out at the subdued group. Martha stood close to Isum, hiding her face in his armpit.

"I don't know what other planters may do in the area, but I'm sure you can imagine that the news of what happened will spread like wildfire and everyone will be on the lookout for the slightest misstep. For your own safety, please be careful. I implore you. It's not safe around here right now."

He sighed as several people nodded and reassured him that of course they'd be careful and would do whatever they could to help.

James drew a breath of relief. "There is one more thing. Someone will have to ride out to warn Pap and to warn the free community. He has a traveling pass but..."

Auntie Ellen hesitated for a moment and said, "Mr. Waynewright, you should ride out yourself with someone so they don't catch them and throw the papers away. You need to be checkin' on the free community to see so nothin' suspicious goin' on there."

James nodded thoughtfully. "You might be right, Auntie Ellen. Let me think about that for a little while. I..."

The barn door opening interrupted him and Jack looking in; he was out of breath having run all the way from the road.

"Excuse me. Massa Burnham and another man comin'. They are ridin' real fast."

James hesitated for just a moment then said, "Jack, go get the other lookout and bring him in here."

Jack looked surprised and hesitated.

"Now, Jack!" James bellowed and Jack disappeared out the door so fast that the barn door slammed into the wall.

When they came back, James took another deep breath and spoke clearly. "I have just told you that I will sell you down south if you so much as try to join any kind of rebellion. I have just told you that you MUST not leave your cabins for any reason at night, you hear?"

"Loud'n clear, Massa." Isum grinned and everyone else nodded in agreement.

James managed a smile. "Thank you. I'm so sorry for this." He glanced at Jack who stood in the corner. "I'm sorry for yellin' at you, Jack. Isum, can you stay back a minute and tell them what I said before. I better go on out and greet Burnham and whoever else is here." James sighed, feeling his jaw clench and his teeth crackling. *I have to stop clenching. One day I'll break my teeth. Oh god, I don't know what to do. I'm scared, and Katherine is going to give birth soon. Maybe we should all just leave, but with seventy people, especially now, how? The plantation is doing so well. They'd catch us and kill us all if we leave. We are trapped, trapped with enemies all around us!*

James' thoughts spun around his head in such a panic that he could barely think straight, but he left the barn and walked toward his house where he saw Burnham and a man he didn't recognize waiting. They were talking to Katherine who stood with the door wide open. She looked tired and her belly seemed enormous. *May God help us,* he thought.

Chapter 11

"Being that your wife is in the family way, we wanted to come here first of all. Not too sure if you have heard the news yet or not," Mr. Burnham said as soon as James was close enough to hear.

James looked at Katherine but he couldn't read her face. *Hadn't she told them already*, he wondered.

"We heard," he said as he walked up the steps. Katherine looked rather pale and he ignored Burnham and the other man, not caring that he hadn't been introduced yet.

"Are you all right, Katherine?"

"I feel a bit tired, James. I think I'll go take a nap."

"Of course, I'll send Auntie Ellen to help you. She'll be on her way up in a minute." James stroked her hand briefly and finally turned to Mr. Burnham and the other man. "Please, do come in. I'm James Waynewright." James shook the man's hand, instead of waiting to be introduced. The man didn't smile, just nodded somberly and said, "Mr. Pierpotter." He didn't mention where he was from or how he knew Burnham.

James showed them the way into the larger sitting room and rang the bell on the wall so that Mary could come and put a log on the fire. He would have done it himself, but he better make it seem as though he had his house negroes under control and have her do it. He didn't want any more comments like he'd had earlier about Pap being absent.

"Have a seat, gentlemen. As soon as we get a log on the fire we'll talk. It's sunny out there but the sun can't quite warm it up in here. Let's just get the chill out of the room. Would you like anything to drink?" he asked them as Mary came in, then told her to put the log on and motioned to the men to let her know what they wanted to drink, but they waved her on, shaking their heads.

"I just spoke to my negroes, had just finished when I saw you arrive. As I said, we did hear of it earlier this mornin'. Awful, isn't it?" James added for good measure.

Mr. Burnham shook his head in disgust. He remained quiet and had a look of outmost concern on his face. He scratched his beard absently and continued to shake his head without a word.

Mr. Pierpotter cleared his throat. "You may wonder who I am and why I'm here, Mr. Waynewright."

"The thought has crossed my mind, I admit," James replied but he kept his eyes on the fireplace. The log wouldn't catch and he rose to stoke the fire.

"Back in '31, after the Turner rebellion, several planters met to find a way to protect our homes should it happen again. Your father was among them. I own the Potter Plantation about an hour from here on the other side of town. Mr. Burnham and I are close friends, and when I got the paper this mornin' I decided to pay him a visit."

"Indeed," Mr. Burnham confirmed. "We would like you to come with us as we ride around and speak to everyone."

James didn't answer at first. It seemed a bit contradictory to round up all the men to talk about how to protect themselves and leave the women home alone.

"I understand your concern, but I don't feel comfortable leaving Katherine alone without me here, especially not in her state. I'm sure you can understand that," *I should go "check" on the free community, too. Should I say that? No, then they'll insist on going with me.*

Mr. Burnham nodded. "I sympathize with your concern, but though news travels fast, I doubt that the negroes have heard about it already and I doubt they'll react so quickly. I'm sure we have a day or two before anything will happen, if it's going to."

"With all due respect, I don't agree. In fact, as I told you, I spoke to my own just now, warnin' them what would happen if they so much as tried to leave my property. Mr. Wilson and Peter Dawson were here this mornin' advising me on it. You may be right that it'll take them a while to think of something, but should we all leave our plantations at the same time, they may seize the opportunity," James continued.

"Hmmm..." Mr. Burnham scratched his beard again and nodded slowly, looking at Mr. Pierpotter who shook his head. "Mr. Waynewright, I must disagree. More than anything, I think it's important that we have a unified front. They caught the guy, but there is no way of knowin' how many others he had with him that right now are lying in wait, preparing to strike again."

"Precisely why I will not leave Katherine alone," James interrupted.

"He does have a point, Aryl," Mr. Burnham said looking at Mr. Pierpotter. "I can certainly understand your predicament. I say that we take James' advice and make sure that there is someone on each plantation that can protect the women. It's blasted really what that traitor has done. We cannot send out our *own* negroes to take a message, nor can we ask them to watch our women. He has basically trapped us on our plantations." He shook his head again with the same look of disgust on his face, and then he rose and stretched his back. "I suggest that I ride over to Dawson. Aryl, you go to your closest neighbor. Whoever has an overseer or sons who can take responsibility meet in the tavern tomorrow mornin' at ten. James...I will take notes and bring them to you afterwards. You are right to stay with the Mrs."

"Thank you. I appreciate it." James hid a yawn and got up to follow them out.

When they left he felt so tired suddenly that he couldn't even muster up the strength to go upstairs and join Katherine. Instead, he leaned his forehead on the doorpost and remained there for several minutes. The polished wood felt cool against his flushed skin as he stood there. *What did this really mean?* he wondered to himself. Harper's Ferry wasn't near here. Could it really cause a rebellion? If it did, how long could he use Katherine's pregnancy as an excuse? Which ranks should he join if it came down to it?

James knew it wasn't a question any longer. He knew in his heart whom he had to join, and they'd name him a traitor too, no better than John Brown.

He fell asleep as soon as he put his head on the pillow and didn't come to until two hours later when Auntie Ellen woke him. She sat down on his bedside and stroked his cheek just as she had when he was a little boy. For the briefest of moments he enjoyed the pleasant memories of childhood mornings. Then he remembered what had happened and he sat straight up. "What time is it?"

"Quarter past three. Mrs. Waynewright told me to wake you. She is worried sick."

"Is she all right? Is it the babies?"

"Sorry, Mr. Waynewright, ain't nothin' like that. They are fine but she worries. I'm worried 'bout Pap, too. What if he...bein' out there on his own with the guards everywhere."

James took her wrinkly, skinny hand in both of his. "I'm goin' to wait until dark and then ride out to the free community. I'll bring him back, I promise. Can you and Mary stay here with Katherine?"

"Of course, and we ask Jack, too."

"Auntie Ellen, what should I do? If there *is* a rebellion, how can I do what's right and protect Katherine at the same time? I'm so tired of all the neighbors comin' by to check on me just because I'm young! I'm getting right irritated over it."

She looked him in the eye without a word. Then she rose and walked to the door. She turned to look at him, "You will do what God tells you. I trust that he will provide you with the right answers. We're all here. We won't let nothin' happen to you, Katherine or the babies. Now go down to your wife and have somethin' to eat before you head out," she said ignoring his comment about his irritation.

A couple of hours later they had eaten dinner and had talked for a little while. Katherine assured him that she would feel comfortable enough with their friends in the house with her. They were hoping that none of the neighbors would come back and wonder why he wasn't home at night since he had said that he wouldn't leave Katherine alone. They couldn't think of a good excuse for why he would leave. Had they only told Peter and Mr. Wilson the truth this morning instead of saying that Pap was sick, he could have just gone about his business with no worry. As it was now, they could only hope that the others felt it safer to be home with their wives and didn't see the need to visit James.

He and Isum set out together. Martha and their little girl went to stay with Jack's wife since Jack was up at the house with Katherine, Mary and Auntie Ellen. Isum assured James that everyone would lay low, stay inside, and not do anything that would draw any attention to themselves, just in case there were patrollers outside.

It was a chilly and clear night. It was dry, the trees rustled and branches cracked with every step. Isum knew the road well. He had helped the six who left for the free community, visited them several times as well and was completely comfortable even though it was dark.

As they were riding, James suddenly realized that neither he nor Katherine had thought to visit Oskar and Ebba. James felt an urgent need to make a detour to let them know, but Isum had no idea about their underground operation and James didn't feel it worth the risk for him to meet them. Showing up at night might give the assumption that Isum was an escapee and James didn't want any misunderstandings. Isum was a nice man and probably someone they could trust, but it was better not to take any chances with the current state of affairs being what they were. Knowing that his former master was a conductor on the railroad would not be an easy thing to keep secret. Katherine and James didn't trust anyone other than Auntie Ellen and her children and Pap, who might have been his dad's closest friend. James remembered Pap and his dad going fishing together by the lake behind the cow pasture. He remembered them sometimes laughing in the study together in the evenings. It hadn't occurred to James until recently how close they were. His father always spoke of Dawson as his friend, but the more James saw of Dawson the more dubious he became of that friendship. Sometimes James wondered what his father would have said if he had told him what he really thought of slavery. Would his father have been willing to do what James was doing had they only spoken about it? Probably not, but sometimes he couldn't help fantasizing about it.

James urged Miss South on to catch up with his riding companion, patting her under her warm mane as if to apologize for rushing her. He had been so deep in thought that he had not noticed that Isum had gone way ahead and was going around a bend in the path and into what looked like a large glen. He could have easily have missed him and gotten lost.

He urged Miss South into a trot and caught up. A ray of moonlight lit up the glen and he could see Isum clearly, when he turned around towards him. "Still have a ways to go, but we're deeper in the woods now. I don' think no one be seein' us here. Another half hour then we reach the swamps," he whispered.

"Thank you, Isum. Look, it's beautiful with the moonlight, isn't it? Like a photograph, you don't see the colors but it's clear."

"Yes, Mr. Waynewright. That moon is holy among my family. We bathe our new babes in the light of the full moon and my grandmama put food out on a rock so it could absorb the moonlight. She live to be almost ninety years old, she did," Isum whispered solemnly.

James shivered at the thought of Isum's grandmother going outside in the dark with the few vegetables they must have planted back in his grandfather's time. He knew that his own father had made vast improvements to the plantation when *his* father died and he probably thought that he was a revolutionary because of it. In fact, his father had given them the right to plant on their little plots outside their cabins that James let them expand.

James could picture a skinny woman with skin black as ebony standing bent over that rock in his mind's eye.

"That is a beautiful thought, Isum. I never knew that."

He nodded, "If you' ever feel weak or scared, the moon will give you strength, just remember that."

"I will," James replied, trying to feel comforted by the silvery light.

They rode on in silence and soon had to ride in single file again as the path narrowed. They were deep inside the swampy woods now. It smelled and looked wet everywhere. The hooves made a sloshing sound, and the few times the moon reached between the trees, its rays glittered on the surface of the water. James felt calm and riding in the dark behind Isum gave him time to reflect on what had happened. As panicked as his neighbors were, he felt vindicated in the knowledge that he was not alone. He was not the only white man down here who was against slavery. James remembered Pastor Beecher's words: *You must do what's right, just as Jesus did. He went against his own community to do what was right.*

Suddenly Isum stopped and waited for James to come up beside him. There was barely enough space for James' horse and she fussed as her hooves kept sliding in the mud.

Isum pointed at something to the right. At first James didn't see anything, but a little further away from where he first gazed, he saw the outline of several buildings, and behind that a cluster of cabins with lamps lit inside.

James took a deep breath. Unbelievable, it was a real village in the middle of the swamps hidden from the outside world. It was as if it had been taken straight from a storybook, only everyone was a freed negro.

"We'll visit Alba 'n Joe first since they live right at the first cabin. What you see here is the stables and the pigsty," Isum said as they approached.

James didn't reply he was full of mixed feelings, what would his former slaves say when they saw him? Would they allow him in here in the first place? What if they had shotguns and shot him as an intruder? James swallowed hard at the thought. What if Alba and Joe were skinny and malnourished? Maybe his father had been right after all and he should not have let them go, what then?

As if to prove him wrong, he heard a door creak just as Isum slid off his horse Alba hurried out, holding a lantern in her hand. She ran past Isum and straight into James who was too surprised and shocked to wrap his arms around her. She stepped back and he could see her eyes narrowing in the flickering light. "Mr. Waynewright, what done took you so long? We been tellin' Isum to bring you for a visit for months and months."

James laughed as he looked her up and down. She certainly did not look malnourished and when he finally hugged her, he felt her warm round flesh against his chilled chest.

"Come inside, Mr. Waynewright, come inside. It's a cold night, it is. I'll put my bean soup on the hearth for you both. Pap was tellin' me there are babies comin' soon. That's wonderful."

James glanced at Isum, he looked moved and motioned for James to follow her into the cabin. "I take the horses Mass...Mr. Waynewright." He said and swallowed hard.

A feeling of home greeted him as soon as he stepped over the threshold. Quilts lined the walls, a sturdy table with a red tablecloth, and leftovers from their supper remained. The spoons still sat in the bowls and a chunk of bread that smelled freshly baked sat in a basket with a checkered towel carelessly thrown on top. A small oil lamp hung from the ceiling above and gave the room a soft pleasant glow.

James felt a lump form in his throat without really being able to put his finger on why.

Alba smiled and pointed to the bench by the wall, "Go on have a seat, Mr. Waynewright, Joe will be home soon. What brings you here to visit in the dead of night?"

She handed him a steaming bowl of soup. It was thick with beans and onion, and smelled delicious.

James cleared his throat and put the bowl down on the table. "Isum and I came to ask Pap to come with us, and to warn everyone. There has been an incident at Harper's Ferry and there are patrollers everywhere."

Alba sat down in front of him with a furrow in between her brows. As he told her, her hand went to her mouth.

"Pap left last night. I thought for sure he be back on the plantation by early this mornin.'"

James stared at her and was just about to ask her if she was sure that Pap had left when she thought he did, when Isum stepped in with Joe.

Joe went right up to him and shook his hand. "Mr. Waynewright, it is an honor havin' you call on us. I'm sorry that there is trouble afoot. Isum just told me."

"Joe," he said and squeezed his hand, at a loss for words for the moment, in shock over the news that Pap had not made it home. He ought to have been home a couple of hours already when Peter and Mr. Wilson visited them this morning.

James cleared his throat. "Isum and I came to warn you, just for you to be aware of..." He hesitated, cleared his throat and looked at Isum, then changed the subject. "Alba told me that Pap left yesterday night. He should have been back already. We should all be careful, all the planters are panicked."

"Did you check his cabin? No one saw him come home did they?" Joe asked

Isum shook his head. "No, Bell wasn't in the stable... I checked when I brought our horses out this evenin'."

"Did Pap say anything about goin' somewhere else?" James asked.

Joe and Alba's eyes met. "No, Mr. Waynewright. He didn't say anything of the sort. He kept talkin' about goin home to see Mrs. Waynewright, tellin' us he was so happy that the babies are coming. Two of them," Alba said as tears were gleaming in her eyes, "are you sayin' something done happened to him?"

James rubbed his neck, "Not necessarily, but it does worry me a bit. Maybe he went somewhere else that none of us know about. He isn't running north is he?"

He shook his head. "Mr. Waynewright, no one on your plantation would run now. We know you're helpin' whoever wants to leave. Besides, Pap won't never leave Ellen," Joe said.

"Pap love that woman. They should have jumped the broom already. Nobody knows what they are waitin' for," Alba added.

James looked at her in surprise. "Auntie Ellen and Pap? Nah, they are just friends. They have been friends for as long as I can remember but I don't think..."

"Then you blind, Mr. Waynewright. Those two had eyes on each other even when her husban' was still alive, but they are both God fearin' people and wouldn't do nothin."

James nodded slowly as the pieces of an old puzzle suddenly came together. "Why haven't I thought of that?"

Joe and Isum both laughed, and for a short moment the laughter kept the fear of Pap's whereabouts at bay, but then Isum brought them back to reality.

"Mr. Waynewright, I had wanted to show you around, but I'm thinkin' maybe we ought to be gettin' back."

James nodded with a sigh and began to get up, but sat down again as Alba pushed his bowl toward him. "You have to eat first, Mr. Waynewright. You too Isum, eat something to get your strength."

Quickly they nodded and spooned up the soup. It had cooled and tasted wonderful.

They rode out in silence, but as soon as they could ride side by side, James nudged Isum's arm. "I don't feel good about this. Do you think that he got lost? What if he is hurt? He might be layin' here somewhere, stuck in the mud or drowned," James whispered.

"Or caught by one of the patrollers who think that he may have started a rebellion," Isum offered. It sent shivers down James' spine.

"I know, I didn't want to acknowledge that out loud." James teeth clenched and he urged his horse on. "Let's hurry home just in case," James mumbled.

He more felt than heard Isum stiffen in the saddle. He was silent for a while and then James could clearly hear the panic in his voice. "Mr. Waynewright, you are right. We got to hurry. If they get something out of him, then they will question everyone and Martha will not handle it. She'll go back to...to..."

Now James clenched his teeth so hard he heard them crunch and it hurt. He kicked Miss South and she leaped forward over a large puddle, her hooves sloshing on the edge of it.

"You are right, Isum, let's go!"

Isum didn't reply, but urged his horse on and got up close behind as they sprinted for home.

It was almost daylight by the time they got to the plantation and James hopped off Miss South throwing her reins to Isum as he ran into the house to make sure that everything was all right. He found it all quiet. Katherine was sound asleep as were Ellen and Mary on the couches in the drawing room with blankets wrapped around them. Jack had been sleeping in one of the easy chairs. He woke up when he heard James and waited for him to come back down after checking on Katherine.

"How is Pap?" he whispered sleepily.

James shook his head and motioned for him to come out into the entranceway, so as not to wake the others. "Something is wrong. He wasn't there. He left late at night the day before yesterday. He should have been back very early yesterday mornin'. No visitors here?"

Jack's eyes popped right open and he just stared at James at first. "Do you think he came back without you knowin'?"

"I'm about to check. Isum and I are riding down there now. I just wanted to check on Katherine first. No one has been here right?" he repeated.

"No, I'm sorry sir. No, thankfully nobody."

James touched his arm and then he was out the door and hurrying to get back on his horse. Isum barely waited for him to get in the saddle before he raced down to the cabins.

Pap wasn't there. They checked the stables, too. There was no sign of him.

Chapter 12

James didn't want to upset Katherine so he called Jack, Isum, Auntie Ellen and Mary to a quick meeting in Auntie Ellen's cabin.

Now more than ever it was clear to him who his friends were and that the color of a man's skin had nothing whatsoever to do with it.

He looked at them as they sat in a semi-circle on Auntie Ellen's chairs. They waited patiently for him to begin speaking, but he just shook his head and said, "I really don't know what to say, but I think it is clear now that someone, that something has happened to him."

"What I don't understand is why they haven't brought him back here. He only need say who he belong to, even if he ain't really yours no more. He would still say it and they bring him back," Jack said jerking his knee nervously. It rattled one of the planks on the floor, but no one seemed to notice.

Pap is protecting me. He won't say anything at all. He doesn't want anyone to come around here looking for rebellious slaves and find the hole right under here in Auntie Ellen's cabin, James thought and caught Mary's eye.

"You are right, Jack. I don't know why either. That's what's worrying me. I'm worried that they just shot him without even bothering to ask." Auntie Ellen's head jerked back as if she had been physically hit and he regretted the words as soon as they left his mouth.

"I'm sorry, Auntie Ellen. I didn't mean to scare you. I might be wrong, there could be all kinds of reasons why they ain't here yet. He could have been caught by an overseer and they might be waiting for the master to speak to him and who knows how long that might take right now, what with everything that's going on."

Isum cleared his throat and got out of the chair, moving behind it and leaning on it before he spoke. "It be fine, Mr. Waynewright. We gonna find him. Pap will never ever say anything 'bout you freein' us or payin' us. He won't, don't you worry'"

"That the truth, Mr. Waynewright. It surely is," Auntie Ellen agreed. She tried to smile, but it didn't really look like a smile. Her chin was quivering as she was trying to hold back tears.

"I hope so. I've been meanin' to remind you, I'm sure you won't forget, but it is crucial now that you call me Master. If someone is nearby, if you don't, if you slipped before I don't think anyone would have done much about it, not more then tell you to mind your mouth and not be uppity, but now it's simply not safe."

"We ought to call you Massa, just the same all the time, just in case someone over hear it, Mr. Waynewright..." then a quick smile, "Massa," Jack offered, glancing at the others. They nodded without hesitation.

James looked pained, but inwardly he drew a sigh of relief in spite of it.

"Thank you. I'm so sorry, but I have a feeling that you are right Jack. At least when we are outside, as we don't know how much the wind carries and what someone may hear as they drive by, at least down by the tobacco close to the road, in the back and down here it's less of a risk." *What if they already have heard?*

He got up, and felt for his vest pocket where he sometimes kept a notebook and a pencil. "I didn't bring anything to write with. Please come with me to my office," he said and gestured at Jack, "I'll write a note sayin' that I left you in charge, and that I trust you completely while I'm gone should anyone come and ask. Then I'll see if Mrs. Petersson can stay with Katherine. No one tells Katherine that Pap is gone, you hear?"

"Understood."

***

James' head was swimming when he took a shortcut and galloped across the edge of the tobacco field behind the main house. Part of him felt like telling everyone the truth, telling the neighbors that he agreed with Brown, telling them that it wasn't right to keep people in bondage and that he was ashamed of them for still doing it when it was clear that others saw the error in their ways. Another part of him was terrified and he wished that he was still in New York and that Katherine and he were safely somewhere in an apartment waiting for their twins. If he had only sold the plantation and freed everyone then he wouldn't have to deal with this now. He really did not know what to do. He didn't know where to look for Pap, and he didn't know what to tell his neighbors about his disappearance. James had taken out Noah instead of Miss South. Just as he jumped over the ditch to the road behind the tobacco fields he saw the Sheriff and another man come full speed toward him.

"Oh, Mr. Waynewright, it's you. We couldn't see from back there. Just wanted to make sure it wasn't some nigger on the run who'd stolen a horse."

"You could surely see that I'm not. I'm not *that* tanned." James said.

The Sheriff and his companion burst out laughing,

"Ha, that'd be the day, when men start tanning themselves!" Both men laughed so loud that the Sheriff's horse's ears twitched nervously as it danced to the side.

The Sheriff stroked it's neck to calm it and turned back to James, "Mr. Waynewright, have you heard that there has been a rebel…"

"I have," James interrupted. "This is why I'm in a hurry to get what I need done before dark, so that I can get home to my wife who is indisposed at the moment."

"Sure thing, keep your eyes open. Report to me should you see somethin'"

James nodded and was about to kick his heels in Noah's sides when he hesitated. "Sheriff, one of my boys is gone. I know he hasn't run away, he had my permission to visit friends, but he ought to have been back by now. Have you seen him?"

"Oh, he ran, I'm sure. Took the chance when he heard bout the rebellion, son. But sure I'll look. Who is it? One of them young ones I'm sure."

"He did *not* run! He is in his late fifties, not a young one," James said hearing how agitated he sounded, but he wasn't able to do anything about it. "It's Pap, my father's favorite. He wouldn't run, Sheriff." The Sheriff laughed aloud again and glanced at his friend, who looked amused at the thought.

"Won't run? There is no telling what niggers will decide to do from one moment to the next. They ain't predictable, and he was your father's favorite you said? What makes you think he'd stay with *you*? I thought you freed all your father's favorites. Well whatever you say son, we have *work* to do, but we will sure keep an eye out for your boy, let you know if we find him. Have a good day now."

He spoke fast out of the corner of his mouth and then he urged his horse on with a loud, "Giddy up!"

James got the distinct feeling that the Sheriff loved what was going on just so that he had something to do. He shivered and chastised himself for saying that Pap was his dad's favorite.

He rode around all day, beginning with a visit with Oskar and Ebba. Ebba immediately saddled a horse and went to stay with Katherine, but Oskar had sprained his ankle badly the day before and was in so much pain that he was bedridden with his foot raised up on a pile of pillows. He would not be able to go with James as he had hoped.

James went around the woods by the stream where the runaways had traveled before he and Katherine drove them, but didn't see Pap or anything that made it seem as if he had been there. He rode into town. If Katherine had not told Peter and Wilson that he was sick the other morning, he could have asked people if they had seen him. He didn't want to contradict himself and draw attention, so he rode around aimlessly, hoping that the Sheriff hadn't asked around on his behalf. Upon reflection, James considered that it might not have been the right move to tell the lawman. He didn't see a single negro outside, not in town, nor on the road. No doubt they had been told by their masters to stay put and not go wandering.

Finally, after several hours of aimless riding, James stopped at the Saloon for a drink.

As soon as he stepped inside he saw Mr. Wilson and right beside him Mr. Burnham. *Now they'll wonder why I left Katherine alone. I should go.* James thought, but it was too late, they had already seen him and he could do nothing but walk up to them and hope that they had forgotten what he said about leaving her. Of course they hadn't.

"Left 'er alone, now did you?" Mr. Burnham said sounding as if he had had a couple already.

James didn't answer at first; instead he got the bartender's attention and ordered a double scotch.

He waited for his drink and had a large sip before he answered. He shrugged playing it off the best he could. "I had to. She is hysterical with fear, scared all the time that some negro will come and take her hostage and that she will have the babies under the threat of a gun. I know it's bad, but I had to take a break. Mrs. Petersson is staying with her a while. I just had to get out."

Mr. Burnham and Wilson began to laugh. "We know how it's like, women folk in the family way, and two, I just heard about that. You have a tough go of it, son," he said and patted James on the shoulder.

"You could say that," James mumbled, swallowing his scotch quickly. He didn't feel like sitting there with the man who had caused the death of his parents, whether it was his fault or not. Seeing him earlier today had been quite enough. He nodded to the bartender, threw some money on the bar, and got up to leave.

"Sorry fellows, but I do have to get back to her. I..."

He heard a commotion behind him and then before he knew it the Sheriff and that companion of his hollered at him from the door,

"Waynewright, we found your runaway! I have him in my cell. Just by chance that I saw your horse outside."

All the air went out of his lungs at once. He had been holding his breath, but hadn't realized it. *Please, please Sheriff don't say that it's Pap. I better get out there before he comes in.*

James moved so fast that the barstool fell backwards and Mr. Burnham caught it with his hand.

"Sheriff, hold on. I'll be out, I'll be right there..."

But he didn't hear it. He marched right across the floor toward them looking important and satisfied with himself.

"Found Pap outside Dawson's plantation. Dawson had him questioned and he was about to send him over to you with the overseer, but since I happen by I brought him with me. I was going to bring him over to you, but since you weren't home I brought him in. My deputy is watching him, I didn't want to leave him alone with the Mrs."

James became ice cold and his heart was hammering uncontrollably in his chest. He tried to say something, but Mr. Burnham touched his shoulder before he had the chance.

"Why didn't you say that you had a runaway, son? We could have helped you. No reason to keep things to yourself."

I'm NOT your son. James thought to himself in the middle of trying to focus on some kind of an excuse. *What did Dawson do to him? What gives him the right?*

"Pap? Isn't he your horseman? Thought your wife told us he was sick this mornin' when our horses were roaming round eating your flowers," Mr. Wilson said, suddenly sounding accusatory and suspicious.

"Actually, Katherine forgot that he felt better and had asked for leave to visit his brother. You know women when they are expecting, it's..."

"Pap has a brother? I didn't know that. What's his name?" Mr. Burnham asked.

"I don't rightly know," James mumbled. In fact, Pap didn't have a brother at all.

The Sheriff looked at James curiously and exchanged a glance with the two older men.

"Mr. Waynewright, you sure it's his brother? I don' recall him havin' one."

God dammit, they all know everything about everyone here, I hate it. James thought desperately.

"Really, fellows, I have to get home and deal with this, and take care of Katherine. Thank you, Sheriff, for finding him for me and for alerting me. Good night gentlemen," James said, deciding to pretend he hadn't heard, and tipped his hat. He didn't wait for a reply but hurried towards the door. He was outside and just about to close it behind him when he heard Wilson.

"Something ain't right with that young man. I can't put my finger on it, but I noticed two days ago when Peter Dawson and I paid him a visit."

James numbly closed the door and walked to his horse. His fingers were shaking when he untied the reins from the hitching post. There was an echoing sound in his ears and panic was threatening to overtake him. He felt as he had that day when he got the letter about Johnnie's murder, or the day when he found out his parents had died. Only now, the enormity of his responsibility of having a wife pregnant with twins and seventy negroes living secretly as free men on his plantation paralyzed him with fear, but he had to deal with it, beginning with getting Pap out of jail.

The Deputy grinned and let him inside as soon as he knocked.

"Ah, there you are. I have your boy right here. I 'gave 'im some water and something stronger. I felt sorry for 'im. Don't tell the Sheriff, will you?"

James shook his head and swallowed. *What did they do to him if he needed a drink and he feels sorry for him?*

James heard the Deputy's keys jingle and the heels of his boots as he quickly went in the back and then the sound of the boots again and softer footsteps. James was relieved that he didn't hear shuffling from Pap's feet. Still he steeled himself for what he would see when Pap was brought out.

He took a deep breath and lifted his eyes.

Pap looked him straight in the eye and he didn't look worse for wear from what James could see.

For one second James looked back at him. Then he played his part,

"Where have you been? You didn't have permission to be gone for more than a day. Do you know what's happened, Pap? We have a curfew now. How *dare* you disobey me like this, having to pick you up from jail?" He almost spit out the last word and grabbed Pap's arm hard, pushing him out in front of him, turning to the Deputy as he did so. "Thank you, Deputy. I'm so sorry about this. I'll keep them on a shorter leash from now on."

"Ah 'is fine, Mr. Waynewright. Negros's ain't trustworthy. You give them your hand and they take your whole arm. Don't be too harsh with him, they can't help it. They don't have the brains for it, you know."

James nodded. He tried to smile, but wasn't very successful at it. He wanted to hurry outside and away from there before the Sheriff came back.

He still held on to Pap's arm for show. "You can ride behind me, okay? Can you get up?"

"Yes, Massa," Pap answered right away and with a steady voice.

James took a deep breath. They were off in just a minute and as soon as they were out of sight of town, James steered the horse off the road and into a little glen in the forest.

"Please jump down," he whispered. "I want to talk here first, if you don't mind. I don't want to upset Katherine. Are you alright? I'm sorry about yellin' at you but—"

Pap slid off gingerly, James held out his hand for him, but he jumped off without taking it.

They leaned their heads close together, each man holding one of their hands on the horse's warm flanks.

"Pap, are you all right? We have been worried sick. Isum and I went to the free community, not sure if you heard what's happened. Everyone is frantic. Are you sure you are all right? Did Dawson hurt you?" James repeated.

"Don't worry, Mr. Waynewright. I know why you scream at me in the jail, got to keep up appearances n'all. I'm just fine. I was on my way home ridin' along when suddenly out of nowhere Dawson himself grab me. I was almost home but I rode a little further. Right along the property line by Dawson's plantation is an old apple tree. I wanted to surprise Ellen. I know it was stupid, bein' in the middle of the night, really too dark to find 'em, but I wanted to, for Ellen."

He paused, clearing his throat. James tried to hide a smile. So there was something between him and Ellen after all. Alba and Joe had been right.

"Suddenly he grabbed me...he had a gun and acted as if I'd run or somethin' even though I know it's the law that if a white man tells you, you have to obey, he know that, too. Still he acted as if I might not know."

James shook his head in disgust.

"He had me ride ahead of him the whole way with the gun at my back," Pap continued, his voice shaking a little now. His voice sounded dry and hoarse. James noticed and pulled out his flask.

"Here, Pap, I'm sorry. You must be thirsty."

Pap took the flask and James heard him drink it down in the darkness and then try to stifle a burp.

"As I was sayin', he brought me all the way to his place and someone took your horse, still has it. The Sheriff had me ride with the deputy and I was tied up'n all. Anyway, Dawson he pushed me into one of the rooms in the overseer's house. Then he started asking me all kind of questions. Where I been, and why I didn't say nothin'. I say I visited a friend and showed him my pass.

"Mr. Waynewright, he ask stuff 'bout how you be runnin' the plantation, said he heard you set some negroes free that Massa Waynewright had promised when he pass on. He say that somethin' was fishy 'bout it, that Massa Waynewright would never had wanted you to set such young ones free and why wasn't I freed then since I was always his favorite. Mr. Waynewright, I didn't know what to tell him. I'm so sorry for gettin' into trouble like this. I didn't mean to, I just wanted to see if there were still apples for Ellen."

James clenched his teeth. The fear and panic was coming at him in waves. He touched Pap's shoulder, "You've done nothin' wrong, nothin' at all. I'm the one who has screwed up." He sighed and told Pap everything, about John Brown, about him lying and saying that Pap visited a brother, about Katherine saying he was sick.

"I'm not alone, Pap, there are more southerners who are on our side, but everyone here has gone crazy. They have all been visiting me thinkin' I'm too young to handle things." He took a deep breath and repeated, "Pap, you are sure he didn't hurt you?"

"No, he didn't. I was scared and he was angry, but no, he didn't hurt me. I'll say I visited a friend that is like a brother to me. I'll say that I call him my brother, should someone ask."

"Did you say you visited the free community?"

"Well, nah. I said that he is free negro livin' over near the swamps in a hut. It's true but there are many huts..."

James nodded. "That's good, Pap. We ought to get back. Should we meet anyone on the road, I'm still mad at you."

Pap smiled and nodded. James managed to smile back, though the fear sat as a stone in the pit of his stomach

Chapter 13

The next morning he woke up early. The stone in his stomach was still there and he knew that he should visit Dawson and ask him what he meant with questioning "his property" without his knowledge or blessing. He ought to find out what he thought was fishy. Dread went through him at the thought. How could he even bring it up? What would he say? How could he answer his questions? Every question would have to be answered with a lie, a lie to protect the people that he loved.

He turned to Katherine and found her lying on her side sleeping peacefully. He gently pushed a strand of her hair away from her face.

It woke her and she looked at him sleepily.

"Sweets, where were you last night? Auntie Ellen said you were out patrolling, but I heard you tell Burnham and that other man...?" She looked at him questioningly, she looked so innocent, and kind and her stomach looked so large. How could he protect her and their children? He should never have brought her here. He should have sold the plantation. He should have known how foolish and dangerous it was.

"Mr. Pierpotter."

"I heard you tell them that you wanted to stay with me, and I noticed how Ellen and Mary were acting. I know you have been looking for Pap. Why wasn't he at the free community? Did you find him?"

James raised his eyebrows, but he shouldn't have been surprised. Katherine had an uncanny ability to know things without anyone telling her.

"We did, Katherine, I apologize. I didn't want to worry."

"In my delicate state," she laughed. "I'm not as delicate as you think, James. I better not be if I'm going to push your sons out of me."

He laughed too and stood up to help her rise and get her legs over the edge of the bed. "Well, Katherine, I think we are havin' one of each, one for you and one for me. I'll take the girl and you take the boy." He kissed her and reached for the robe that lay folded over the chair.

"Yes, we found him," he said, then hesitated, "since you are sayin' that you are strong enough, I might as well tell you everything."

Katherine went pale, especially when he told her what Mr. Wilson said in the Saloon. She began to breathe heavily and reached for his arm. He didn't want to tell her about Dawson and Pap, but as usual she could read him like a book.

She stood a minute to get her bearings, holding her hands around her stomach as if to protect their children from what he was about to say.

"What else, James?"

He told her. She sat right back down again.

"They are on to us Katherine. What are we gonna do?" James said, not being able to hide the panic in his voice.

"James, that is not necessarily true. We really don't know that. Yes, Dawson told Pap that there is something fishy about it, but that doesn't make it true. It means that Dawson is a nincompoop who gets nervous because you run things differently and with a modern eye. His old ways of doing things doesn't par up with yours. He may be a nincompoop, but he isn't stupid. He rides by here several times a week, and he sees our fields, sees the growth and he sees how everyone is obedient and hardworking. He is jealous, James. It's as simple as that."

James looked at her. He hadn't thought of that. Katherine patted his arm with her left hand. She wasn't wearing her rings as her hands were swollen from her pregnancy. It moved him, seeing her body change to carry his babies. Suddenly the memory of a poem one of the professors had read at the College of Physicians and Surgeons came to him. *These hands are the hands of God. You can heal yourself and the world with them.*

He shivered and took them into his own and kissed them.

"Katherine, you are right. You are so wise. What would I do without you?" "You'd manage, sweet James. Let's go down, no, let's ring the bell and have breakfast up here. We'll talk to Ellen about it. See what she thinks we should do. She knows Dawson better than any of us, I think, having been here so long."

James cleared his throat, "That is a wonderful idea. I'll send Matilda to help Jack. I think I heard her downstairs."

"She is here for her reading lesson. She is progressing splendidly, she is a fast learner."

"Katherine, you can't do that!" James voice sounded harsher than he'd meant and she looked at him with surprise.

"I mean, I think that right now when everyone is snoopin' around asking questions, it's not wise. If they ask her, she is only a child and if she tells them, they would... I don't know what they'd do, but what I heard the last couple of days doesn't make me think they'd be nice."

Katherine swallowed, holding her hands protectively over her belly again. "You are right, James, you are correct in this. I...Martha is coming for her lesson as well."

She looked overwhelmed, tears began to fall down her cheeks, and he almost regretted what he said.

"Katherine, please don't cry. It won't be forever, just until this blows over. I'm sorry if I sounded harsh."

Half an hour later, they had had breakfast in bed and Auntie Ellen and Mary joined them, each of them pulling up a chair to the bed.

Auntie Ellen sat pensive and still for several moments before she spoke.

"I can't say I know him well, but I sure been round long enough to know that Mr. Dawson ain't someone to be messin' with. I remember him comin' over here many a night spendin' time with Massa Waynewright. I never understood what my Massa saw in him. Guess they been friends so long that they stopped questioning each other."

"From what you are tellin' me, I think the best way would be for you to pay him a visit an ask why he be questioning your negroes. Ask him what he did, getting your wife worried 'bout her favorite slave in her state. Ask what he mean doin' that to your property. I can't help but enjoy the thought that he ain't got no idea what really be goin' on over here. That man a cruel bastard. Pap ain't said nothin' to him at all, I know that's a fact."

James caught Katherine's eye and touched Auntie Ellen's hand. "I wish I was as confident as you, Auntie Ellen," James said. "You are probably right, though. I should go over an..."

"You tell him that you have made a lot of improvements to your plantation, just like you told Mr. Gilbert," Katherine interrupted him. "I told James that Dawson is just jealous of him, jealous that we have such great crops and good working, obedient *slaves.*"

Mary looked at Katherine, hesitating for a moment before she spoke,

"When Massa Waynewright bought Timmy and his Tobias from Dawson, it wasn't long before they told me that they all slowed down their work there all the time. Dawson was a hard Massa but they tried in their own way to defy him." She nodded for emphasis.

"So then my theory makes perfect sense, doesn't it James? He sees how well our people work and it confuses him, and again, it makes him jealous. I think that Auntie Ellen is right. The best thing for you is to head over there right away and ask him why he has made me hysterical." Katherine patted her stomach, "Don't you worry little ones. Daddy is going to go yell at the man who hurts your friends."

***

James handed his horse to Isaac, who appeared as soon as he approached Dawson's home.

"Is Master Dawson inside?"

"No, Massa Waynewright. He is down at the overseer. Shall I have somebody call for him?"

"That would be great, Isaac. Thank you." He smiled at him, but Isaac's eyes were lowered, focusing somewhere on James' throat and he didn't see his smile. *Did ours do that before, too? I don't remember.*

James waited outside. He walked over to the side of the main house and looked at the lake behind it. It was windy and the water looked grey and cold. Small waves lapped at the beach and a boat was bobbing up and down. James took a deep breath to calm himself as he tried to think of what to say. He had several conversations in his head on the ride over but now he couldn't form a single thought.

He heard steps on the gravel and as he turned he saw Dawson hurry toward him after getting out of his carriage. His plantation was so large that he had a special driver whose only assignment was to drive him around the grounds.

He looked determined, bending forward slightly in the wind. He held up his hand to stop him when James began to walk toward him.

James realized that he wouldn't be invited inside. They'd remain outside by the cold lake. His chest constricted.

Dawson touched James' shoulder; he didn't smile. His hand remained there as he gently pushed him toward the lake. It did not feel friendly.

"Let's talk down here for a while. I have something I'd like to speak to you about. I'm glad you came calling."

"I do too, actually," James said stiffly and hid both of his hands behind his back so that Dawson wouldn't see them shake.

"You do, do you? Well why don't you begin then," Dawson said harshly. It sent chills down James' back. No wonder his negroes were afraid of him.

"Well, I would like to know why you held my Pap for several hours questioning him about me. Really, Mr. Dawson, kindly explain your purpose. Katherine was hysterical with worry. She still has almost a month left, I was afraid her time would come early."

"Are you sure there is a month left? Maybe the baby ain't yours? Could be Pap's if she is so hysterical. The way you run your plantation I'd not be surprised."

James cocked his head to the side. He *must* have misheard him. Did he really say what he thought he said? He heard a faint ringing in his ears.

"Excuse me?"

"You heard me. We all know that something ain't right over at the Waynewright plantation. Mr. Wilson was here last night informin' me about a couple of things. For one, he caught you lying to the Sheriff about your nigger's brother. Only your nigger told me himself he'd been visitin' a friend, apparently your wife had said he was sick. If you don't know where he was and your wife's tale is different from yours, it's not hard to draw the conclusion that your wife and your nigger are a couple of perverts."

James was utterly dumbfounded. He stared at him with his mouth open, wondering if he was actually dreaming still. In none of his imagined conversations had he even remotely come close to this.

"Is this some kind of sick, twisted joke?"

"It certainly is *not*," Dawson answered curtly.

James laughed, it sounded shrill in his ears, but he couldn't control it.

"Pap is close to sixty years old and a *negro*. Katherine is twenty-two. I don't think you need to worry about anything in that department, Dawson. I know where my wife is at night." He laughed again, "I... well Dawson, I don't quite know what to say. This accusation is so ridiculous that it barely deserves to be dignified with a response." He shook his head trying to focus on what it was he was going to say.

"If we could go back to the real matter at hand, instead, why did you question Pap without my permission? Having to leave my wife in the hands of a neighbor at a time like this, and then spend time pickin' him up from jail? Really, Mr. Dawson, don't you think you are overreacting just a little, and overreaching, too? Pap told me everything. How you think that there is something fishy about how I run things. So why don't you clear that up, with me, instead of with one of my niggers," James' voice was steady, more confident, fueled by his anger.

Dawson looked taken aback, but it lasted for only a fraction of a second.

"Well, I tell ya James. There have been rumors goin' 'round in town for a long time, your father being so soft and you spendin' time in New York with these abolitionist sympathizers. Then seeing your wife and you fraternizing with your negroes on the porch, and your *wife* servin' wine." He paused as if he had to swallow the distaste that was spewing out of his mouth.

"No matter what you told the Sheriff about your father's will, settin' young bucks and fertile females free like that, well it's more than a bit unusual, to say the least. Quite honestly, I don't believe that your father wrote that will. I think that you have been influenced by northern bullshit."

The ringing echoed in James ears again and he clenched his teeth, heard and felt the crunching in the same tooth as before.

"Enough, enough with your bloody insults; how dare you!" James almost lost his breath as he had screamed without realizing it.

"This is bloody unbelievable, really, but I'll tell you, because apparently you have a wild imagination. I don't know what hurts me more, that you have perverse thoughts about my wife, or that you disrespect my father's memory like this, my father that was your best friend since you were both children. Did you really think that my father planned to die when he was so young? Did it cross your mind that when he was an old man his favorites wouldn't be so damn young anymore?"

There was a slight crack in Dawson's angry mask, just long enough for James to have the strength to go on.

"I'll tell you, yes, I *did* learn a couple of things in the North, you *are* right about that. Seein' my father in-law's paid servants made me realize that a carrot can go a long way. I have made many improvements to my plantation. For one thing, I have given each negro more land and more seed for planting… I have added improvements to their cabins. I have given more benefits at the end of the year, more clothes, utensils and the like." *And share cropping, if you only knew, idiot.* "As a result of this, Dawson, I have a very good crop, my negroes are happy and work hard. Yeah I did learn a lot up North. The negroes that I freed, well Dawson, I don't question my father. I'm sorry that you see the need to, but if my father wanted them free, I'm sure he had a reason for it and that reason is none of your god damned business."

James stopped and took a deep breath, and then he looked Dawson right in the eye,

"How DARE you insult my *wife*, you son of a bitch!"

He didn't wait for a reply. He turned around, leaving Dawson where he stood and hurried up the hill, whistling for Isaac to bring his horse.

The wind brought tears of anger to his eyes.

Chapter 14

James went straight into his office when he got home. He didn't see anyone downstairs, and hurried through the rooms before he could be spotted.

He poured himself a scotch. His hands were shaking so badly that he spilled some on the ivory surface. He ignored the small golden puddle and brought the bottle with him as he sat down behind his desk. His heart was beating fast and irregularly. He swallowed the contents of his glass and immediately poured a second glass.

Finally, after finishing almost half of the second glass, he was able to relax and focus his thoughts. After a while he began to think that that Dawson probably had nothing on him at all. If he had, he would have provided some of the facts, such as him hiding fugitives, instead of coming with ridiculous notions of his wife and Pap having an improper relationship. Though Dawson did voice some suspicion over James being influenced by the North, he obviously had nothing concrete. James took a deep breath, feeling a little calmer. He let his eyes gaze out the window. Without him noticing, it had become dark and he couldn't see much out there, not inside either come to think of it. He pulled out a match and lit the lamp on his desk, having to squint for a moment as his eyes adjusted to the sudden warm light.

Once adjusted, he noticed two letters on his desk. One was from one of his merchants in New York, and another from Katherine's uncle. James raised an eyebrow. *Why would he be writing to me?* He wondered.

As he slid open the envelope he found a small note that read:

> ***With the political climate and your location we thought it safer if I addressed the envelope, this is actually from Will.***
>
> ***Sincerely, Peter Greenfield***

James drew a breath and took another sip of the scotch. He felt slightly inebriated and laughed out loud.

Dear Mr. Waynewright,

I got so much to tell you that I don't know where to start.

Peter have been incrediblle. I live in a room in his apartment but I suit myself and do whatever I want. I even have my own key!

I work in the workshop every day escept Saturday afternoon and Sunday unless we have customers then I might work on those days too.

Peter treat me like an equal tbat took some getteeing used to.

It was very overwalming when I first came here. I was shy and scaired of all the noise and so many white people when I walked alone, but they don't pay me no mind. No one ask me who I belong to or how I could be walking by myself. Funny houw quick a person get used to things, cause now I walk around never thinkin' about it.

I have been reading and writing more. Practicing a bit each evening.

Here James paused, remembering Katherine's insistence that they could read already but weren't telling them. She had been right. If it hadn't been clear before, it was very clear now as evidenced by this letter. There were spelling mistakes, but that was certainly expected of someone who didn't have formal schooling.

Peter and I have been goin to listen to speeches, and yesteday we met Fredrick Douglass. He is an incredible man, grew up a slave hisself! He was not well treated at all, even whipped on a daily basis by a man known for braeking us negroes.

Now he is free, has traveleed the whole country talkin bout his experiences and has even written a book.

Well, I could go on for a long time, but I will end it for now. Please tell my dear Mama and Mary that I love them.

Almost forgot, Hettie is doen very well, she has taken emploimen as a housekeeper for a family on Long Island. We are sad we ainn't together but Peter nos this family and said she would be happy there with good people. They are involved with abolition and she will be joining their childrens lessons.

Sincerely Will

James cleared his throat as he put the letter down on the desk. So very much had changed, only a few years ago his father had owned Will, then *he* had owned him and now he was reading his letter. James swallowed hard. His world had been turned upside down more than once.

James wished that Will was still here, he missed him. He would have confided in him now, not needing to heed his mother's advice of not doing that too much.

James picked up his glass of scotch. It was late. He needed to find Katherine and tell her that she had been right about Dawson's jealousy. He would simply have to wait to tell her everything until after the birth, or maybe not tell her that part at all.

Chapter 15

With the help of Auntie Ellen, who had helped James' mother and numerous other women on the plantation, their twins were born on a cold and windy afternoon. It was November 26, 1859, one little boy and one little girl, so tiny and pink. They named them Wilbur and Elisabeth after James' parents.

They were not invited to the Winter Ball this year. They told themselves that it was to be expected since they had newborn twins and had a wonderful dinner with the Peterssons and their workers instead.

Visits had been curiously absent even after the birth of their children. Not a card had they received, not a single gift from anyone of their neighbors except for Oskar and Ebba.

James felt as if danger was silently waiting outside the door, waiting to pounce. He couldn't say anything, couldn't do anything. Instead, he tiptoed around his little newborn babies and his beautiful wife.

The political climate in the country was brewing to the point of boiling over. There was even some talk of secession if the southern states couldn't keep their slaves. The secret debates that had only seemed present in James and Katherine's life in New York were now debated everywhere, in the saloons and in the newspapers all over the country. James had overheard many a conversation when he had errands in town.

Katherine was horrified at the thought of being separated from her own family by a border and if they hadn't had four month old twins, she surely would have asked him to go back up north.

One name that kept appearing in the paper and on peoples' lips was Lincoln, Abraham Lincoln, a very tall and scrawny sort of a fellow with a deeply lined face. Katherine thought him downright ugly when she saw a likeness of him in the paper.

One afternoon in March, James and Katherine sat by the fire with the babies sleeping soundly beside them in their wicker basinets. James read aloud that Lincoln believed not only in hard work, but that *all*, including black men, should have the opportunity to work hard to better themselves. He grabbed Katherine's hand and continued; 'When one starts poor, as most do in the race of life, free society is such that he knows that he can better his own condition; for he knows that there is no fixed condition of labor, for his whole life. I am not ashamed to confess that twenty-five years ago I was a hired laborer, mauling rails, at work on a flat boat—just what might happen to any poor man's son! I want every man to have the chance—and I believe a black man is entitled to it—in which he can better his condition. When he may look forward and hope to be a hired laborer this year and the next, work for himself afterward, and finally to hire men to work for him! That is the true system.'

Katherine let go of his hand and turned so she could look at him. "Who *is* this man? It's not the first time we have read of him," she said.

"No, it's not, Katherine. There is a rumor that he might even run for president, and he is Republican and is staunchly against slavery." James smiled as if to himself and said, "There are those who are sayin' that they belittle our own bondage down here but fail to see the white slavery in the factories up in the North East. People work fourteen hours a day and their employers don't have a personal investment in them as we have here. It *is* a worthy argument."

Katherine hesitated before answering, "Yes, it *is*, but only until you start to truly look at it, and only if you compare it to slave owners who *do* take real care of their people, such as your parents. Even then, the difference is that no matter how good someone is to you and even if you have all your needs taken care of, if you cannot leave when you want, a cage is still a cage even if it's made of gold."

"Indeed, I didn't say I agreed, just that it is debated."

Katherine leaned into James and rested her head on his shoulder, "As strange as it may sound, I feel relieved that we are estranged from our neighbors with all this going on."

"It's crossed my mind, too. Can you imagine what Dawson is saying if he is readin' this?"

Katherine shook her head and looked to Wilbur who scrunched his little face in his sleep as if he was about to cry. She picked him up and held him against her chest, glancing at Elisabeth who was still sleeping peacefully. "What do you think will happen if he runs for President?"

James opened his mouth to speak, but closed it again and just shrugged.

Then there was a loud knock from the door clapper.

James' first thought was that Mary had decided to come for a visit. Just yesterday, he and Mary had had a conversation about the door clapper. She told him that it was one of those things of prestige that she and her friends sometimes used to fantasize about, one of those little things that only white people had the privilege of owning or using when they went visiting. James had laughed and told her about Dr. McCune Smith and that he was sure that he owned one. He also invited her to use it whenever she wanted to as long as she knew that they were home alone.

"It's just Mary, I'll get it," he said and winked.

"Mary?" Katherine looked surprised. She carefully stood up, still holding Wilbur and followed James.

It wasn't Mary. Instead, they found Oskar, Ebba, and a man whom they had never seen before. He had dark eyes and rather prominent eyebrows that moved upward when he smiled at them.

"Sorry to come unannounced like this, but this man here is one I knew you would be delighted to meet," Oskar said with a conspiratorial look in his eyes. "This is Minister Conway, a fellow Virginian. He is visiting us all the way from Cincinnati where he resides now." With a gentle gesture he looked to James and Katherine. "Mrs. and Mr. Waynewright."

"Do come in, please." James stood aside but Ebba blocked the way and started cooing at Wilbur. "Oh dear, what a darlin'. My you have grown since last time! And your little chubby cheeks...ohh, where is your brother?" she squealed getting real close.

Katherine moved backwards, pulling Ebba with her so that everyone else would be able to pass through the door. "This is Wilbur, Elisabeth is still sleeping."

"Oh darlin', I'm sorry, " Ebba cooed,. "May I?" she said and held out her arms so Katherine could give her the baby.

Minister Conway chuckled, "Moncure Conway is my name. I'm delighted to make your acquaintance Mrs. Waynewright and the little man, how old can he be?"

"Four months," Katherine beamed as they made their way into the small living room.

"There we have the beautiful sister sleepin' happily through this entire ruckus," Oskar said and sat himself down right next to the basinet and peered inside.

"I take it we are alone tonight?" Oskar asked just a moment after they all sat down.

"Indeed, just us," James said. He picked up his pipe and pointed to his father's box, "Please."

"Thank you, sir." Minister Conway gently touched the beautifully carved lid before he opened it. He had strong and well-manicured fingers, but he was not wearing cuff links James observed.

"Nicely done; the lions are done just right. Family crest I take it?" Minister Conway asked with his forefinger still on top of the raised crest in the middle of the lid.

"It is, yes. According to my father this crest was made *before* my Great Grandfather was knighted by George the II," James said sarcastically, getting an odd look from Ebba.

"James, that is *wonderful*. I didn't know your grandfather was a knight?"

"Well," James began, but paused for a second. "My father didn't believe it. Supposedly he had the King's orders to begin tobacco planting over here in the new world, but my father always thought he made it up," James said.

"You don't say!" Minister Conway said with a bemused smile. "Cedar isn't it? The carving is beautiful," he said. He traced his finger over the two lions standing on two legs guarding the family name with their paws. "Thank you. I'll be happy to have some of your tobacco, knowin' it has been grown by free negroes."

James and Katherine glanced at each other.

"Minister Conway here is of our convictions. You and he have much in common," Oskar said noticing their look.

"From what I've heard, we have somewhat of a similar background. I, too, grew up with servants...if you will," he said, hesitating at the word servants, "but I came to realize that it is immoral and inhumane. I used to be the pastor of First Unitarian Church of Washington, D.C., but my abolitionist ideas were not respected, you could say," he chuckled. "Well, well, one has to do what God tells one to do. I'm ministering in Cincinnati now, where I'm among those of us with the right compassions."

James listened interestedly as Minister Conway spoke, but remained cautious.

"Just as Pastor Beecher, a man with passions for what is true and right!" Katherine exclaimed and didn't notice James' cautionary glance in her direction.

"Indeed," Minister Conway said as he carefully stuffed his pipe with James' tobacco and leaned forward so that James could light it without further comment on Beecher.

"Ah very nice," he said and leaned back on the couch and puffed again.

Ebba, who had silently been snuggling little Wilbur on her lap, finally looked up. "Oskar and Minister Conway have known each other a long time. Oskar's barge took in water on the Rappahannock and he stayed with Minister Conway's family for two days when it was gettin' fixed. Had me worried sick before he was finally back home several days too late. That was the day they met and I guess you could say that we were lucky that he took in water that day."

"I remember it well. I was still living with my parents and our servants then," Minister Conway nodded slowly, puffing pleasantly.

James nodded too, but paused for a moment and discretely got Katherine's attention, "Will you get us some refreshments?" Turning to Minister Conway again he asked, "What brings you all the way over to our parts? Where on the river is your family home?"

"Falmouth. I'm not on friendly terms with family; my brothers and my father have very strong opinions, and let us just say that we do not agree on the issue of slavery."

James relaxed a little more and finally felt that he could say something, "It's not easy, that's for sure. I have had to keep my views secret in these parts. None of our neighbors know anything. They have made it very clear that they would not approve. It would not be safe for our workers or for my wife and children were we to be open about it. Not that I'm that surprised, them being planters and all, but somehow I had thought there would be room for *some* right to a different opinion."

"That there ain't!" Oskar said, pressing his lips together and shaking his head.

"Things are changing, are they not? If Lincoln runs, then everything will be different," Minister Conway added seriously.

"I was just reading about this right before you came," James said and picked up the newspaper, he handed it to Oskar who reached out for it. "If he does, or even if someone else with similar convictions would come on stage, then it would sure be another world."

Minister Conway nodded. "My congregation is hearing all kinds of rumors; there is talk of splitting our great nation in two."

"People are speaking of it, but I wonder if it would really come to that?" James said, chewing on his pipe stem.

"We will see what will come of all this, but as a man of an older generation than you two, I see real change a comin, real change indeed. We used to feel completely alone in our anti-slavery convictions, Ebba and I. It wasn't easy," Oskar said looking thoughtful as he remembered the past.

"Well, as did I. As an illustration, I didn't have the courage to write about it to Oskar for years," Minister Conway said, "we both avoided the subject in our letters until we met in Richmond one year and overheard a conversation by some very loud Democrats and then none of us could keep it to ourselves anymore. You can imagine our relief when we realized that we both felt exactly the same!"

James laughed, "Surely must have been a relief. I daresay that both the Peterssons and us had a similar experience."

Ebba turned to Katherine when she reappeared with a tray of tea and biscuits.

"Did Ellen and Mary go home already?"

"Yes, they have Sunday off. There is no need for them. We are fine alone. Lucy helps on Sundays sometimes, but she has not been needed today," Katherine said.

"I figured, but I would love for Minister Conway to meet Ellen and Mary. Do you think they'd want to join us?"

James caught Katherine's eye as he listened, and Oskar seeing their hesitation shook his head, "There is no reason to hide anything here. Moncure has known about our involvement since that conversation in Richmond so long ago. In fact, he has been sendin' us funds from his church in Cincinnati. He knows about Ellen, though he has never met her. I apologize, James. I should have mentioned my friend here earlier, but he came calling to surprise me and, well, I didn't think of it. I don't mean to put you in an uncomfortable situation."

James hesitated for just a moment longer and then he nodded, "No harm done. It's nice to meet someone who is in agreement and if things change, then we will need each other."

James went to the room adjoining the living room, opened the porch door, and slammed it three times. He waited a few minutes and then there was the sound of an owl hooting.

When he got back to the living room Katherine was serving tea.

Ebba suddenly got up and carefully grabbed the kettle from Katherine. "Dear, I ought to be ashamed of myself. Please sit and rest. I could have gotten the tea ready. You a new mother with two babies, you should rest yourself."

Katherine smiled,"No need, I'm fine. It's nice to move about. I..."

"Nonsense," Ebba said and continued to pour.

Only a few minutes later Auntie Ellen and Mary appeared.

They both looked bewildered when they found Minister Conway sitting there but Minister Conway immediately stood up and went to greet them, "Very nice to meet you Mrs., Miss? ... I'm Minister Conway, Moncure Conway. I'm delighted to meet you."

He is addressing her as Mrs. I should do that, too. She IS a widow. I have never done that. James thought and caught Katherine's eye. She looked as if she had thought the same thing.

Auntie Ellen looked delighted as they shook hands. "Ellen will do jus' fine, Minister Conway. This is my daughter, Miss Mary." At that she looked happily at James. He smiled, feeling embarrassed.

"You sit," Ebba said and disappeared to the kitchen to get more teacups.

Minister Conway smiled widely exposing a row of crooked teeth. "I see I have indeed arrived among friends, us seated together like this."

"Minister Conway is a Pastor of a Unitarian Church in Cincinnati," Katherine informed them.

"So I take it that Minister Conway ain't the one who need our help getting' North today?"

James almost laughed before he understood that she was serious.

"Oh, I do apologize, No, Auntie Ellen, he simply wanted to meet you. I wasn't thinkin' when I used our signal. Minister Conway is close to Oskar and Ebba and has been outspoken against slavery for years."

"Yes, he already knew about you and your brave work and he wanted to get to meet you," Ebba added.

Auntie Ellen smiled shyly but didn't say anything and neither did Mary.

James realized that the curtains were open and got up to pull them. It looked still and quiet out there, the sky darkening as the sun was going down. He turned to his guests and smiled apologetically, "Not that anyone comes here anymore, but as a precaution, it's better that we ain't seen together like this."

"Such are the times, such are the times," Minister Conway said.

Auntie Ellen, who was sitting with her hands clasped together in her lap, immediately unclasped them and made a motion to get up when Ebba came back with another tray. Her hands were so large and calloused and the fingertips were flattened. James felt a wave of tenderness and gently touched her arm, "Please, Auntie Ellen, you just sit back and rest."

"Indeed, you don't do a thing. You work hard enough, Ellen, no need to get up," Ebba said as she placed cups and saucers in front of her and Mary.

"Ain't no trouble workin' for my family," Auntie Ellen said. Mary's eyes were filling with tears.

"Mary? Are you unwell?" James said when Katherine handed Mary a handkerchief.

"Just happy, Mr. Waynewright, just happy that we're all together like this."

James felt foolish.

"That reminds me," Katherine said, "James will you go get the letters from Will?"

Auntie Ellen's face lit up, "Ah, there are letters?"

"One from Hettie and two from Will, I apologize, Minister Conway. I don't mean to distract from our conversation by personal matters, it's just that I thought of it now."

"Of course not, I'm happy to see that you are both readers. Unfortunately this important skill is so often denied to you."

"Indeed it is," Auntie Ellen answered as she took the letters from James. She put both of them in her pocket.

Silence filled the room as they sipped tea and ate their biscuits. Wilbur had fallen back to sleep and Elisabeth was still sleeping soundly. James looked at Katherine, wishing he could reach out across the table to grasp her hand.

Then there was a loud knock at the front door.

This time James had no illusions of their friends trying out the door clapper. He swallowed hard and hissed, "Auntie Ellen, go open the door. Mary go upstairs and start dusting."

Mary rose silently without hesitation.

Another loud knock and then James heard Mr. Wilson's voice in the hallway.

"Get Mr. Waynewright!"

"Certainly, Massa Wilson, just a moment," they heard Auntie Ellen reply cheerfully, not even a hint of fear in her voice.

Mr. Wilson didn't wait for her to get James. He followed her and found them sitting down with their tea. He nodded as he took in the scene.

"Please Mrs. Waynewright, don't get up. The babies look..."

At first James thought that Mr. Wilson became silent because he realized that their little ones were sleeping and maybe he did at first, but then he froze and stared at Minister Conway as if he had seen a ghost. He looked surprised and confused.

Auntie Ellen cleared her throat, "Massa, do you need anythin' else, more tea?"

"Certainly, Auntie Ellen."

Auntie Ellen leaned over the table to get the kettle.

Mr. Wilson eyes widened at the sight of Auntie Ellen's pocket where the edge of Will and Hettie's letters were visible.

James felt a dull pain in his tooth as he clenched his teeth, but turned to Mr. Wilson and said, "This is Minister Conway and you have already made the acquaintance of Mr. and Mrs. Petersson."

Mr. Wilson completely ignored Minister Conway's hand and instead sat down in the spot where Mary had sat just a moment before.

"Who else did I miss at this gatherin'?" he asked, his eyes like steel as he saw Mary and Auntie Ellen's half-full teacups.

Chapter 16

It felt as if time slowed down. James heard a ringing in his ears as he looked from one face to another. Katherine had become visibly pale and Ebba and Oskar had moved closer together.

He couldn't read the look in Minister Conway's face at first. It wasn't until later he realized that what he had seen there was a mix of guilt and regret.

Elisabeth let out a piercing howl and all at once time moved at normal speed again.

"Who else was here?" Mr. Wilson asked again.

"No one, those are our teacups. We left them there yesterday night and Mary forgot to get them this morning," Katherine said as she bent down to pick up Elisabeth, hiding her face in the basinet and didn't see what happened next.

James looked on in horror as Mr. Wilson leaned forward and touched the still warm teacups. The ringing in his ears become louder, a dull but steady tone as if someone had hit a cymbal.

James was at a loss for words and before anyone else got a chance, Mr. Wilson stood up.

"I came calling to let you know that there is a meetin' in town on Wednesday, but I see here that you are entertainin' abolitionists instead, so I gather you ain't interested in protecting us planters." The look of disdain was obvious.

"Abolitionist?" James tried numbly.

"Well, well," Minister Conway interjected with a much stronger and different voice than what he used earlier.

"I see that I have been found out here. I had preferred that my friend Oskar and his wife Ebba wouldn't find out, but I see that I might as well be honest now. I take it you have heard of me, heard why I had to leave my church in Washington, D.C. Perhaps also heard that I'm not following Jesus enough, but quote Emerson. Seen my photograph perhaps?"

"This is why you saw fit to have high tea at a plantation, is it?" Mr. Wilson said and glanced briefly at Minister Conway and then stared hard at James. "I knew it, *Mister* Waynewright. I could smell it. Something ain't right here, wasn't addin' up after the Brown raid. I could feel it. Dawson said so too, and you freein' young healthy bucks..." He shook his head again. "I'll see myself out."

No one said a word. James could feel his heart race and he forced himself not to clench his teeth, afraid it would hurt, as if a tooth was important in this situation.

Oskar was the first one to move, he went to the window, and peered out behind the curtain.

"I see him. He is off already, riding down your lane."

"See if he makes a right or a left," James said. His mouth was so dry that it came out as a whisper.

"He made a left."

"Then he is riding straight to Dawson!" Katherine almost screamed and sat down next to Ebba and began to cry with Elisabeth in her arms.

Auntie Ellen and Mary must have been listening from upstairs and came clambering down the stairs as fast as they could.

"Oh Lord, oh Lord," Mary cried wringing her hands. Auntie Ellen looked angry.

"I never liked that man. He act like he such a stand up man, treat his negroes fair, but underneath there's somethin' that he's hiding. He almost scarier that Dawson, I use to have a friend visit me from his plantation, she told me everything."

"Mama, please," Mary said and looked desperately at James who again was at a complete loss.

"I'm so very sorry, James and Katherine. It was inexcusable for us to come here unannounced like this," Oskar said, Minister Conway nodded in agreement.

"No, no one has visited us in months. It makes no difference, but that he could show up at the same time, it always seem to happen like that, doesn't it? It's like the devil is conspiring against us," Katherine said. "What is going to happen? What do you think they will do?"

"They can't do *anything*. They have no proof of anything one way or the other. Thank you, Minister Conway, for trying to rescue the situation with what you said," James said, but he didn't feel as confident as he made it sound. Rather his knees felt weak and he sat down next to Katherine, but she stood up as soon as he did.

"I have to go feed her, she is very hungry. Will you bring Wilbur to me when he wakes?" she asked, her eyes pleading with him to hide in their upper sanctum with their babies.

"Of course."

James waited until she had left with Elisabeth and then he looked at Oskar and almost whispered, "I have to go to that meetin' on Wednesday. If I don't, it will just confirm his suspicions about me."

"I think we should leave as soon as possible. We should all leave tonight, else they come and take us from you," Auntie Ellen said.

James swallowed and ignored her. He was thinking that he ought to hide their freedom papers. He had them signed and ready in the drawer in his office desk. It was locked, but could easily be opened. If he had freed them, he didn't actually own them anymore and having stayed in the state for so long without registering with the town clerk meant that they were basically free for the taking. He tried to calm himself down, hiding the fear that was threatening to overtake him completely.

"Mary, I'm not sure if that is the wisest choice right now, but a warning is probably in order. Please stay inside tonight," he said finally.

Uncharacteristically, Auntie Ellen let out a sob, and pleaded, "Mr. Waynewright, please can Pap, Mary and I sleep here tonight? I'm too scared sleepin' down in the quarters."

"Certainly, Auntie Ellen."

Oskar and Minister Conway looked at each other. "We ought to stay here as well, just to make sure you are safe," Oskar said.

James wanted to say yes, yes please stay. I cannot protect my family alone. But he swallowed hard and said,"No, it would just seem suspicious. It would be best if you leave. Minister Conway you ought not to stay with them tonight after your revelation. You must act as if you want nothin' to do with him, Oskar. I would not put it past Dawson and Wilson having spies out at night. Watch what you say to each other. You never know who might overhear it."

Oskar nodded reluctantly. "I will call on you tomorrow. Not sure how I feel 'bout you going to that meetin'. A man has the right of difference in opinion. It's your right, there is no crime in it."

"Not so sure, not so sure, my wife made the terrible mistake of hugging and kissing a young negro girl. My family still has not forgiven her and we are not on speaking terms. If they would suspect, your neighbors I mean, I wouldn't advise..." Minister Conway mumbled, speaking as if to himself.

"If I don't go, it's as if I'm hiding something." James wanted to speak about Dawson's outrageous comment about Pap and Katherine, but he didn't feel comfortable with Minister Conway there.

Oskar and Minister Conway rose at the same time.

"We ought to leave, the sooner the better, then you ought to leave, I suppose." Oskar looked insecure. "I hope it's safe, but I gather James is right."

They looked at each other and for a moment fear and panic threatened to take over but it subsided and Oskar, Ebba and Minister Conway quickly took their leave without saying so much as a word.

Auntie Ellen and Mary approached James nervously as soon as they left, saying that they changed their minds and thought it more important that they stay close to their friends in the quarters.

James picked up his son and walked up the stairs to join his wife.

Chapter 16.5

So many had never left at once, nor had anyone from their own plantation left. Not like this anyway.

Auntie Ellen looked into the eyes of her family and friends, squeezing each hand as they asked God to bless her and Pap, as well as Mr. and Mrs. Waynewright.

Then she handed out ten signed papers from Mr. Waynewright's desk drawer. Many years earlier, Old Massa Waynewright had lost his key in the tobacco fields. Auntie Ellen was the only one who saw it. She, having been a young woman then with three little babies, picked it up pretending that something was itchy and quickly hid it in her undergarments.

Yesterday she snuck into Mr. Waynewright's office to try it. It still fit. *That old Massa Waynewright must have had a spare,* she had thought to herself.

"You must walk in the cold stream, a long time, three, four hours. Just go, find your own way." She hesitated. She didn't know the route. Oskar and Ebba would have told her passenger where to go next, but she couldn't risk any spies on their farm. Wilson surely suspected them as well. "It ain't safe for Mr. and Mrs. Waynewright to know this. We must protect them. Should you get caught, don't show the papers unless you know is nobody from here that can get Mr. Waynewright in trouble. You gotta hide durin' the day the best you can. Run in the night. Put the horseradish and pepper pouches on your shoes, just keep them dry when you walk the streams, follow the drinkin' gourd to the North Star." Her voice broke but she continued, "Don't show no one the papers until you're far away, please."

Martha, Isum and little Eva, Jack and seven others looked back at her with tears in their eyes. Jack hugged her and Pap, then he took both their hands in his at the same time. "We will guard these papers with our life. We not betray Mr. Waynewright!" he said fiercely, locking eyes with Ellen for a split second before he turned to the others. They waved one last time and then they crept out in the night and disappeared.

"Follow the Drinking Gourd. For the old man is waiting to carry you to freedom. If you follow the Drinking Gourd. The River Bank…" Pap sang quietly and put his arm around Auntie Ellen's back as she whispered, "*Run!* Run where no whip shall ever touch you!"

Chapter 17

When James arrived, the meeting had been going on for a while. Not having known when it started since Wilson left without telling him, he had just assumed it would be at two as most town meetings were held at that time.

As it was, he opened the creaking door to the meetinghouse and found Dawson pausing in midsentence, frowning.

"As I was sayin'," he continued when James had found his seat in the empty row behind everyone else, "People are starting to question our way of life, the very basis for our livelihoods. We *NEED* to organize, we have to have a *Unified Front!"* he exclaimed, shaking his fist in the air for effect. "All this talk in the North, all these newspapers are speakin' of a change and of a hatred for us planters who provide our country men up there with *their sustenance*!" Again he shook his fist, getting a cheer and several fists in the air from the men listening.

James tried to concentrate on what he said, but he found himself looking at the backs of the heads of the men in front of him. They were all there, Mr. Wilson, Mr. Burnham, Peter Dawson, Mr. Pierpotter and some who he did not recognize. People must have traveled from everywhere to participate. Mr. Pierpotter hung on every word and nodded several times. Mr. Wilson was taking notes, writing furiously in a book that he had placed over his crossed knee.

James let his eyes wander around the room. On the wall to his right, he found several large paintings of negroes in harmonious scenes on their plantations. One showed a dance at a wedding with the Master and Mistress happily looking at the dancing couple. Another had a Mistress tending to a sickly child. As much as he tried he couldn't remember if these had been there the last time he was here. Right behind the podium someone had hung a handwritten sign with a quote from Ephesians 6:5 and this he knew had not hung there before.

Slaves, obey your earthly masters with deep respect and fear. Serve them sincerely as you would serve Christ, it said.

A little piece of the left corner suddenly started sagging as James was looking on. Little by little it slid down, right behind Dawson who didn't notice anything.

He kept talking about the northern propaganda and the importance of keeping their negroes ignorant so as not to have a rebellion on their hands.

Just then, the sign fell down, the right side snapped off the wall with sudden force and it sailed in the air for a short moment and then landed on Dawson's head.

A sound of surprise and embarrassment escaped from Dawson's lips.

James bit down hard to keep himself from laughing. There was a sharp pain as his sore tooth finally broke in half and blood filled his mouth.

For a moment James felt as though he was about to get sick, but he managed to keep his face still as he felt for his handkerchief in his pockets, then he discretely spit out his tooth. He didn't dare to look at it but sliding his tongue over the tooth he could feel the fracture and a deep cavity in the gum. His mouth steadily filled with blood and he had to spit again so that he wouldn't gag on it.

When James looked up again Dawson had made light of the situation and had rolled up the sign. He handed it to one of the men that James didn't recognize.

"I take it that it's time for me to stop talkin' now," Dawson said with a grin as he straightened himself up. He smoothed his hair, but it was still messy with a big strand sticking straight out on the side like an oddly shaped cow horn.

Mr. Wilson pretended to smooth his own hair as a way to bring it to Dawson's attention, but he didn't notice.

"Well, well," he said, his hair slowly losing the odd shape. "I will stop shortly. I just want to urge everyone here to stay unified and pray that that odd-looking radical Lincoln will not win the nomination. God help us all if he should run for president."

"Amen," was heard from every man in the room except from James who sat silently with his heart pounding as Dawson elegantly jumped off the podium and walked straight toward him. At the last minute he steered off and went in the direction of Mr. Wilson instead.

Mr. Pierpotter turned around in his seat and smiled at James.

"Hello there, Mr. Waynewright. Didn't see you until now. How are you faring? New father and all I assume now, from my last visit."

So Wilson hasn't informed you about our company the other night, James thought as he tried to smile. It felt odd as the inside of his cheek touched the broken tooth.

"I'm fine, my wife is doing wonderfully and our twins are thwinging."

"Excuse me?" Mr. Pierpotter looked at him oddly as he slurred, probably thinking that he was drunk.

James spit a little more in the handkerchief and was able to speak a little more clearly, "Forgive me, I have a broken tooth." He opened his mouth and pointed to it.

"Oh dear, you need that pulled, son."

"I know," James agreed as out of the corner of his eye he saw both Wilson and Dawson stop talking and turn towards them. They both looked angry.

James steeled himself as he expected them to come talk to him, but Wilson shook his head and took Dawson by the arm. Instead, they walked toward the back door with their heads bent together talking quietly amongst themselves. Passing them on the left, Dawson glanced at James with a raised eyebrow.

James swallowed and tried to suppress his fear as he pretended to listen to whatever it was that Mr. Pierpotter was still talking about, turning slightly in the direction of the backdoor he saw Dawson gesture to Mr. Burnham, urging him to follow them outside.

"What *are* your feelings on this situation Mr. Waynewright?" Mr. Pierpotter looked at him intently.

"I'm sorry, sir, could you please repeat that? I got distracted. I keep scraping my tongue on my tooth. Funny how such a little thing can irritate you so much, isn't it?" James said, trying to sound as normal as he could and doing his best to try to focus on Pierpotter instead of what Dawson and the others were most likely talking about outside.

"When did it break?"

"Just now durin' the meetin', it's been bothering me for a while but it chooses this fine moment to come apart."

"Oh, right now, no wonder. As I was saying, how do you feel about the Northern threat, if you can in fact call it that? The radicals up there certainly cannot number that many, can they? We provide so much for them, cotton, tobacco, sugar... they would be shootin' themselves in the foot if they continue with their propaganda and the South will have to secede, don't you think?"

"I'm not sure. It worries both Katherine, especially Katherine as her whole family is in New York, and me. It would be awful if..."

"That is right, you have family there. We have to pray for the best and stick together." With that, he abruptly stood up and began to pat down his pants as if they were dirty. "Sorry, James. I better get going." He was staring over James' head at something and James didn't need to turn his head to figure out that Dawson and Wilson were getting his attention. With a quick nod, Mr. Pierpotter left the hall.

James felt shaken and remained for a few minutes to collect himself. He was scared of leaving and facing the men outside. He was alone now. The only one left was a short and stocky negro who was sweeping the podium. James wondered if he had been listening in the background and would go home to his family and report back. Just as he thought that, he looked at him. They stared at each other and then he picked up his broom and left. James saw light fill the podium as a back door opened.

James froze. Was this a sign from God, or from the sweeper? Did he know who he was? He had never realized that there was a back door. If he snuck out that way he could leave unnoticed and wouldn't have to face Dawson and the others who surely waited to confront him. It might be the safest thing to do. He would end up just behind the trees and might possibly be able to signal to Pap to drive back around and meet him out of sight. He had left Pap in front of the post office a few paces away from everybody else and it may be possible that he could get away unnoticed.

James kept staring at the door as he stood up and felt his body prepare to move in that direction, but then at the last moment he realized that it would seem suspicious. He had come to this meeting for the sole purpose of seeming normal. Leaving surreptitiously would make the whole visit a waste of time.

He took a deep breath and silently asked God to protect him.

James had to squint as the afternoon light hit his face before he had a chance to put his hat back on, and at first he didn't see anything and walked straight into Dawson's crossed arms.

Mr. Wilson and Burnham were both standing wide legged right beside him.

"I hear you have had abolitionist visitors at your home. Care to explain that?" Dawson practically snarled at him and James felt spit hitting him in the face.

"Hasn't Mr. Wilson already done that?" he said coldly, hoping his voice was steady.

"He sure has, sayin' that you had him drinkin' tea and that two other men had been there drinkin' with you, but must have gotten nose of Wilson approaching and left in haste. Who were those men?"

James looked Dawson straight in the eye, "We had no men at our house. If you ask Mr. Wilson *again*, he can tell you that it *was he* who recognized who our guest was. I had no inklings of his political leanings. We were simply havin' tea with the Peterssons and Minister Conway. We were all in for quite the shock when Mr. Wilson informed us of this little curiosity. Mrs. Petersson is quite poorly because of it. She and her husband have known the minister for years, not knowin' anything about it. I'm sure you can imagine the shock. She is an old frail woman!"

Dawson didn't waver, just kept staring at him with cold eyes. They reminded James of that day when he had threatened Adam with the cigar cutter, but then he surprised James and suddenly waved his hand in the air and turned around right in front of him and walked away. James began to draw a long breath of relief when Mr. Wilson stepped closer, almost pushing him back into the door out of which he came. James clenched his jaw and flinched when the pain shot through his cheek again, as he did so his head involuntary turned to the right and James noticed that Mr. Pierpotter was walking straight to Pap, and Dawson was running to catch up.

This is practically an ambush. I should never have come here! That's why Dawson suddenly left. He wants to interrogate Pap!

"You seem nervous, son. I was hesitant to believe what Mr. Wilson and Mr. Dawson told me but now I have to say that you are certainly acting oddly," Mr. Burnham said.

At that James felt a surge of anger flooding his system.

"I'm tired of you old men acting like jealous toddlers. You should be ashamed of yourself. You all runnin' around checking on me, hopin' to see me fail since I'm so *young,* having to deal with my plantation all by myself, being so *young* and all. You're all jealous of our thriving tobacco crop. It's pathetic!" James was screaming now but he couldn't stop. "If you are so damn curious, for god's sake ask me what it is that I'm doin' to get such a good crop. Not one of you has visited us, not one of your wives has visited Katherine after our twins were born. She came here all alone from New York. The *only* people who have made her feel welcome are the Peterssons."

Mr. Burnham looked taken aback. "Son, there is no need to get one's self agitated, but there are a couple of things that ought to be cleared up. People are talkin', James. Mr. Dawson feels that your father would never have freed the young bucks you claim he had promised. You are having your boys run round in the middle of the night and your stories ain't matching up. We live in dangerous times," he said and glanced at Wilson, who with ice in his voice added, "Those tea cups your wife said had been left there since the night before still had hot tea in them. You are hidin' something and I don't believe you. I think you became abolitionist in New York."

James laughed nervously. "Don't be ridiculous, I own my own negroes."

"Only because you inherited them," Mr. Burnham said.

"YOU of all people do NOT have the right to speak of my parent's death!" James exclaimed without being able to hide the disgust in his voice. He pushed himself past them and hurried toward Pap. His blood was boiling and he thanked God that he didn't have his rifle with him, or he would probably have used it on Burnham at that moment.

The adrenalin was surging and he was too angry to fully comprehend that in all likelihood he and Katherine had been found out.

Pap looked scared when James approached. He was standing stiffly next to the carriage wriggling his hands together.

"I know nothin' of the sort, Massa Dawson. I ain't seen nothin' like that. Massa Waynewright is a fair Massa," he said, raising his eyes and looking pleadingly at James. Dawson and Pierpotter followed his gaze and stood quietly waiting until James had walked up.

"Seems your boy here is ignorant of what went on last night. I'm surprised that you freed one of them and then just sent him out in the night. Knowin' of your abolitionist leanings I'd think you'd put them in first class on the steamboat."

James stared at him and tried to process what he had said. His heart was thumping loudly, distracting him.

"You look surprised? You really should have put him on that boat, or at least given him a horse. As it is now, I'm happy to take him, since you don't want him!"

James glanced at Pap, but he was looking down into his hands, nervously moving from foot to foot.

"What the hell are you talking about, Dawson?" James said finally, ignoring his comment about him being an abolitionist.

Mr. Pierpotter suddenly left Dawson's side and came close to James. He was very tall and stared down at him. "Don't play stupid, Young Waynewright. We know what you are doin'. You might as well admit it now."

"Admit what?"

"Oh Jesus, James. For God's sake!" Dawson screamed so loud that the horse began to trample and Pap had to jump to get her bridle. The carriage made a squeaky sound as it was pulled forward with the brake on.

"We know that you freed Jack. I have your signed paper at home. It took a lot but I finally got Jack to tell me the truth."

In the split second before James answered he saw Pap's reaction, saw how all the blood drained from his face and saw him steady himself by grabbing Ballerina's neck.

James felt the same anger he had felt earlier begin to take hold of him and he took a step closer to Dawson forcing Pierpotter to move out of his way.

"What the *hell* are you talking about, Dawson. What have you done to Jack? Where is he?" Somewhere in the back of his mind James tried to grasp what Dawson meant by the freedom papers, but he couldn't focus on it.

There was a threatening feel to the air, as if they were surrounded by walls that kept closing in on them. Pap had jumped up on the seat with reins in hands ready to move, but James didn't dare to look at him to acknowledge it.

"Why would you care, James? You signed for his freedom. Like I said, if you don't want him, I'll take him, but from what he told me, you freed more than him last night."

"I have not freed anyone, what have you done with Jack? What gives you the right to mess with my property? It's not the first time, either," James said and gestured in Pap's direction. "What the hell is going on here? I'm tired of your perverse thought patterns and your meddling." He took another step closer to Dawson, so close that he could smell his sour breath and see the tiny hair sacks that were already darkening with stubble from this morning's shave.

"Perverse?" Pierpotter mumbled, but no one took notice.

"Where is Jack!?" James was so angry now that he pushed Dawson backwards and grabbed on to his collar. He fell back on the carriage leaning precariously and sliding down when Ballerina moved. James, still holding on to his collar, straightened him angrily almost shaking him. He was surprised by his own strength.

"Hey, Mr. Waynewright, calm down, calm down will you. Let Mr. Dawson go. Let's talk about this like men."

Mr. Pierpotter pushed himself between them and tried to loosen James' grip on Dawson. It was hard to discern what he was thinking; he looked bewildered, almost sad.

James took a deep breath and let go of his grip and spit a clump of saliva mixed with blood on the ground.

"You need to explain what it is you are accusing me of and what the hell you are doing with my property," James said and glanced at Pap who sat stock still on the driver's seat. Only his hands moved. They were shaking uncontrollably.

"Very well, I was ridin' around my grounds yesterday when I found your Jack wandering round the woods, or hoppin' I should say. He had broken his foot and seemed delirious from the pain. I hurried over to help, but instead of being grateful that there was someone there to take care of him he panicked and tried to run," Dawson paused and grinned, "well, it was certainly a funny sight to see him try."

"Jesus, Mr. Dawson. Why didn't you bring him home to me so we could call for the doctor?"

Dawson ignored James and looked to Pierpotter as if it was a funny story that the two of them shared.

"I caught him, of course. I always carry chains so as to be prepared should I come upon a runaway. I took him home and at first he insisted that he just felt like strollin' round at night and was on his way home. I was just about to believe him and send him on his way..."

"You were about to send him on his way with a broken foot?" James looked at him in disgust.

Again Dawson ignored him. "He acted oddly and suspiciously so I lashed him."

"You what?" James started towards him but was stopped by Pierpotter who put his hand on his chest.

"Well, it was lucky because he had something hidden on his person, a small pouch with ginger root, horseradish and pepper around his feet, to confuse the dogs apparently. Amazing what they get into their dumb heads. There was something else in that pouch too, James, an official document with *your* signature. Jack Waynewright a free man as of October *'58!* Needless to say, I lashed him a bit more. Amazing what a little abuse can get out of a nigger." Dawson was grinning with glee now.

"See, James, I *knew* it. I could tell that something weren't right. You have acted suspicious and pansy ever since you came back from New York."

James felt ice cold and strangely calm. "People say anything when they are tortured. You send Jack home to me immediately, or I will have the Sheriff arrest you for theft."

James took one step and was in the carriage. "Let's go!" he hissed.

"I can't steal something that no one owns. *People?* Jesus," Dawson muttered as they drove away.

Chapter 18

At first he only heard the rushing and crunching of the wheels on the road. He was surprised at his own calm and composure. It was almost as if he was relieved that he didn't have to pretend anymore, but then he was sick with worry for Jack and in the midst of his calmness almost nauseous at the thought of what had been done to him. He would have to file a report with the Sheriff and get a lawyer. It was the second time now that Dawson had been threatening his negroes. The first time he had hurt one of them, though.

He tried to figure out what Dawson had meant with the freedom papers. It didn't make sense. He had the papers locked up in his desk drawer. He fingered the key ring in his pants and felt for the key; it was still there.

The odd thing, though was that Dawson had the date correct. Had Jack falsified his signature?

Suddenly James became aware of another persistent sound; sniveling. Pap was crying.

"Pap, please stop the carriage. Talk to me."

Pap did so immediately and quickly looked around to see if they were alone on the road, then he steered Ballerina on to the side and over the grassy edge.

"Massa Waynewright, I'm so sorry. I'm so sorry we panic and now we put you in danger. I..." He stopped and to James' astonishment he jumped off the seat and prostrated himself on the ground next to the carriage. "Please Massa, please. We meant no harm, please we..."

James stared at him in bewilderment.

"Pap, what are you doin'? Get up. What are you doin'?"

Pap slowly pulled himself up and looked at James. Pieces of pine needle had stuck to his wrinkly brown check, glued there by his tears.

Again he looked around and then he gently took James' hands between his own. They felt cool and calloused against his skin.

"Dear, Mr. Waynewright, we, Ellen...she, Oh God I'm so sorry... I ain't..." His voice broke and he cried openly not trying to hold back.

James was too stunned to say anything.

"We panicked. Some of your people set off last night; they were too scared to stay on. We shouldn't have done it, but the papers... Oh God I'm so sorry we took the papers..."

James got a sinking feeling as his heart lurched in his chest.

"Pap, what are you talking about?"

"Ellen, she had a key... Isum and Martha they couldn't face trouble again, they jus' couldn't. They had to get out they were so sorry, but it was too much. They had been plannin' on leavin' soon anyway. Jack, his wife Karissa and some other followed..."

"Oh sweet, Jesus, Ebba and Oskar, did they?" James exclaimed without finishing his thought.

"No, Ellen didn't send them on that route, they're on their own. Jack must have decided to go back after hurtin' himself." Pap's tears were still falling down his cheeks as he told him everything.

"We have to get home to Katherine and my babies," James said hoarsely when Pap finished. "Then we will see what we should do."

They continued in silence. Fast. Ballerina's flanks were wet from sweat as they turned into the lane. The sun was lower in the sky and it was getting dark under the trees. As Ballerina trotted out from underneath the shadows, he could see a murder of crows lift suddenly from the large maple behind the house and scatter in panic across the sky. Something felt oddly warm in his chest.

Then he heard Katherine scream.

PART IV

Chapter 01

She heard the shot echo between the house and the barns, annoyed that someone would be hunting so close to the house waking the babies, just as she saw Pap and James arrive. She had been anxious to talk to them about how it went.

At first she thought James must have been leaning sideways to get a better view of her and she lifted her hand to wave at him, smiling at his antics.

Her smile faded as he kept sliding and fell headfirst straight down off the carriage.

She screamed.

She lifted her skirts and ran, pushing the glass door to the large living room so hard that it slammed into the wall and cracked. She didn't notice it.

Breathing heavily, she turned the knob and pushed on the front door. It didn't open. She pushed as hard as she could, frantically turning the doorknob in the other direction at the same time. Still it wouldn't budge. She forced herself to stop, pulled the door towards her instead and tried again. It didn't open. Tears of frustration and nightmarish panic were falling down her cheeks before she realized that it was locked and she only had to turn the key. The door opened easily now and she lifted her skirts and ran down the stairs. She heard herself breathing laboriously and heard the crunching of her boots on the ground. It felt like it had been hours since she first saw James fall, when in fact it had been less than a minute. Pap was just getting down from the driver's seat when she reached James.

He had fallen over on his side, his legs bent as if they thought he was still sitting. His shirt and jacket were red with blood that was dripping down and had already begun to pool on the ground.

There was so much blood!

She sank to her knees and shoved Pap aside without thinking, frantically grabbing James face and screaming into his staring eyes. She patted his cheeks and neck as blood started to bubble out of his mouth. It felt hot, burning her ice-cold hands.

"No, no, Nooo! This isn't real, Jaaames! James. " She kept hitting him in the face and on his chest as if she could wake him up. The blood splattered on her dress and on the carriage as she slapped him.

Pap sat still beside her, kneeling in the gravel, staring in front of him with unseeing eyes, almost as if he had been shot, too.

Then she saw Mary's round hand grab her wrist. "Katherine, sweetie..." Using her first name for the first time, Mary gently pulled Katherine to her feet. She wrapped her right arm around her waist and pulled her with her, "Come inside child, you come with me and set yourself down."

Katherine looked at her hoping that Mary would tell her that it was all a dream and that she was acting crazy, hoping she was hallucinating. Mary's eyes were full of tears. Her eyes looked unnaturally large and black, full of panic. Still she had the strength to take care of Katherine. Auntie Ellen, who had been upstairs minding the babies and hadn't noticed until now, rushed past them and flung herself into Pap's arms.

It would be days before Katherine thought to question what Pap said.

"It's our fault, the papers, we should never have gotten have papers."

Mary sat down next to Katherine on the chairs in the small dining room behind the kitchen. She held Katherine's hands in hers, gently caressing them with her thumbs.

They were both silent. All they heard was the clock ticking on the wall. Ticking even though time had stopped and nothing would ever be the same again.

Then Elisabeth and Wilbur began to cry upstairs. Without a word, Mary let go of Katherine's hands and rose to get them.

Katherine remained there, staring in front of her. She felt confused, she kept thinking of that day in the park when James first told her who he really was. She saw the fear in his eyes, remembered the feeling of his gloved hands around her own. Remembered how she ran from his side. It broke her heart. How could she have left him alone in the cold? How could she have run from him when he asked to kiss her? Now he was dead and she would never be able to undo it.

She must have cried out because suddenly both Auntie Ellen and Pap were by her side.

She collapsed into Auntie Ellen's arms.

Chapter 02

Two days later, Katherine woke when Ebba stroked her forehead.

"Katherine, dear, you must wake up now and start dealing with this. The Sheriff is here, and Jack...Jack is back, too. He isn't well, he may not survive, but he insists that he wants to talk to you before..." Her voice broke as she stifled a sob.

Katherine began to speak but her voice was too dry. Silently Ebba handed her a glass of water.

"Is James, is he dead?"

Ebba looked at her silently for a long moment and then she nodded,

"Yes, Katherine, he is. I'm so very sorry."

"He was murdered. I was waiting for him, standing by the window then someone just shot him. Who shot him, Ebba? He fell down, he..."

"I know I know my dear child. Mary has told me everythin'. I'm *so* very sorry. We're all grieving for him, he was a great man. The nicest young man I have ever met."

Katherine fell sobbing into her arms and as she leaned on her she noticed how full and painful her breasts were, so much so that they leaked on Ebba's skirts. Embarrassed, she sat up realizing that she had not fed her babies in a long time.

"Sorry, my...they must be hungry how long have I...?"

"It's all right, no need to worry. Ellen and I have been feedin' them watered down cow's milk. They were fine. They were hungrier, ate more often than usual, and had a bit of stomach trouble, but they will be happy to see you again. Why don't I go get them and tell the Sheriff that you will be down when the babies have finished?"

She nodded and waited quietly for Ebba to bring her children. Her children who were fatherless now, someone had killed their father, leaving her all alone. A few minutes later Auntie Ellen who brought them instead. She looked extremely distraught. Her eyes were red and swollen and her curly grey hair, which she always kept so neat in a tight bun, was unkempt.

She looked timidly at Katherine as if she was scared of looking at her. "Mrs. Waynewright, I wait out here in the upper parlor. You jus' call me when you're done and I'll take them so you can talk to the Sheriff."

Katherine didn't reply. She put both babies to her breasts at the same time. It was awkward but they were still small enough that she could do it by letting them rest on her arms and pillows on both side of her with their heads touching as they nursed. In the evenings when they were alone, James had used to love to watch them eat.

Had used to.

Auntie Ellen took the babies and Ebba helped Katherine down stairs. The Sheriff was waiting on the couch in the living room. Mary or Auntie Ellen had already covered the mirrors and the windows for mourning.

He stood up and nodded somberly, "My deepest condolences, Mrs. Waynewright."

"Thank you." It seemed unreal, as if she was playing a role. *How could this be happening?* She wondered. She hadn't been married long and she had two little babies. *My condolences?*

"Mrs. Waynewright, may I sit? I'm afraid that I must ask you a couple of questions."

She nodded numbly and sat down herself on the edge of the seat.

"Do you have any inklin' of who may have done this?"

"Yes, it's probably Dawson," she blurted out.

The sheriff gave her a shocked look, "Mr. Dawson? Surely he would not have shot your husband, Mrs. Waynewright. Are you saying it was a huntin' accident? Mr. Petersson said it happened right here in front. No one hunts so close to people's homes. Are you quite well?"

"It may have been Mr. Wilson. He is mad at us, as well. He didn't like our company the other day, but seeing him go straight in the direction of Mr. Dawson who is an evil and hateful man who...he...has hurt Jack, too. I'm not really sure. I..." She burst into tears as she remembered that Jack lay hurt somewhere and wanted to see her. The Sheriff was keeping her from him.

The Sheriff looked confused. "Mrs. Waynewright, please calm down. Who is Jack exactly?"

"He...he is one of our workers. He..."

"You have a white man working for you, an overseer?"

Out of the corner of her eye she saw Ebba hurry to her side. She gently squeezed her shoulder. "Mrs. Waynewright is still in shock as you can see, sir. She is talking about one of their negroes. Mr. Dawson found him on his property and *lashed* him to bits. I have never liked that man, Sheriff. He has always been cruel to his negroes, it ain't right. You should take care of those who can't fend for themselves, says so right in the Holy Word. Mr. Dawson is misusin' his responsibility."

The Sheriff scratched his head and looked at them both.

"I'm sorry, Mrs. Petersson, could you perhaps call your husband so he can help Mrs. Waynewright and explain what it is that is going on around here?"

"That may be a good idea, sir." Ebba turned around to Mary who was sitting on a chair in the hallway should they need anything. "Get my husband, Mary," she ordered. If it hadn't been for the circumstances, Mary would have smiled at Ebba's tone, so different from the friendliness it resonated with when they were alone.

Oskar sat down and looked gravely at the Sheriff just a moment later.

"Truth to be told, Mr. Dawson and the other planters round here have not been welcoming to Mr. Waynewright. He has been accusing Mrs. Waynewright and Pap of the vilest acts, among other things. Both Mr. and Mrs. Waynewright have been confiding in me that they feel uncomfortable around here, saying that Mr. Dawson and Mr. Wilson have been acting oddly and accusatory."

"You don't say?" the Sheriff said incredulously.

"Yes."

Oskar who had been discussing what to say with Auntie Ellen, Pap, Ebba and Mary, was well prepared. He explained everything, leaving out their involvement with the Anti Slavery Society and the railroad. Going with the story that James had learned a lot from the Northern custom of having Irish help at home that were paid, and because of this philosophy had given more incentive and more benefits, which had made the negroes work harder. He invited the Sheriff to take a walk and see for himself, telling him that Dawson especially had been jealous of their strong crop. He also gave an obfuscated version of their visit with Minister Conway, explaining that Mr. Wilson had misunderstood the situation, and went on to tell him how Pap had witnessed them acting threateningly to James a short while before he was shot.

The Sheriff sat silent for a long time after Oskar had finished, and when he finally spoke it was clear that he was uncomfortable.

"Hrmm, well I...I will have to speak with Mr. Dawson and Mr. Wilson, of course. I will speak with Pap too, but surely a negro will say anythin', especially if he is talkin' about someone who has just been lashing his friend. He isn't gonna to be able to be unbiased in a situation like that Mr. Petersson."

Katherine stared at him, feeling gall rise in her throat, "I can vouch for Pap speaking truthfully. The fact remains that Dawson has *no* right, *no* right to touch our property. Jack is *ours.* Mrs. Petersson is right, Mr. Dawson is a vile, vile man and I *know* he shot James. If not him personally, he had it done on his behalf."

"I highly doubt that, Mrs. Waynewright. Mr. Dawson has a high standing in our community and was a dear friend of your late father-in-law. There is no possibility that he would shoot someone who is like a son to him."

He stopped and looked sternly at her as if she was an insolent child. Then he took his hat and saw himself out, pausing briefly to look at Katherine with genuine pity and sorrow, "My sincerest condolences again, Mrs. Waynewright."

Ebba, Oskar and Mary looked at each other as he left. "There ain't nothin' a mere woman or a negro can do when a white man speaks," Mary said looking resigned.

Ebba acknowledged her with an exasperated nod and then took Katherine by the hand. "Dear, you need to speak with Jack, and I think it is time you hear the whole story. Pap will tell you."

Katherine would never forget it. Jack laid on his stomach with his broken back exposed. Henry shielded him with a blanket, but she still saw. He was ravaged by fever and could barely hold his head up when Katherine came to sit by him.

He grabbed her hand, and she could feel that it was burning.

"Who did this to you, Jack?" she asked but he just shook his head as if it was of no matter. "'I'm so sorry, Mrs. Waynewright, it's my fault. I should have burned the letter when I turned back, but my foot hurt so bad I forgot. Then he caught me, I tried to be quiet, I really tried but he...it hurt so bad and I couldn't. Then he done saw the paper and Mr. Waynewright' signature. He got SO angry he...you have to watch out Mrs. Waynewright, that's an evil man...he...please be careful, I didn't mean, I'm so sorry..."

She stroked his hand, but she was too grief stricken to speak. There was too much happening for her to absorb. Auntie Ellen and Pap had told her everything. Auntie Ellen could barely look at her, knowing that had she not stolen those papers James would probably still be alive and Jack would not be so hurt.

Katherine stared at him. What could she say to the poor man? It wasn't his fault, neither was it Auntie Ellen's. She had meant well, trying to protect the people whom she loved who were completely vulnerable and scared of losing control. Had she only asked them to help.

Henry who was sitting with Jack, looked at her and shook his head sadly.

"Did you tell him that James had freed you and that everyone who is living here does so of their own free will?"

Jack nodded, tears burning in his eyes. Katherine looked down into her lap and sat quietly before she answered. "You did nothing wrong; you told nothing but the truth."

Chapter 03

They had the funeral and buried James next to his parents.

The sun was shining from a bright blue sky and it was warm and balmy already even though it was still only the end of March. Katherine was too numb to feel anything. The Preacher was clearly uncomfortable. He must have heard about what the neighbors really suspected. For a man of God, he didn't seem overly concerned that one of his congregants had been murdered in cold blood.

The morning after the funeral, Ebba and Oskar sat down with Katherine in the small dining room. Oskar took her hand in his and said, "Katherine, we need to discuss your future. What are you plannin' to do?"

"What do you mean?" she said in such a low and weak voice that it was barely audible.

Oskar looked to his wife who swallowed hard but didn't say anything, and he continued,

"Katherine, you are a widow with two little babies, land and a tobacco plantation. Most of all, you have about sixty-four negroes left. Negroes whom your dead husband signed papers for, something I'm sure everybody in the community knows about now. Do you realize what this means?"

Katherine shook her head. She was too numb with grief to comprehend the complicated legacy that they had been left with because of James murder.

Ebba looked pained as her husband spoke and clasped her hands in her lap and said a silent prayer asking God to help Katherine stay safe through this terrible time.

"What it means is that your people have been free for over a year and stayin' in Virginia without registering with the Sheriff which means that they can become re-enslaved at any minute," Oskar said and cleared his throat. "A widow's word ain't nothin' against a man's signature."

"I don't understand, Oskar," Katherine whispered.

"What I'm saying is, that I think if Dawson or Wilson decided to come here and take your friends they could. You don't own them anymore since James freed them, and since they have not legally registered with the Sheriff they are free for the takin'. May not be entirely legal, or maybe it would be. I ain't too sure, but I sure don't want to bet on it. I think the safest and most sensible thing to do would be for you all to leave as soon as possible."

Katherine stared at Oskar as the gravity of the situation became clear.

"You are saying that we should send them on the railroad, all sixty-four of our friends? Sixty-four people cannot sneak away unnoticed in the middle of the night. That is an absurd notion."

Ebba sighed. "We don't know what the future holds, but people ain't thinkin' the same on slavery anymore. Things could change. If Virginia secedes, you would live all alone in a country different from your family, with hostile neighbors all around you."

"Do you really suggest that I leave our home with two little babies... and...James' resting place..." Katherine cried and was not able to finish her thought.

"Dawson had James killed already. The best thing in my opinion is to leave with everyone and then come back down when the negroes are all safe in the north. Come back with your father and a lawyer and sell the plantation, or possibly hire some young yeomen to work the tobacco and a trusted overseer that can protect your property and stay far away from these evil people down here!" Oskar abruptly got up and banged his fist on the table with such force that the vase with greens and early pink flowers that Ebba had brought for Katherine toppled over and all the water spilled on the floor. Ebba just sighed and patted Oskar's shoulder. "I'll go get a rag."

"I'm so tired, Oskar. I can't. I—" She began to sob. What Oskar was advising her to do was an insurmountable ordeal. How would they be able to do something like that? Not even Moses herself had ever taken so many people at once. There would be spies everywhere, to be sure. They would all be caught.

Oskar grabbed the vase and put the flowers back in place. The water was spilling over the table, dripping down over the edge and down on the floor. It reminded Katherine of James' blood. She stared at it for a minute and then she left the room. Unable to think clearly and reliving the moment when James lay bleeding on the ground, she went to the mantelpiece and began to pull on a brick that had come loose. Isum was supposed to restore it just a couple of days ago, but instead he had left in panic without saying goodbye.

Katherine felt something crack within her and she grabbed the brick with both hands pulling as a sound like that of a wounded animal escaped from her throat. She understood that the sound came from within her, but it scared her and she fell sobbing to her knees. The brick slipped out of the wall and fell in front of her. It crumbled as if it was made of sawdust.

Auntie Ellen, who had just come up to the house after spending all morning in her cabin with Mary wondering what they ought to do, found Katherine just as the brick came out.

Katherine felt her sit down next to her on the floor. She didn't touch her, just sat there quietly waiting. Glancing a little to the right without fully opening her eyes, she recognized Auntie Ellen's skinny knees and the striped blue and grey pinafore that she usually wore.

Katherine kept crying, listening to herself with mild surprise. She had never cried like this before about anything. It was as if there was something inside her that had to get out and she couldn't stop it; it just kept going on its own until she felt her throat swallow and it ended. She fully opened her eyes and looked at Auntie Ellen who was still sitting beside her on the floor but had shifted her weight so that she was leaning back on the wall next to the fireplace.

"Here," she said simply and handed Katherine a handkerchief from her own pocket.

It was threadbare and thin. An image of Auntie Ellen carefully washing and drying it on a little line over her sink in her cabin came before Katherine and then out of nowhere she saw Auntie Ellen sneak in to James' drawer and take the papers. Jack had had one of those in his pocket when Dawson found him. It was because of that paper that her husband was dead.

She pulled herself up from the floor and left Auntie Ellen sitting there. She dropped the handkerchief back in her lap.

"You come here now, come and sit in a comfortable place instead."

Katherine turned toward Ebba's voice and saw her and Oskar standing in the door. Ebba had both babies in her arms. Wilbur was sucking his thumb loudly and Elisabeth was looking around the room with wide eyes, as if she was looking at it for the first time.

"I can't believe I broke the fireplace," Katherine said and took Wilbur from Ebba. "Thank you for helping me and taking care of everything. I'm not myself."

"How could you be? You need not to thank us," Ebba said. Her eyes too were red from crying. Oskar nodded and stroked Katherine's cheek. "We are here for you. You and James are the only sane white people roun' here," he said before he realized his mistake.

"You...I'm sorry Katherine."

"I can't believe it, either. I have known James since he was a little babe. I helped 'im into the world, nursed him for almost two years. Never would I have thought that I'd see him with more blood on 'im than when he came into the world," Auntie Ellen said and took another handkerchief from her skirts and blew her nose.

Katherine swallowed her tears, took Elisabeth and walked in to the parlor to sit down.

She nursed Wilbur while Elisabeth lay next to her on the couch. She was feeling completely comfortable with Oskar in the room. It seemed ridiculous to hide away from an old man after James' murder, insignificant and ridiculous. Oskar paid the situation no mind.

Katherine was still too much in shock and too grief stricken to think clearly, but Oskar and Ebba felt as if the plantation was vibrating with urgency, a tangible threat that hung over them all. The significance of the fact that not a single person had called on Katherine after the gruesome death of her husband, not one of the wives came calling on her, a widow with infant twins, spoke loud and clear.

Oskar was nervous but determined to get everyone up north safely. How he would manage to get sixty-four negroes and a woman with infants up there safely he didn't know, but he knew he had to manage it somehow. There was no one he could trust. If only Minster Conway had stayed a couple of days longer he could have used his help and his contacts, but he had left at first light the next morning and must be safely back in Cincinnati by now. For a while Oskar had thought that they could sit tight and wait for letters to arrive to Katherine's family and to Minister Conway and other abolitionists. He could even write to Fredrick Douglass, or Thomas Garret, but he didn't trust the postal worker. The Sheriff, that rude bastard, had made it perfectly clear where the town and his people stood. They were hopelessly and helplessly alone.

"No we ain't!" Oskar said suddenly and rose from his chair startling Wilbur so that he let go of Katherine's nipple and began to wail.

"What?" Katherine asked as she put Wilbur on her shoulder to comfort and burp him. She patted Elisabeth's back where she lay next to her before she began to cry as well.

"We ain't alone. There are almost seventy of us. We simply need to get weapons, then we can leave. They can never overtake such a large group."

"What are you sayin', dear?" Ebba looked at her husband and pulled on his arm to get him to sit down again. Auntie Ellen blew her nose loudly before she sat down next to Katherine on the smaller of the two couches.

James and she had used to love to sit here together. How in the world could he be dead? Gone forever from her and her babies. She forced the thoughts away and focused on what Oskar was saying.

"I'm sayin' that we should walk, just go. If Tubman can, so can we. Do you know the way to the free community, Ellen? Do they have guns there? How many guns does James have, Katherine? Not only that, I've been ponderin' what to do about Jack, and I think the best way is to bring him to the free community. When we do, we can ask about weapons."

"You cannot be serious? We cannot all walk to New York. It would take weeks, or months, I have little babies to think of. Where would we sleep?"

Oskar remained silent for a minute, searching for words, "You are right, it would, but we may not need to walk to New York all at once. There are a couple of large Quaker communities a few days walk northeast of here. The church is right on the border of Maryland and Pennsylvania, if we could just get there. It's far enough from here, away from Old Woodbank and our surroundings. Then we could spread out, get help from others, people whom you might stay with until we can get a letter safely to your father. You, Ebba and the babies can take a carriage and meet us there with the signed emancipation papers from James. The rest of us will travel through the woods, stoppin' at the same station that we send our own travelers to." Oskar paused, sounding a little out of breath, but he smiled, looking relieved that he had thought of a viable plan.

"Negroes got to have a license... I mean free negroes got to have a license to be carryin' a weapon. Slaves can be killed on the spot if they carry 'em, Mr. Petersson," Auntie Ellen said quietly.

Oskar and Katherine looked at each other. "We'll have to hope that we never need to show anyone our rifles. Katherine, you never answered my question. How many does, I mean...*did* James have?"

"I'm not sure. I think there are four maybe, three carbines and a musket, in the cabinet in his office. I think that's what he had mentioned."

Katherine and Auntie Ellen stared at each other, their eyes locking with an expression of both disbelief and of determination.

"What will happen with the plantation if we leave it? All the animals, all our horses?"

"I have thought of this, Katherine. It's warm enough already that we can put them out in their pastures. It's risky, but we have no other choice."

"We could take the horses. If some ride it'll be faster," Ebba said.

"It be noisier too, though," Auntie Ellen filled in.

They went back and forth with the debate for hours. The only people who remembered to eat were the babies, but finally they figured it all out.

Pap and Oskar would ride with some people to the free community in the swamps. They would bring Jack. His fever was gone, and his back was slowly healing, as was his foot, Auntie Ellen had wrapped it the best she could. The community was secluded enough and from Pap's last visit they had learned that no one had found them or at least cared that they were there after the Harper's Ferry incident in spite of all the scouts scrutinizing the area. They would see if they might trade for some more ammunition and rifles there as Mary and Ellen cooked food that would be suitable to bring on a very long journey.

They would leave a carbine with Katherine and ask John and Carl to stay in the house and keep watch. An irony to all this was that the murders kept Wilson, Dawson, Pierpotter and the others from snooping around the plantation. Most likely they stayed put in their homes trying to act as "normal" as possible. Both John and Carl were strong, but didn't know how to shoot. No one did. Negroes were not allowed to hunt, even with their masters, and it would be too noisy to practice now. Oskar would show them how to aim, shoot and reload, and then they had to pray that they would actually hit the right place if they tried. Mostly they would pray that they didn't need to shoot at all.

The plantation turned into a place of chaos. Everyone was up and down between the quarters and the main house as they carefully planned their escape.

Katherine and Ebba would take a carriage ride ahead and try to find the Quakers. They would ride during the day, pray and hope that no one stopped them.

Then all the rest, Oskar and the sixty-two others would leave. They would leave in groups of ten, since they realized that the likelihood of a station having space to hide more than ten people at once would be small. It was their hope that the stations would be able to do so six times in quick succession, but that wasn't very likely. Nevertheless, maybe they could at least stop and ask for some food, and for directions onward.

Then there was the question of how to find their way if no one was home at the station after Peterssons', or if they didn't find it. Neither Auntie Ellen nor the Peterssons knew what lay beyond the station they sent people to. Auntie Ellen had known how to send people to the Peterssons' and they had known how to send people to a retired farrier named Bowen who lived by himself in the woods. His son worked in his shop in town now and lived in a little room on the second floor. Ironically, the shop was right next to the Sheriff's office. Oskar and Ebba didn't think that he knew what his father did out in the woods. He had never shown that he did in any way whatsoever when they had used his services.

They did not know who manned the stations before Auntie Ellen, or whom the farrier sent the runaways to. Oskar was hoping that the Quaker church on the border was the station after Bowen's, but he couldn't be sure. It may be further than he thought.

If not, they would be following the North Star and hope to see a house with a candle in the window, or a quilt on the line, trudging through the darkness hiding from white people, hiding from snakes, wolves, mountain lions...

Katherine felt numb with fear. Ebba had an old map and hoped that she would be able to find the way to the Quaker church, but she wasn't sure the place on the map was the right one. Katherine felt more and more reluctant. She didn't want to leave her people behind to get to safety first. Could she trudge through the woods with two four-month-old babies? It would obviously not be safe. James would have been adamantly against it.

Still she couldn't see herself leaving ahead of everyone else. Everything inside of her was telling her not to.

So she took a deep breath and went to speak to Ebba. She was sitting on the porch with a cup of coffee in her lap, looking straight at the spot where James had been shot.

Katherine went to stand in front of her so that she didn't need to see it and looked Ebba straight in the eye trying to convey a confidence that she didn't really have.

"Ebba, I'm not going to leave my friends. I won't do it."

Ebba stared at her for a moment and shook her head, "Katherine, that is foolish talk. You *have* to, dear. It's not safe any other way."

"No matter, I cannot leave them behind, I..." She stopped and took a deep breath and pulled the other rocking chair towards her so that she could sit in it with her back turned away from the memory.

"You ain't leaving anyone behind, they are going too," Ebba interrupted her. She looked annoyed, as if Katherine was a young child that had come and disturbed her when she was trying to have a moment to herself.

"I know, Ebba, I know. I can't explain it. I just can't leave them. I feel responsible. I...if I had not met James and influenced him so that he became abolitionist, everyone would be safe and alive. Yes, I know they'd be slaves but they would be with a nice master who would never...and he, he would be alive," she stifled a sob.

Ebba's eyebrows shot upward, making her forehead crease with wrinkles so thick you could have put a pencil inside one of them and it would have stayed there.

"You wish you never met your husband and had your children so that all of your friends would be slaves so that they would be safe? That you lived a nice sheltered life up in New York and shut your eyes and didn't see what's happenin' to your fellow human beings down here?"

She sounded angry and Katherine swallowed hard. "Well, I might not shut my eyes. I would still be against slavery, but..."

Ebba almost looked disgusted. "Don't dishonor your husband's memory in this way. He died a brave man, a true martyr for the cause. We need to honor that and his memory. Never regret anything, Katherine. It's better to die bravely than blind and indifferent to what's wrong."

She didn't know how to respond, but then she almost smiled. "So then how can you say that I should take the cowardly way out, if it is so important to be brave?"

Ebba looked at her and said simply, "Because you are grieving and you have two little babies. How can you walk through the woods with them both in your arms?"

"Because it's the right thing to do, Ebba, we made a vow when we set them free that if they didn't want to leave or couldn't, and if we would have to move we would all move together. You can ask Auntie Ellen and Mary. We made a vow, Ebba," she tried to explain it the best she could.

Ebba took a deep breath and pulled herself out of the chair, "I think it's a selfish thing to do, just to still your own conscience. James would want his children and wife to stay safe, no matter what."

"Riding out in the open isn't safe either. Dawson killed James in broad daylight, and the Sheriff won't lift a hand."

"Yes, but you are a woman with two little babies. Not even Dawson is that cruel."

Katherine looked at her for a long moment and then she nodded.

"I pray that you are right," she said. "We'll take the carriage with you."

Chapter 04

Katherine took Auntie Ellen's strong, skinny hands in hers, looking into her face, searching for something meaningful to say as they spoke their goodbyes.

Auntie Ellen swallowed hard and said, "I have ruined everythin', all this is my fault. Had I not taken the papers..., I'm the one who responsible for James' death," she said and bent her head as tears rolled down her face dripping on to her breast. Katherine felt her hands shake as she held them.

Katherine firmly shook her head, "No, Auntie Ellen. You did what you thought was the right thing to do in a panicked situation. You helped people move north, people who were already free. Those papers belonged to them, not to us. James always said that whoever was ready only needed to ask and they could leave. Dawson is the one whose fault this is. Not yours. Dawson is a murderer."

"But I should have asked, not just taken them."

Yes you should have, why didn't *you? Oh God why?* Katherine thought but said, "You were panicked, and so were Martha and Isum. They had been through enough." Auntie Ellen sobbed,. "Bless you for your kindness. I don't deserve it."

Katherine tried to reply, but she couldn't. She just squeezed her hands again and then she turned away and walked towards Ebba who was sitting in the carriage with the babies in her arms.

Katherine didn't look back. She sat next to Ebba, concentrating on Ballerina's strong muscles as she pulled them away from her home.

She was petrified and shook as if she was cold. The smallest sounds, a broken twig crunching under the wheels, or a bird escaping from a tree sent her heart racing in her throat.

It was still early and sunny and she had a perfect view of the road ahead. Two large horses pulling a load full of timber were ahead of them, but she couldn't see if it was someone she knew. Ebba kept a steady pace in spite of it, chewing on her lower lip as she looked straight ahead.

Wilbur squirmed on her shoulder trying to pull his arm free from the shawl that held him and his sister tied to their mother. He must have been feeling Katherine's nerves and he let out a wail.

She patted his back, but he kept crying, making Ballerina nervous. She too must feel that this wasn't an ordinary outing, her ears twitched and she fell out of pace, galloping to the side of the road. It was only a step or two, but enough to cause Katherine to lose her balance for a moment and Ebba had to grab her to steady her.

"Calm down, Katherine. You have to calm yourself. It's only a couple of hours and then we will stay at Bowen's for the night."

"Are you sure it's safe? Is he really one of us?"

Ebba patted her arm, "We have sent people to him for years. You have nothin' to worry 'bout," she whispered and grabbed the reins with both hands again.

Katherine remained quiet, holding her babies' backs firmly as they each leaned their soft, warm heads on her shoulders.

After a while she calmed down. They had left Old Woodbank behind them and were heading into the forest on a much narrower road. They had only seen four other people. A young couple in a rather fancy carriage driven by an elderly negro dressed in livery, and later, a man riding alone on his horse.

They wished them a nice day and didn't react to the fact that Ebba and Katherine were out there alone.

After a while, they had to stop so that Katherine could nurse. Ebba held Elisabeth as Katherine nursed and Ebba left the reins slack and allowed Ballerina to chew on some of the tall grasses on the side of the road.

Ebba smiled at Katherine and kissed Elisabeth on the head. "Everything is going according to plan. Do you see the small clearing there on the left," she said and pointed, "that is the road to Bowen."

Just then, they heard a scream from a hawk. It was loud and it startled Wilbur causing him to let go of her nipple with a cry. At the same time, Katherine saw it swoop down and immediately after it flapped its wings as it struggled upward with a large squirrel between its talons.

Then everything happened fast. Ballerina looked up at the sky with long pieces of grass in her mouth. She looked surprised and stood with her hoof lifted for a split second. Then she reared and bolted. Somehow, Ebba managed to hand Elisabeth to Katherine and in one sweeping movement, she got hold of the reins and pulled as hard as she could, but it was of no use. Ballerina galloped in full panic down the road as Katherine desperately held on to her babies, widening her legs to steady herself, leaning into the corner of the seat and the armrest to have some sort of support. It seemed like she ran a long time, but it couldn't have been more than a minute.

Ballerina stopped but her eyes were staring in panic and she began to walk backwards forcing the carriage sideways into the ditch at an odd angle. Katherine slid sideways towards Ebba as they lay leaning precariously with two wheels still above the edge.

Ebba quickly clambered over Katherine and pulled herself off the seat and onto the road. She took the babies from her and then Katherine managed to climb out as well. She would never remember how she did it, only that she stood on the road; her legs were shaking as Ballerina continued backwards, now with more ease since the carriage was empty. There was a loud crack as something in the carriage broke and then Ballerina slid into the ditch and landed on all fours albeit at an odd angle.

Ebba took one look around her and then bore her eyes in Katherine's, "You stay there, I'll get her up."

Ballerina looked at them and if a horse could feel embarrassed, she did, as well as defeated. She stayed calm as Ebba unbuckled her from the harness and was able to get her out of the ditch.

Ebba took a deep breath, "Are you all right? This could have been the end of all of us. Thank God you are still in one piece."

"Yes," Katherine was too stunned to say any more and just stood there numbly hugging her crying babies as tears flowed down her own cheeks.

"No matter, we ain't far now. We'll leave the carriage and walk. I'll grab the satchel."

With a quick look to the heavens, she let go of the Ballerina's bit, clambered down in the ditch and pulled the satchel out.

They left the carriage behind them, and walked, with Ballerina limping next to Ebba.

"It looks like you got your will after all, Katherine. You may have to walk the rest of the way with everyone else, unless Bowen's son is there with his horse."

"He doesn't have horses? But he is a farrier," Katherine said, knowing that she sounded completely distraught.

"Not anymore. He is too old to work now. He just has a small cottage and an old empty stable. He is a bit of an eccentric, paints mostly when he's not aiding runaways."

Mr. Bowen met them in the clearing as they came walking in, running toward them as if he was a young man when he saw Ballerina's limp.

"She ain't fit for anymore travelin'," he said immediately. "That's a severe sprain."

"I thought so," Ebba replied gravely as she caught Katherine's eye.

When they woke the next morning, they found that the first two groups had arrived safely, including Oskar. Seventeen people and one horse had quietly been shuffled into Bowen's empty and rather dilapidated stable.

The next night, Katherine and Ebba would walk with some of them. Farrier Bowen would keep Ballerina and treat her injury as well as fetching the carriage and repairing it.

Chapter 05

They set out as soon as it was dark. Katherine walked with horseradish, mint and gingerroot in pouches sewn on to the side of her shoes to confuse tracking dogs. She and Ebba walked with Pap, Auntie Ellen, Mary, Abraham, Fanny, Ned and Robert.

Auntie Ellen smeared soot from Bowen's hearth into hers and her babies' faces. Ebba's face was dark from the sun and wouldn't stand out as much in the darkness.

Katherine took one last look behind her before they slipped into the woods behind Bowen's cottage, wondering if she had tempted destiny too much by arguing that she wanted to walk like everyone else.

It was dark and moonless and she could barely make out the outline of the house and barns in the darkness. It was moist and cold; the air had a raw feel to it that had already crept into her skin in spite of several layers of skirts and sweaters. *Ideal weather for running*, Auntie Ellen had told her earlier. Had it been dry their footsteps would make more noise. Mary and Fanny carried her babies for her, both adamant that they should do it instead of her as they were used to much more physical activity. She would have enough just concentrating on walking and keeping up.

Their group left first, walking parallel to the same stream that flowed past their plantation, Peterssons' farm and Bowen's cottage. They walked east of it, away now from the plantations and into the forest. Katherine didn't understand how Pap and Robert could know the way, but they slowly and steadily moved forward without hesitation.

Katherine listened to every sound, every branch moving, and every rustling of the wind in the trees. She heard the calm strong breathing of her friends walking steadily behind and ahead of her. Her eyes slowly got used to the darkness and she saw shadows everywhere. She had to focus to keep the panic away.

They had only been walking for a little over two hours and she had already begun to regret her decision, thinking that had she not been so insistent a couple of days ago, Ebba might have suggested that she stay with Bowen.

She thought that she, Ebba and Oskar must be the only white people who had ever traveled the railroad. She worried about the other groups that were somewhere behind them, having left their plantation by now heading in their direction, and the last three groups that wouldn't leave until the next night. What if Dawson or the Sheriff went to check on their plantation? It had been a whole week since James died. It might be about time that they decide to check in on her or to come and take the friends from her. Tears began to fill her eyes as she thought about it and she began to pray, asking God to protect everyone and to carry them all to safety.

Praying occupied her mind so that she was lost in thought and she didn't notice that everyone had stopped until she walked right into Mary who had turned around and was waiting for her.

"You need to feed Elisabeth, she is beginnin' to stir," she whispered and gestured with her head toward a tree stump on the side. She must have been waiting for a good place to stop and had probably tried to distract Elisabeth until she found it.

Katherine nodded and helped Mary pull her out of the blanket and sat down. It was a hard and uneven seat, but it was as fine a place as any. Elisabeth began nursing hungrily, completely oblivious to her surroundings. *Thank God that they are still babies. How do people escape with whiny two year olds?* Katherine thought.

Mary silently handed her a flask of water and she drank thirstily. Nodding in thanks, she wondered if Mary was as scared as she was. She was leaving the only home she had ever known, venturing out into a world she knew nothing about. Katherine remembered the first couple of weeks after James and she had told them that they were free and she had showed her the globe. Even though Mary had dusted it weekly since she was ten years old, never having had the world explained to her, she thought it was just a ball with funny patterns and strange words on it. Having learned to read a bit in secret, the names of the places on it made no sense to her as they related to nothing in her life. It had never crossed her mind that it was actually the world on which she lived.

Katherine remembered her astonishment as she had tried to explain that they lived on a sphere and that the world was enormously large, so large that neither Old Woodbank, Richmond nor Charlottesville were deemed important enough to be written on it.

When Katherine showed her how far away Africa was, and how large the body of water that her ancestors had been forced to travel across, she had burst into tears.

Katherine wordlessly grabbed Mary's hand and squeezed it, suddenly overcome with emotion.

Mary thought it was because of exhaustion and whispered that they would find a place to hide soon. If they didn't, it meant that they would have to sleep somewhere in the woods in broad daylight with two babies who had been lulled to sleep in Fanny's and Mary's arms all night. Her babies would be awake for a good part of the day. Wilbur slept more than Elisabeth, but Elisabeth was often awake all morning and wouldn't sleep after the morning feeding, sometimes only taking a short nap after the midday feeding. Wilbur could sleep for four hours straight without a peep.

"What are we going to do? Elisabeth will be up all day," Katherine whispered as Fanny handed her Wilbur. Mary took Elisabeth and put her to her shoulder and she burped almost immediately. It sounded extremely loud to their ears as if it almost echoed through the woods. The three women looked at each other in fear but none of the others who silently waited among the trees around them noticed.

"We will have to take turns with sleepin' and entertainin' them. It'll be fine, by the time daybreak come, we'll be far away. No one knows we're gone, no one knows," Fanny repeated as if to convince herself.

Katherine nodded. She glanced around and saw only thick trees and swampy land. There could be snakes swimming around. She wondered if she should really lay down her head and sleep in a place like this during the day when the snakes were warm and active.

Half hour later they set off again. Now the path, if you could call it that, was more precarious. Wet branches and leaves scratched her face and Katherine was nervous that the black smudge would come off and make her white skin shine unnaturally in the dark. They had to walk over moss-clad logs, through icy water so deep that it reached to her knees. Then Pap suddenly made a sharp left turn, up ahead, and she could feel rather than hear several people around her take a sigh of relief. She didn't understand but she was too far away from anyone else to dare to raise her voice enough to ask.

Katherine began to feel extremely fatigued. Her feet hurt and there was something hard in her boot that irritated the skin on her heel, but she wouldn't stop. She had slowed everyone down enough by insisting on walking with them and by having to nurse.

Suddenly everyone stopped. There was a rather large body of water up ahead. At first she thought it was a lake, but in the darkness her eyes had played a trick on her. They were back by the stream now, only further north. That was why Pap had turned. Ned and Robert stood side by side by the water's edge ready to help everyone across it. Katherine felt her heart lurch in her chest as she wondered how cold and deep it was.

She would never forget the look in Ned's eyes as she took his warm hand and he walked her into the water. His eyes remained steadily in hers, a look of surprised astonishment and joy that the world had changed so much that he was on equal terms with his former mistress, a white woman who could have sold him at her whim; instead they journeyed together in the night. Then the reality of why they were out there came back. The reality that James had been murdered; that in other people's eyes they were still property like runaway cattle that needed to be herded in.

She concentrated on hoisting her skirts far enough up so that they didn't get wet and still being decent in front of everyone. It was quite hard as the water reached well beyond her knees. She could feel pieces of something hit her legs as it was floating along in the water. She didn't know if it was snakes, weeds or small branches that had fallen from the trees. She told herself that it was too early in the year for snakes. Prayed and willed it to be true.

Finally she was across and Ned nodded as she took the first step on the other bank, then he turned around to help Mary and Elisabeth.

They had just come halfway across when there was a loud crackling sound behind them, the sound of hooves trampling through branches, galloping through the woods.

Everyone froze. Mary pressed Elisabeth close to her chest and stood stock still in the water, locking eyes with Katherine. Ned was still holding Mary's hand and Robert instinctually pushed Ebba's face downward as he motioned for Katherine to do the same. She didn't realize why at first, but still bent her neck. She could see her skirts bellow slightly in the wind. Then she realized that the smear on her face must have come off and her white skin was too visible, Ebba's too. They had been wrong not to smear Ebba's as well. She was so used to the darkness now that she didn't think about how faces look in the dark. She remembered the first time she and James had helped a runaway, how they could barely see him as he approached their wagon in the dark, how ghostly white James' face had looked.

The trampling became louder and louder and soon it was right on top of them. Katherine wanted to swallow but she didn't dare make any sound at all as she pictured Dawson and his men on horses with guns aimed right at them. Her heart beat so hard in her chest that her pulse sounded like a drum in her ears. Then suddenly two large deer took the stream in one leap just a couple of feet away from them and continued running.

Katherine just caught Mary's broad smile of relief before she bent forward and retched right where she stood. She felt ashamed, but no one seemed to be upset. Ned gently put his hand on her shoulder.

She smiled gratefully but nodded and made a motion that she could go on. Pap waved them all forward as if nothing had happened. No one said a word.

They never made it to the Quaker church. The sky began to lighten and they had to find a safe resting place. Katherine had been scared of the dark since she was a little girl, and had never been able to even use the chamber pot under the bed in the dark without lighting the lamp. In the beginning of their marriage it had woken James up and he had wanted her to get used to going in the dark, but she never could.

Now as she saw the sky above her brighten, and as the trees became more visible in the dawn, the light scared her.

They began to look around themselves to find a place to hide. She had felt as if she walked in a closed space surrounded by trees and boulders on all sides, but it was a lot more open and airy than it had seemed in the dark.

They were standing at the rim of a small valley with pines, cedars and oaks fighting each other as their branches reached for the light in the sky.

They could see small light green buds just beginning to sprout. The evergreens had begun to grow shoots of soft light green needles and the ground was covered in a carpet of the brown pine needles that had been shed to make room for the new. It looked soft enough to sleep on, but the forest wasn't dense enough for them to hide in plain sight.

What if there was a game hunter about or worse, a bounty hunter? Katherine wondered silently.

Katherine had never been so tired, and she could have fallen asleep standing up leaning on a tree, but Pap led them further still. Slowly they crept along the rim, all eyes and all ears poised and ready to either flee or attack. Then by the grace of God himself, they were given a miracle.

Right in front of them, just slightly above the rim was a group of boulders, at least ten of them loosely standing together and creating spaces between them large enough for several people to hide. Ebba did a silent little dance with her hands in the air making everyone break out in broad smiles. They would have all laughed had they dared make a sound.

They crawled in, hiding tightly together in the middle so as not to be seen from the outside. They were not quite able to lie down but were comfortable enough if they leaned on each other. Katherine sat snug in between Ebba and Mary. Auntie Ellen who sat next to Mary reached across her legs for Katherine's hand and gently patted it. They had barely laid eyes on each other during the whole trek as Auntie Ellen had walked in the back. Katherine was ashamed to admit to herself that she had barely thought of her. She had been so occupied with herself and her babies that somehow she had forgotten her.

Now she silently looked into her face and strong brown eyes and felt in awe of the strength radiating from her. This skinny old woman who had helped so many people flee, who had loved James his whole life and was now comforting *her*.

Katherine smiled as tears fell from her eyes, blurring her vision. Just a moment later, she fell into an exhausted sleep.

Chapter 06

When she woke up the last time, after drowsily feeding her babies throughout the day, the sun was already low in the sky. Auntie Ellen lay curled on her side, pressed in between peoples legs like a little child. Her hands lay flat under her cheek for support. Katherine's eyes yet again filled with tears at the sight of her. She was so beautiful and old. Old women shouldn't have to sleep on rocks at night hiding from evil men that thought they had the right to own them just because of the color of their skin.

James died for her; he died protecting those he loved. He realized that the world is wrong. How can I live without you? How, James? Katherine thought, she couldn't control herself anymore and began to sob. She tried to do it quietly but the sobs forced themselves upon her.

Suddenly someone slapped her hard across the cheek. Stunned, Katherine stared into Mary's round face. She stared back at her and held a finger to her mouth.

"I'm so sorry, you are right, it's dangerous." Katherine whispered as low as she could but so that Mary could still hear it.

Mary's brow was furrowed but then her face broadened into a grin. Her eyes twinkled and she put her hand to her mouth.

"What?"

Mary kept shaking her head behind her palm and wouldn't answer.

Auntie Ellen had woken up and seen the whole thing. She sat up and shook her head at them. "She ain't never hit a white woman before," she whispered it, but Pap and Ned heard. Ned stared angrily at them and shook his finger.

Katherine felt an overwhelming urge to giggle but swallowed and forced it down, casting another glance at Mary. Their eyes locked in understanding before Katherine turned to Wilbur and Elisabeth who slept on the ground next to her. As she moved to get a better look, she felt how sore and stiff her body was. Her back felt rigid and achy and when she moved her foot she felt a sharp pain on the inside of her arch. When she leaned forward, the movement made her want to cry out in pain, but she stifled it and untied her boot and sock. She had a big water-filled blister right above the heel.

Her heart sank. How could she have been so stupid and not taken care of this yesterday? She had felt that there was something irritating her foot, but she had insisted on pushing on. Now she would have to pay the price. She reached for her bag and pulled out a piece of cloth and a bandage that she could wrap around it. It would be tight inside her footwear, but if she didn't do it the blister would burst and cause even more pain. She felt cold to the bone and restless. It would be a long while before the sun was down and they could go on. It could be one or two days walk until they found the church on the border. Oskar and Pap had looked at a map with Bowen who had explained how they would walk and what to look for. Pap said that he had a general idea. He was able to look at the moss on the trees, which way the foliage turned and by following the stars.

Katherine wondered how Ebba felt being separated from her husband who had come with the second group during the night and would have left a couple of hours after them.

She was sitting with her face to the evening sun now, eyes closed. Ned, Robert and Fanny sat sideways in front of her in another section within the boulders. Katherine could see Ned's muscular leg and Robert's shirtsleeve from where she sat. Everything was quiet. They heard birds chirp and trees moving in the wind, but no footsteps or sounds from horses moving.

Ebba caught her eye and cautiously crawled over on all fours.

She nodded and smiled at her, Auntie Ellen and Mary in greeting and then she motioned for them to put their heads together so that they would hear. Whispering low, but slow and clear she said, "We ought to be prepared for sounds as dusk comes. Lot a' animals come out at that time, they like to graze before they hide away for the night. We may hear sounds, but we have to be real still. There could be hunters out as well. We should eat now. We can't be making any noise later. Katherine, you should try to nurse when dusk comes so that they are busy suckling and won't cry."

"Good plan, that is sound. I go tell it to Pap," Auntie Ellen said but remained where she was, managing to get her point across through a series of signs and gestures.

Ebba had been right. Just as the sun began to go down, they heard rustling and trampling all around them. The birds, too, began to sing loudly and frantically. A mourning dove called hauntingly just as four deer walked past them. The last female stopped for a second and stared at them with her large moist eyes. Then she calmly continued on her way.

Elisabeth stirred and Katherine put her to her breast, wrapping a blanket over her, feeling conscious of being in a closed space with Robert, Ned and Abraham.

They waited until it was completely dark and then they carefully filed out of the rock formation and began walking. The blister made itself known but it was not too painful.

By now, the last group was probably beginning to leave the plantation. Katherine could picture them as they snuck out, hurrying up from their quarters, up through the tobacco fields and around the main house and behind the horse pastures. How did they feel leaving the place where they'd been enslaved their whole life?

Katherine wondered how it would be if she had been negro, not allowed to learn to read or study anything and looked down upon by all. Still, here they walked, each as vulnerable, taking the same risk, running from the same enemy.

They kept walking in silence. Ned and Robert holding the babies this time as Mary and Fanny had complained of aching backs and arms from last night's ordeal.

Elisabeth and Wilbur were completely comfortable in their strong muscular arms, although both Ned and Robert looked a little nervous. Ned was right in front of Katherine and she could see how tenderly he held little Wilbur's head so that he would be safe. He looked over his shoulder and back at Katherine and smiled; the same feeling that had passed between them as he helped her over the stream yesterday gleamed in his eye. Then he nodded and turned to look in front of him.

They had had to move a little more east to avoid an area full of uprooted trees and low but cumbersome underbrush. Here the path was relatively flat and easy to walk, and they moved quickly for several hours. She had a feeling that the group who had left two hours after them could not be that far behind since she had had to stop and nurse. She listened for them but didn't hear anything. She had just heard the whinnying of a horse and a dog bark in the distance. At first, the reality didn't register and she was surprised at a collective gasp of fear from everyone else. She walked straight into Ned as he had stopped to listen and she had to remain with her face in his coarse coat as she understood and heard it again, this time too scared to move. Closer this time, a distinct sound of hoofs beating rhythmically against uneven ground. Hearing it now, she realized that it was a much different sound than yesterday when they *thought* they had heard horses. This time it was unmistakably clear.

No one moved a muscle. Katherine moved her eyes to her right and her left but didn't dare to turn her head. She sensed Abraham and Pap slowly and quietly getting their guns out of their satchels.

Ned's coat scratched her cheek, but she remained where she was. She could hear him breathing fast, heard the softer calmer breathing of her son, and heard hoof beats come closer and closer. They were not as deep in the woods as they had been earlier, but were closer to an empty field on the right. There was a sliver of a moon that made it fairly visible. The sounds came from the left. If they ran out into the field to get away whoever was riding would see them immediately. If they continued straight on into the rather thick wood they would surely make too much noise.

The dog barked again, loudly; then there was a second bark different from the first one. There were two dogs out, possibly sniffing and tracking for them. Even though everyone's feet were covered in strong smelling herbs, surely after walking for three days they must be giving off a pungent smell that would easily be picked up by a dog. Did this mean that they had visited the plantation and found it abandoned? Or was it just a late hunter hurrying home with his dogs?

The tension was arresting and felt as one among them all.

Finally the horse was so close that they could hear its heavy breathing and the dogs pant. Katherine glanced to the right, looking out into the field just so that she didn't have to see what was coming for her. There was a cluster of bushes in the middle and something moved, maybe a deer awakened by the sound of dogs barking. Something suddenly flew out of the bushes. It was too dark to see what it was, but there was a movement and a loud thump as it fell down a couple of paces ahead of where she had seen the movement. Then it happened again, another movement and as a cloud steered clear of the moon she saw a large branch fly with force across the field and land with another thump, then a third time. They heard the horse and dogs stop, and then a man's voice urging the horse on. The sounds came closer for a moment and then dissipated. Just ahead of them and a little to the right they saw the flank of a horse between the trees. Then the rider urged it away from them toward the sound of whatever it was that had been thrown in the field.

Katherine stood silently praying harder than she ever had, even when James was shot, that her little babies would stay asleep. Suddenly she felt Auntie Ellen's strong hands grab the sides of her head and gently bend it to the right so she could see. Something moved fast, she couldn't make out more than a shadow, hurrying away from the bushes to the protection and the density of the trees on the south side of the field.

Auntie Ellen's mouth came very close to Katherine's ear. She could feel her warm fast breath, and heard her whisper, "It was Moses, I know it was. She saw us and she saved us, I know she did."

Chapter 07

They waited in the same spot for a long time. It felt like at least an hour, and then they slowly and cautiously moved forward again. No other words were spoken and by the grace of God, Elisabeth and Wilbur stayed asleep.

It was almost dawn when Fanny spotted a light glimmering in the darkness. Hung high on a pole a lantern swayed slightly in the wind. As they slowly walked toward it and their eyes became used to the darkness again after looking at the light, they could see a little church. It sat stoutly in a glen, hidden behind the trees surrounding it.

Katherine sank to her knees as she saw a little candle lit in the window of a smaller building next to the church.

Pap stopped and lifted his finger to his mouth, then motioned for Ellen to come towards him. Without speaking, they understood that the two of them would knock while the others hid among the trees.

The church was made of round cut stones. There were bushes growing along its sides and a small gravel path led to low steps and a large arched entrance way. The door looked either green or blue, but it was too hard to determine in the low light. Katherine could perceive a picket fence on the right side of the church; dark shadows loomed behind it. They were gravestones, looking like people and children standing still in the dark. She shivered.

Pap and Auntie Ellen slowly walked up the path and then they made a left to the building with the candle in the window. The outlines of their bodies contrasted with the light colored wood paneling. They stood there a long time. She couldn't see if they knocked again or not, but then the door opened wide and they were quickly pulled inside. The door closed without a sound.

Katherine swallowed and took Elisabeth from Robert's arms feeling the urgent need to hold her. Everyone stood silently and close together staring intently at the house. *How could they trust that the people were who they were supposed to be? What were they doing with Pap and Auntie Ellen?* Katherine thought wordlessly.

Then the door opened and someone held a lantern up high and walked quickly towards them.

An old man with a face full of wrinkles and small eyes peered at them from behind his lantern. His hair was hidden under a gray nightcap that he hadn't bothered to take off after getting roused from his sleep. A skinny chest was visible where the unbuttoned coat exposed a grey nightshirt.

His eyes went from face to face and widened in surprise as he stared at Katherine and Ebba, their white faces looking at him among all the black.

He gently waved them forward and silently stood aside as they passed him one by one, looking up in surprise yet again as Ned passed him with little Wilbur sleeping in his arms.

Katherine looked him straight in the eye and he nodded and whispered, "Welcome, all of you. Welcome to Pennsylvania, you are safe now."

Epilogue

They stayed with Mr. and Mrs. Solvo, the kindly old caretakers of the church. They waited for the rest of the former Waynewright slaves to join them. Hours or sometimes a couple of days apart each group appeared. They were hungry and tired, wet and scared, but all safe.

During the following weeks they slowly regrouped. The Quaker community helped with housing and traveling. Some chose to stay at one of their larger farms and became members of their congregation. Others moved to a negro settlement just north of the Pennsylvania-Maryland border.

Katherine sent a letter to her father and she, Pap, Auntie Ellen, Mary, Ned and Fanny waited for him and her uncle to come down from New York so that they could travel back safely with them.

Fifteen people decided to continue following the secret railroad all the way up to Canada, their freedom papers safely hidden within the folds of their clothing.

After what happened to Jack, they didn't feel safe traveling in the open. It was just a piece of paper after all. A paper that could easily be taken and destroyed and they would have no recourse whatsoever.

Until the day Katherine died, many years later, she hoped to hear from them, but she never did, nor did she hear from Imus and Martha, or little Eva and Mathilda. She could only hope they made it there safely and that Jack and Karissa had reunited somehow.

The Peterssons went back home and remained custodians of the Waynewright Plantation until it was sold in a somewhat dilapidated condition after the war.

They could never prove that it was Dawson who shot James, or who hired the man who did. Katherine's father and Uncle made inquiries with the county judge, the Sheriff and the neighbors, but they found nothing.

They say what goes around comes around.

Dawson sent his wife and daughters north during the war while he and Peter stayed, forcing their slaves to stand guard with clubs should the Union Army approach, but loyalty only runs so deep. When the Union soldiers came, Dawson's slaves laid down their weapons and told the Union solders that they wanted to join their side. As this was not yet legal, Colonel Smith declined. The army raided the coffers of valuables, food and weapons and took his horses. Dawson and his son were killed when they tried to stop them. Then they burned Dawson's barns and mansion to the ground.

Rumor had it that on their way out, Adam stopped briefly and asked them to leave the Waynewright plantation alone.

It was left intact.

Katherine Waynewright lived out her life in New York City. Pap and Auntie Ellen lived in a small apartment near her and married. Mary joined her sister and began teaching at a negro school. Will married and had four sons.

Elisabeth married and had seven children, teaching them all the importance of equality. One of her sons was influenced by W.E.B. Du Bois and helped to found the NAACP in 1909.

Wilbur studied medicine, finishing what his father had started. He kept a framed picture in his office with an old thumbed photo of his father. Underneath it said:

In Memory of Mr. James Waynewright, standing like a beacon of light in the darkness, forever shining upon us reminding us to do what is right.

59906511R00223

Made in the USA
Middletown, DE
22 December 2017